DECONSTRUCTING SOCIAL PSYCHOLOGY

DECONSTRUCTING
SOCIAL PSYCHOLOGY

Edited by
IAN PARKER
and
JOHN SHOTTER

ROUTLEDGE
London and New York

First published in 1990
by Routledge
11 New Fetter Lane, London EC4P 4EE
Simultaneously published in the USA and Canada
by Routledge
a division of Routledge, Chapman and Hall, Inc.
29 West 35th Street, New York, NY 10001

Typeset by LaserScript Limited, Mitcham, Surrey.
Printed and bound in Great Britain by
Biddles Ltd, Guildford and King's Lynn

British Library Cataloguing in Publication Data

Deconstructing social psychology.
1. Social psychology
I. Shotter, John II. Parker, Ian, 1956 –
302

Library of Congress Cataloging in Publication Data
Deconstructing social psychology / Ian Parker and John Shotter,
editors.
p. cm.
Bibliography: p.
Includes index.
1. Social psychology. 2. Deconstruction. I. Parker, Ian, 1956–
II. Shotter, John.
HM251.D3584 1989
302—dc20
89–10472
CIP

ISBN 0-415-01077-2
ISBN 0-415-01074-8 (pbk)

CONTENTS

CONTRIBUTORS

Kum-Kum Bhavnani is currently a visiting Associate Professor at Oberlin College, Oberlin, Ohio, 44074. She is based at the University of Bradford, and her previous publications include (with Margaret Coulson) work on the challenge of racism for feminism, and (with Reena Bhavnani) work on racism and resistance in Britain.

Michael Billig is a professor at the Department of Social Sciences, Loughborough University, Loughborough, Leicestershire, LE11 3TU. He is the author of *Arguing and Thinking: A Rhetorical Approach to Social Psychology* (1987) and co-author of *Ideological Dilemmas: A Social Psychology of Everyday Thinking* (1988).

Erica Burman is a lecturer in psychology at the Department of Psychology and Speech Pathology, Manchester Polytechnic, Elizabeth Gaskell, Hathersage Road, Manchester, M13 OJA. She is editor of *Feminists and Psychological Practice* (1990).

John Bowers is a lecturer in psychology in the Department of Psychology, University of Nottingham, University Park, Nottingham, NG7 2RD. He has worked on problems in cognitive psychology, and on issues raised by post-structuralism.

Antony Easthope is a lecturer in English at the Department of English and History, Manchester Polytechnic, Ormond Building, Lower Ormond Street, Manchester, M15 6BX. He is author of *British Post-Structuralism: Since 1968* (1988).

Celia Kitzinger is a lecturer in psychology at the Department of Psychology, Polytechnic of East London, Romford Road, Stratford, London, E15 4LZ. She is author of *The Social Construction of Lesbianism* (1987).

Mike Michael is a researcher at the Centre for Science Studies and Science Policy, Lonsdale College, Lancaster University, Bailrigg, Lancaster, LA1 4YN. He has worked on questions of social psychology to do with gender and masculinity.

Ian Parker is a lecturer in social and abnormal psychology at the Department of Psychology and Speech Pathology, Manchester Polytechnic, Elizabeth Gaskell, Hathersage Road, Manchester, M13 OJA. He is author of *The Crisis in Modern Social Psychology, And How To End It* (1989).

David Pilgrim is a lecturer in the Department of Psychology, Roehampton Institute, Digby Stuart College, Roehampton Lane, London, SW15 5PH. He has worked as a Principal Clinical Psychologist at a Special Hospital, and is currently researching radical responses to changes in mental health practice.

Nikolas Rose is a lecturer in the Department of Human Sciences, Brunel University of West London, Uxbridge, Middlesex, UB8 3PH. He is author of *Governing the Soul: Technologies of Human Subjectivity* (1989).

Edward E. Sampson is a professor of psychology in the School of Social and Behavioral Sciences, California State University Northridge, Northridge, California, 91330. He is author of *Justice and the Critique of Pure Psychology* (1983).

Janet Sayers is a lecturer in psychology in the Faculty of Social Sciences, Keynes College, The University of Kent, Canterbury, Kent, CT2 7NP. She is author of *Sexual Contradictions: Psychology, Psychoanalysis and Feminism* (1986).

John Shotter is a professor of Interdisciplinary Social Sciences at Vakgroep Ontwikkeling en Socialisatie, Rijkuniversiteit Utrecht, Heidelberglaan 2, 3584 Utrecht, Netherlands. He is author of *Social Accountability and Selfhood* (1984).

Corinne Squire is working at the Center for the Study of Women and Society, The Graduate School and University Center, The City University, Box 135–192, 25 West 43 Street, New York, NY 10036–8099. She is author of *Significant Differences: Women in Psychology* (1989).

Peter Stringer is a professor in the Policy Research Institute, The Queen's University of Belfast and the University of Ulster, 105

Botanic Avenue, Belfast, BT7 INN, N. Ireland. He is the co-author of *Social Texts and Context: Literature and Social Psychology* (1984).

INTRODUCTION

Ian Parker and John Shotter

This book follows in the wake of *Reconstructing Social Psychology* (Armistead 1974) – an influential collection of papers published more than a decade and a half ago which was critical of the theories and assumptions in the discipline. Then, social psychology appeared to be in the middle of a resolvable crisis. Now we realise the problems were more deeply rooted. For the crisis is not to be found just in the theories and assumptions of social psychology, but in a whole set of 'crises' to do with the very character of the conduct of western intellectual life. They are implicit in the *practices* and *institutions* within which not only social psychological knowledge, but all our knowledge, is produced. It is these practices which must be criticised and changed if these crises are to be resolved. We need to press forward the critical dynamic which *Reconstructing Social Psychology* encouraged, and to draw upon contemporary theoretical debates to unravel the ways in which the very nature of our knowledge-producing practices and institutions entrap us, and lead us into simply reproducing unchanged what in fact we thought we were reconstructing.

DECONSTRUCTION AND SOCIAL PSYCHOLOGY'S CONSTRUCTION OF ITS OWN SUBJECT MATTER

What is 'deconstruction', and why is a movement in literary criticism (which, to the extent that it uses literary devices in its conduct, has dared even to criticise philosophy) of relevance at all to the crisis in social psychology? While philosophy may be vulnerable to such a form of criticism, why should a concern with

1

the nature of the literary and rhetorical devices constituting the structure of a *text* be of concern to *scientific* psychologists?

We have no doubts at all about the powers of language as a story-telling medium. We all know we can be moved to tears of pity or joy in contemplating the actions and sufferings of a fictional character in a non-existent world; that people can easily tell us lies and deceive us; that we can easily deceive ourselves. Hence our concern in psychology with trying to be scientific: we are aware of the persuasive force of language alone, and attempt to guard ourselves against its powers to mislead us by taking account in our formulations of publicly available evidence and observations. Second, the fact is that until now we have ignored (or repressed) the degree to which social psychology is textually constituted. Whatever else is involved in the doing of a science, a central activity is the writing and publishing of textual material. Indeed, just as this book illustrates, without written texts, social psychology would be not only unable to formulate and instruct its practitioners in its theories, methods and procedures, and to argue for their correctness, it would also be unable to be self-critical, and to entertain alternative versions of itself.

Thus we once again face the anxiety we had hoped to avoid by using our concern with observation and evidence. Could it be that our scientifically acquired knowledge of the world and ourselves is not determined by our and the world's 'natures' to anything like the degree we have believed (and hoped) in the past; and that instead our knowledge is influenced by the 'ways', the literary and textual means, we use in formulating our concerns (Gergen 1985)? To go further: could it be that we spend our time researching into fictions of our own making? These are the questions 'deconstruction' faces us with. They arise out of the peculiar nature of academic textual communication.

The strange and special thing about an academic text, which makes it quite different from everyday face-to-face talk, is that by the use of certain strategies and devices, as well as already predetermined meanings, one is able to construct a text which can be understood (by those who are a party to such 'moves') in a way divorced from any reference to any local and immediate contexts. Textual communication can be (relatively) *decontextualised.* Everyday talk, on the other hand, is marked by its vagueness and openness, by the fact that only those taking part in it can understand its drift; the meanings concerned are not wholly predetermined, they are negotiated by those involved, on the spot, in relation to the circumstances in which they are involved (see Shotter, this volume, Chapter 11). Everyday talk is *situated* or *contextualised*, and relies upon its situation (its circumstances) for its sense. But more than that, its use is for practical purposes, and it is understood 'practically', i.e. each statement is responded to in terms of its practical import in the immediate (but symbolic) context of its utterance – hence, the opacity of written transcripts of such talk. To the uninvolved reader, they are disorderly, they lack coherence; the reader lacks access to the 'background' in terms of which the recorded utterances make sense. Academic texts are different: they do make sense to the reflective, uninvolved reader. Irrespective of their surrounding circumstances, in their reading of the text, readers seem able to construct a new context (from the syntactically related parts of the text), an *intralinguistic* context, in terms of which the text itself makes sense.

VARIETIES OF DECONSTRUCTION

In discussing the 'deconstruction' of such textual based activities, we should make clear that in this book, there are at least three different senses in which this term is employed. The first is that derived from the work of Jacques Derrida (1976, 1978, 1982b), who offers a series of techniques and examples which show how texts – *systematic* texts of a philosophical, scientific, or of any everyday kind – can, so to speak, be subverted. They can all be revealed as containing 'hidden', internal contradictions, and the absent or 'repressed' meanings can be made visible. Derrida's spectre hangs over the discussions (and destructions) of texts, narratives, and rhetorics in the chapters making up Part 1 of this book. But, as Erica Burman points out in Chapter 15, this form of deconstruction does not automatically lead to reconstruction. Allowing repressed terms a voice within a discourse is not the same as them speaking within a discourse of their own.

This leads us on to the second sense in which 'deconstruction' is used in this book, the sense which in fact predominates. It is concerned with what Foucault (1977, 1980, 1981) calls the *genealogy* of a social formation, whether it be an academic discipline, a social technology it legitimates, or the form of subjectivity it induces within the form of social control it institutes. In taking a genealogical approach, Foucault subverts the privilege classically afforded *systematicity* in academic analyses. He wants to uncover the working not of abstract principles and universal laws, but the particular and local (i.e. irregular and discontinuous) operation of the actual power relations at work in structuring social forms in the modern world. This emphasis upon revealing the 'workings' of disciplines (whether academic or otherwise), of power and its resistance, is present in Part 2. Yet, although there are important differences between Derridian and Foucauldian forms of 'deconstruction', both can be used to make visible the otherwise 'hidden' social and political processes in the *orderly* products of academics. But are such revelations enough?

This brings us to a third sense of the term, one which reveals in fact a degree of resistance to the rather elitist and alienating language of post-structuralism itself. To 'deconstruct' in this final, third sense, is not just to unravel hidden assumptions and to uncover repressed meanings, but to bring to the fore concerns altogether different from those implicated in the discourses concerned. It is here, for example, that feminist work on the social construction of gender is situated. Psychoanalytic notions (often, but not always drawing upon Lacan's post-structuralist ideas) – to the extent that they afford a space for the exploration of an 'other' in a more radical sense than a mere polar contrary – are prominent here. It is this third sense which is represented in Part 3, and it is here that an approach to politics in terms of a political economy of voice and silence is stressed.

For this we feel, in the end, is the subject matter of politics: a struggle to do with a scarcity of opportunities to be someone, i.e. of opportunities to speak about who and what one is, and about what one feels one needs in one's future in continuing to be oneself, and to have what one says taken seriously and responded to by the others around one. Only in such circumstances, in which one can play an influential part in determining one's own future, can one be said to be leading one's own life and not to be oppressed.

DECONSTRUCTION AND RHETORIC

In the rest of this Introduction we would like to begin with an account of the first (Derridian) sense of deconstruction, and some of the general issues of textuality and power this work raises. We will draw attention to links with other useful work on meaning, and develop arguments about the role of contemporary discourses in psychology, here making use of the second, looser sense of deconstruction. Later, however, we shall inevitably find ourselves in the realm of politics, and our deconstruction widens out into the third sense we discussed above – to do with attempts to resist some of the hidden powers and forces at work in currently, unreconstructed versions of social psychology.

To turn then to the nature of the processes by which social psychology produces a new, *intralinguistic* reality to research into, to replace the actual, everyday world of social life. What is the general nature of the linguistic and textual strategies and devices by which this effect is achieved?

First, it is necessary to emphasise that, as most theorists of language since Saussure (1974) have claimed, language does not work by combining a set of isolated, unchanging, atomic elements, but by making and marking *differences* within a global, temporally developing totality (of speech sounds, for example). Thus what something 'is', can only ever be characterised linguistically in terms of its distinctive features: it owes the kind of distinctiveness we perceive it as having in our lives, its significance, not only to its relations with (and thus differences from) other 'parts' or 'aspects' of a present totality, but also to some 'part' of a totality in the past, out of which it was differentiated. (If this is all too abstract, think of the child's development of speech sounds, as he or she learns to articulate within the otherwise vague sounds they make, some clear differences.) Thus any attempt to talk about a particular part of such a system, assumes that *always already* the whole system is on hand as an 'invisible' background. For any use of a 'difference' remains a mere 'promise' of a contrast, until reference to the other polarity of the contrast is ultimately and actually made. However, as Derrida (1978) points out, this reference may be *deferred* in time, sometimes indefinitely. (Deconstruction also, we must add, subverts the notion of 'totality' which we are using here as a step in our account.)

This reliance upon differences, *whilst* deferring reference to both sides of the polarity constituting the significance of a text, is where all our problems lie. For no element of a text can function as a sign without relating to another element, one which is not itself actually present. These problems become particularly acute in supposedly *systematic writing*, the type of writing common in scientific social psychology, which assumes that a 'bit' of experience can be discussed independently both of whose experience it is and the context in which it occurs. The aim in such writing is to construct a system of dependencies (or dominations), a set of scientific laws of behaviour. Within language itself, however, no one would ever claim, for instance, that just because the sound signifying /m/ *depends* for its signification upon its relations to the sound signifying /n/, that /m/ *dominates* /n/ – for /n/ clearly also depends upon /m/. Yet people *do* try to suggest in their textually expressed theories, that certain terms, instead of being mutually interdependent, are 'logically' dependent upon others, i.e. they are derived from them, or are dominated by them.

It is here that Derrida's (1976) attack upon the 'ruling illusion' of Western ways of thinking and philosophising – that they can somehow proceed without taking their reliance upon writing into account, and can simply present themselves as a matter of orderly and systematic *thought* – which has proved particularly devastating. For what he has shown, by subjecting philosophical texts to literary analysis, is their essential *differential* structure, and how this structure undermines any claim that they can provide indubitable foundations for knowledge. He shows all such structures to be unstable, for all the relations of one-way dependency relations are in reality (just as in the example of a language's sound system above) two-way ones; the claims to truth made could just as equally be the other way round. Indeed, he goes a step further and, following Nietzsche, he unmasks the claims to systematic knowledge made in the dominant texts of our culture, as elaborate schemes for preserving and disguising the intellectual will-to- power.

TEXTUAL TRICKS AND STRATEGIES

In their attempts to represent the open, vague, temporally changing nature of the world as closed, well-defined, and unchanging, they have made use of certain textual and rhetorical strategies to construct a closed set of intralinguistic references. In other words, in moving from an ordinary conversational use of language to the construction of such systematic texts, there is a transition from a reliance on practical meaning, upon reference to the immediate context, to a reliance upon links with what has already been, or with what might be said. In essence, there is a decrease of reference to what 'is' with a consequent increase of reference to what 'might be', in other words, to fictions. Such a consequence, however, requires the development of methods for *warranting* in the course of one's talk one's claims about what 'might be' as being what 'is'. It is by appeal to such methods to give support to one's claims, that those who know such procedures can construct their statements as factual statements – and claim authority for them as revealing a special 'true' reality behind appearances – without any reference to the everyday context of their claims. About such textually structured ways of talking, Dreyfus and Rabinow (1982), in their discussion of Foucault, say:

> This exotic species of speech act flourished in especially pure form in Greece around 300 BC, when Plato became explicitly interested in the rules that enabled speakers to be taken seriously, and, by extrapolating the relative context independence of such speech acts to total independence, invented pure theory.
>
> *(Dreyfus and Rabinow 1982: 48)*

What this means (now just as much as then) is that certain speakers, those with a training in certain special techniques – supposedly to do with the powers of the mind to make contact with reality – are privileged to speak with authority beyond the range of their merely personal experience.

Let us examine what some of these special techniques are: First, we should mention Marx and Engels's (1977: 66–7) account of the tricks involved in the production of 'ruling illusions' – their concern here is with how something *imaginary* can be posited as 'ruling' our lives and with how we can become victims of fictions of our own devising. The three tricks involved are discussed in Shotter (this volume), so we will not mention them further here, except to remark upon their resemblance to the 'controls' required for the collecting and relating of data to theory in the doing of experiments. The second textual process we would like to draw attention to has been called by Ossorio (1981) the *ex post facto* fact fallacy: it is to do with the concealing or hiding of the social origins of 'ruling illusions'. The general form of the temporal sequence of events involved is as follows:

(a) First, a statement is formulated as a description of a state of affairs which, although we may not realise at the time, is *open* to a number of possible interpretations.

(b) We are then tempted to accept the statement as true.

(c) By its very nature the statement then 'affords' or 'permits' the making of further statements, now of a more well articulated nature.

(d) The initial interpretation (already accepted as true) is now perceived *retrospectively* as owing its now quite definite character to its place 'within' the now well-specified context produced by the later statements – it has been 'given' or 'lent' a determinate character in their terms which it did not, in its original *openness*, actually have.

Someone who has studied its nature in relation to scientific developments, is Fleck (1979). He comments upon the general nature of the process as follows:

> Once a statement is published it constitutes part of the social forces which form concepts and create habits of thought. Together with all other statements it determines 'what cannot be thought of in any other way'. Even if a particular statement is contested, we grow up with its uncertainty which, circulating in society, reinforces its social effect. It becomes a self- evident reality which, in turn, conditions our further acts of cognition. There emerges a closed, harmonious system within which the logical origin of individual elements can no longer be traced.
>
> *(Fleck 1979: 37)*

In attempting retrospectively to understand the origins and development (and the current movement) of our thought, we describe their nature within our to an extent now finished and systematic schematisms. But the trouble is, once 'inside' such systems, it is extremely difficult to escape from them. We can, as Stolzenberg (1978) puts it, become 'entrapped' within them in the following sense: that 'an objective demonstration that certain of the beliefs are incorrect' can exist, but 'certain of the attitudes and habits of thought prevent this from being recognised' (1978: 224). And the attitudes and habits of thought which prevent those within the system from recognising its inadequacies arise out of them ignoring what Stolzenberg (1978: 224) calls 'those considerations of standpoint that have the effect of *maintaining* the system.'

In other words, their plight arises, not just from them ignoring the fact that they have located themselves within a particular discursive or intralinguistic reality (sustained by a discourse couched within a particular idiom), but also from the fact that their (self-contained, systematic) way of talking does not 'afford' or 'permit' the formulation of questions about its relations to its socio-historical surroundings. Syntax masquerades as meaning to such an effect, that, as Wittgenstein (1953, no. 104) points out, 'We predicate of the thing what lies in the method of representing it . . . .'

PROFESSIONAL DISCOURSES

To learn to speak these professional discourses is to learn a vocabulary and a set of analytic procedures for 'seeing' what is going on (in the everyday activities under study) in the appropriate professional terms. For we must see only the partially ordered affairs of everyday life, which are open to many interpretations (see the *ex post facto* facts fallacy above), *as if* they are events of a certain well defined kind. But to 'see' in the 'theory-laden' kind of way, we require training. For, to the extent that all theoretical writing claims that things are not what they ordinarily seem to be, but are 'in reality' something else, the terms of a theory are not intelligible in the same way as terms in ordinary language. They need a special form of introduction: if people want to be taken seriously as making *scientific* claims, they need to be 'instructed' (and now even 'chartered', i.e. officially certified and qualified) in how to see various social phenomena *as* having a certain psychological character, e.g. how to see them as 'social representations', *as* 'prejudices', *as* 'attitudes', *as* 'attributions', *as* 'learned helplessness', etc. The effect of this 'transformation' – of an everyday world, in which ordinary people act according to their own reasons, into a professional world of behaviours, readily categorised for study as to their causes – is the construction of a world in which only the voice of the professional has currency, while the voices of those outside are rendered silent.

To put the matter in Garfinkel's (1967) terms, the activities of everyday life are, quite literally, *made* 'rationally-visible-and-reportable' within the institutional order of the profession, and quite literally, *made* 'rationally-*in*visible' within their own terms. But more than that, as the various forms of deconstruction displayed in this book reveal, much that has been rendered 'invisible' has also been *repressed* – by being embedded within larger, all embracing orders. These larger orders achieve their influence whenever any breakdowns or puzzling circumstances arise: for it is then, in making repairs, or in formulating explanations, clarifications, etc., i.e. giving accounts of 'what is happening', that reference to such orders is made. They provide the final court of appeal. So, although social psychology's most important practice might seem to be its explicit 'methodology', within the actual day-to-day conduct of social psychology as a professional enterprise, this 'methodology' only has sense, and only makes sense, in the context of the use and production of *written texts* and the professionalised images of human beings they purvey. All professional psychology and social psychology moves from text to text, usually beginning with the reading of already written texts, and ending in the writing of further texts. Hence, all the problems identified by Derrida, to do with the sources of a text's authority, apply in Social Psychology. Whether it is to be found in certain, special scientific techniques within the profession, or outside in the practices of everyday life, is according to him an undecidable question. How should claims to truth now be warranted?

This same confusion and undecidability is readily apparent also, in a brief but crucial section in a report prepared for the British Psychological Society (BPS 1988: 45–6) on the future of the psychological sciences. It states in para. 12.1: '[A]Chartered psychologist, should be able to indicate clearly the extent to which the procedures they adopt have been validated . . . . [But] what are the criteria for legitimate claims?' How should one warrant one's claims? Even within the BPS itself there are, as the report says, 'clearly . . .grounds for controversy,' for the fact is that:

> If, in addition to quantification, objectivity, and openness, 'scientific' should be taken to mean the control of all salient variables, then clearly many practical aspects of psychology cannot be evaluated from a strictly scientific point of

view . . . . Many applied psychologists believe that the validity of their practice can only be established by extra-scientific procedures.

(para. 12.2)

In discussing how they might proceed in the future, psychologists were undecided:

A fair proportion of the submissions to the Working Party noted that while psychology may have established its credibility on the basis of its scientific approach, an over-reliance in the future on such an approach may serve to lessen the impact of psychology in the public domain. Nevertheless, other submissions coherently argued that the scientific approach had served psychology well and that it should remain the dominant model.

(para. 12.3)

Either way it would seem that the criteria to which one should appeal for deciding the legitimacy of one's claims should now be discussed in terms not of truth, but of professional interest (see section 18 of the report: *The Marketing of Psychology*, especially para. 18.10, the marketing analogy; and para. 18.11, delivering the goods to other professions). Deconstruction, on the other hand, with its associated return to rhetoric, gives us another way: public discussion and political action.

CONSEQUENCES

Garfinkel (1967: 44–65) discusses the feelings of anger occasioned by the 'experiments' he had his students do upon unsuspecting people, in which they transgressed, in an attempt to make them explicit, the rights and duties, the 'moralities' (Sabini and Silver 1982) implicit in everyday conversational interchanges. The anger occurs because the nature of such 'open' interchanges is such that those involved in them should have to negotiate in 'making sense' of their common circumstances (see Shotter, this volume, Chapter 11). To 'close' negotiations prematurely by imposing a set of already determined meanings, is to deny people these rights. Such feelings of anger at being 'silenced' are now beginning to be extensively reported in the writings of women, and of colonised peoples (Smith 1988; Spender 1980; Thiong'o 1987). The deconstruction of the theoretical texts in social psychology, which fail to give a voice to oppressed people, has to be linked with a deconstruction of the institutional apparatus of psychology. This much is clear from the following bizarre paragraph from the BPS future of the psychological sciences report:

> Para. 21.1. *A Significant Intervention at the Harrogate Conference.* During a discussion period at the Harrogate conference a female (*sic*) participant made a vigorous contribution .... She suggested that the language we use affects the way we think and that sexist language had a distorting effect both on the nature of psychology and the nature of personal relations. The reaction of the audience was not easy to interpret, but it is safe to say that it was not overtly positive or supportive of her views.
>
> (*BPS 1988: 77*)

No matter how benevolent one as a psychologist may be towards those one studies, no matter how concerned with 'their' liberation, with 'their' betterment, with preventing 'their' victimisation, etc., the fact is that 'their' lives are made sense of in terms which do not in fact make sense to 'them'. They only make sense, as Smith (1988) points out, within the 'ruling apparatuses' of the State, e.g. within schools, universities, polytechnics, the law and the police, health care, social welfare policy, etc. In such apparatuses the 'relations of ruling', as we might call them, are mediated by various discourses, texts, or idioms, certain accepted, proper, or professional ways of talking within which one can only properly have a place by being 'licenced', by gaining the appropriate credentials – otherwise, one runs the risk of having what one says not taken seriously, ignored as 'unprofessional'.

These, then, are some of the dilemmas we face: although one may pride oneself upon one's radical stance, upon one's attempts to subvert oppressive projects, upon one's ability to reveal the moral scandals and hypocrisy at the heart of 'their' activities, if one wants to speak as a professional, the fact remains that one usually continues to participate in the very discipline that makes those activities impossible. (It *could* also be argued that professional psychology does provide some powerful 'tools' for human betterment; and it would be foolish to recommend their destruction.)

What seems to be required is the deconstruction of the whole (Enlightenment) project of an intellectual élite discovering the basic principles of mind and society. Instead, the intellectual class might be seen as society's 'psychological instrument' (Vygotsky 1966) makers, and an attempt made to reconstruct the aim of social studies as a rhetorical enterprise in which the voices of those who are other than professional 'scientists' can also be heard. Then it might be possible to construct a real (as opposed to counterfeit) set of analytic procedures and terms, for a proper emancipatory social psychology. To a first approximation, the task is, we feel, as stated by Clifford Geertz:

> The problem of the integration of social life becomes one of making it possible for people inhabiting different worlds to have genuine, and reciprocal, impact upon one another. If it is true that insofar as there is a general consciousness it consists in the interplay of a disorderly crowd of not wholly commensurable visions, then the vitality of that conscious-ness depends upon creating conditions under which such interplay will occur. And for that, the first step is surely to accept the depth of the differences; the second to under-stand what these differences are; and the third to construct some sort of vocabulary in which they can be publicly formulated.
>
> (*Geertz 1983: 161*)

But it is at this point we must break off Geertz's account, for he then goes on simply to list the *academic disciplines* which would then be enabled to give 'a credible account of themselves to one another'.

But the problem is more than a purely academic one; it is a practical–political one too: that of devising the kind of analytic vocabularies and arenas in public life for their use, in which all can participate in the interplay of which Geertz speaks. And this is why we feel the processes of deconstruction displayed in this book are important. For deconstruction cannot lead to a proper pluralism, nor is Geertz's vision of the interplay of a disorderly crowd of not wholly commensurable visions possible, while present power relations remain intact. Thus, as we see it, although deconstruc-tion does work against the repression of both concepts and subjects in psychology, it is only *one* strategy among others. It is necessary for critical opposition to be plural and many-faceted, and to be open to different tactics at different times. But this task is much easier to describe in theory than to achieve in practice.

Part One

TEXTS AND RHETORIC

Social psychology is a collection of texts and practices. The five chapters in Part 1 focus on texts, and the ways in which these texts attempt to produce and guarantee 'truth' in the discipline. Peter Stringer opens the set with an overview of introductions to social psychology textbooks. The introduction to a textbook attempts to account for the spread of different, contradictory theories and 'discoveries' about social behaviour that the reader will find. It is a good place to start in a deconstruction of social psychology, for the introduction foregrounds some of the (dubious) assumptions that the writer is making about what a social psychologist should be doing. These assumptions can be unravelled further by distinguishing between different narratives that run through the enterprise holding its texts together. Corinne Squire draws attention to the detective story, autobiography, and science fiction story narratives which organise social psychology's search for truth, enlightenment and progress. This scathing attack helps expose the falsities which masquerade as facts, as a narrative grips the writer and reader and draws them into the discipline.

There is a risk, of course, that critics of traditional social psychology might attack the texts as fictional accounts only to be caught in the trap of positing their own 'true' account. Worse, they may start conceding that there are true descriptions in social psychology which have to be sorted out from the false ones. Here, of course, radicals can all too quickly be drawn by an undertow, straight back into the discipline. One of the characteristics of a deconstructive approach to texts is that the contradictions and oppositions that it sets up are simply *strategic* devices to help us escape from the dominant concepts. When we draw attention to the rhetorical nature of social psychology, for example, we are making a point about *all* texts, including our own. Michael Billig, then, emphasises that there are argumentative aspects to all accounts of social activity. A reflexive outcome of this position is to say that a radical social psychology would be deliberately rhetorical. Celia Kitzinger drives home the point by showing how the opposition between 'pseudoscience' (a merely rhetorical, and therefore false science) and 'true science' has the effect of reinstating some very nasty 'truths' and unpleasant scientific norms. The opposition between true and false science is rhetorical. It is a textual and – to anticipate themes taken up later in the book – a political matter.

Matters would be so much easier if we could judge the truth of a text by finding out what the position and intentions of the author were. Social psychologists do, in fact, often labour under the illusion that it is possible to untangle rhetoric and textual devices free from the individual who produced it. Deconstruction takes off, however, from the text itself, and Antony Easthope draws on Derrida to show why this is so. He offers an example of the deconstruction of a text in which theories of intention are especially important. We have arrived at the point where the theory of writing, of *différance*, that deconstruction works with becomes relevant. The turn to rhetoric, and the deconstruction of the opposition between slippery rhetoric and perfect communication, are crucial to an understanding of how social psychology operates.

16

Chapter One

PREFACING SOCIAL PSYCHOLOGY:
A TEXTBOOK EXAMPLE

Peter Stringer

In this chapter I should like to be able to persuade you of two points: first, that in reflections on the discipline of social psychology, both generally and more particularly with respect to its teaching practices, textbooks deserve a different kind of attention than they have yet received; and, second, that by exposing textbooks, and eventually other social psychological texts, not to conventional psychological analyses, but to the kind of close reading which is suggested by recent literary theory, it is possible to reveal something of what is involved in the representation and transmission of social psychology as a body of knowledge and as a practice.

BACKGROUND

'Textbook' is intended here to refer to those fairly weighty volumes which are often used to introduce social psychology to students. Well-known examples are those by Kretch and Crutchfield, Brown, Secord and Backman, Hollander, Wrightsman, and so on. The observations which follow are based on an examination of nearly thirty distinct textbooks, all published between 1976 and 1981. The dates are a matter of convenience and autobiography. I collected the books in 1982–3; and produced the first draft of this chapter as a conference paper early in 1984. For the sake of homogeneity, they are all North American books, which aim to give a global overview of social psychology from a psychological (rather than sociological) perspective.

Readings which are influenced by recent literary theory should be contrasted with conventional psychological analyses of texts.

The latter would, for example, investigate the effect of texts on readers – their readability, communication effectiveness, and so on; how readers process information in a text; or attempt explanations of the text in terms of the author's intentions and values. The former approach, on the other hand, has the virtue of not only drawing on a rich, broad-ranging and continually developing intellectual resource, but most importantly of avoiding the use of the same analytic resources as the subject of study. It works from post-structuralist or deconstructionist literary theory, or more broadly from certain areas of discourse analysis. I say 'from', and not 'within'. It is a matter of being influenced by, rather than strictly applying, a set of ideas. Elsewhere in this volume (Chapter 12), Michael says: 'Deconstruction's task is to recover the excluded term by which the present(ed) term is formulated'. I shall use the justifications which are adopted in textbook prefaces to indicate what is in fact excluded by the textbooks, despite their prefaced claims. Varieties of the approach have been adopted at length elsewhere with reference to historiography (White 1978), philosophical writing (Norris 1983), sociology (Edmondson 1984), and the human sciences generally (Simons 1989). I have used it myself in a volume on literature and social psychology (Potter, Stringer, and Wetherell 1984) for an analysis of the 'reading practice' of the social psychologist, Irving Janis, as revealed through his *Victims of Groupthink*.

Any written text is of interest because texts are one of the forms of discourse of which social psychology consists. Discourse is both the content and medium of social psychology. For this reason, no social psychological text can be interpreted as a straightforward, literal account of its subject matter. Texts are persuasive; and a writer's principal aim, and difficulty, is to produce a simple, coherent account which will persuade the reader of its acceptability – that that is indeed how matters stand. Of particular interest is the means by which persuasiveness is constructed. Arguments at various points in this volume suggest that writing a persuasive social psychological textbook, within the mainstream of the discipline, would be an unusually difficult project, because of the complexity, incoherence, and reflexivity of social psychological material.

Another feature of the broad approach followed in this chapter is a refusal to allow certain kinds of text to take a privileged position. Thus, textbooks may be taken as being as significant as the *Journal of Personality and Social Psychology*, if one wants to understand what social psychology is about and how it works. Even the sociology of science, which is interested in the procedures of academic practice, has tended to ignore textbooks as a source of material. It has privileged empirical and theoretical research reports over other texts as data for study, and has treated research as more fundamental than teaching.

Textbooks

The number of social psychology textbooks which appeared in 1976–81 is fairly remarkable – there were probably more than the thirty at which I looked. Social psychology is clearly presented to relatively large numbers of students through that medium. If your reaction is that texts of this kind are insignificant or trivial to the discipline, then you are both discounting the experience of many hundreds of thousands of people, and ignoring the wider aspects of the representation of social psychology. North American textbooks are probably the medium for a large part of the social psychology which is taught throughout the world.

The importance of this latter point is reflected in the interesting argument of Moghaddam (1987) that there are Three Worlds of Psychology, with unequal capacities for producing and disseminating psychological knowledge. The first consists of the United States and the Soviet Union. He interprets the 'crisis' in western social psychology as partly arising from an attempt by (some parts of) the second world – developed countries – to establish a social psychology which is independent of the United States. A Third-World psychology has to challenge the domination by the other two worlds in Third-World developing countries. Textbooks and their contents are one means by which domination is exercised.

Yet a revolutionary textbook which deliberately seeks to undermine the received versions seems to be a difficult notion to accept. Both Gergen and Sampson, for example, have in their writings made striking contributions to the reformulation of social psychology; but they have produced textbooks which depart rather little from the basic form and content of their competitors. More critical approaches to social psychology (e.g. Archibald 1978;

Wexler 1983) tend to come from a predominantly sociological orientation. An exception is Antti Eskola's (1971) textbook. It has been translated into Dutch and reprinted several times in the Netherlands; but not, I believe, into English. This book, however, should not lead us to believe that 'normal' social psychology textbooks are as innocent as they appear. Like all texts, they seek with particular devices to persuade readers of the relevance, interest, and validity of their own perspective on human affairs. They can be treated as constructing a version of social reality for their readers, just as much as conveying the elements of a discipline for analysing social life.

The examination of textbooks as instruments for teaching psychology is not intended to throw light upon teaching as a separate activity within the discipline, but on something which in academic institutions constitutes an essential element of its practice; and through that, on the nature of social psychological practice itself. Textbooks reveal some of the personal and social contingencies, which, in addition to the theories and investigations which are foregrounded on their pages, go to make up 'what social psychology is'.

Textbooks work at two levels at least. They seek explicitly to give a comprehensible account of the discipline: they formally, and with claims to expertise, say what social psychology is and what social psychologists have achieved. They are presented as if they were direct and privileged descriptions of what the writer's fellow-scientists had done and seen. Yet for many reasons they cannot have that status. For example, their variability – which is something other than their relative (in-)accuracy – refutes it. They are many steps removed from the ultimate subject which they purport to explain. To mention only a few of those removes: they refer to books and articles which may be summaries of other texts, which refer to results, which are drawn from data, which are elicited from subjects.

In the accounting process, and in their own practice of social psychology, textbooks give an alternative set of (covert) information about its nature. The authoritative content of textbooks may of necessity be of interest to students; but here their 'how' rather than their 'what' is more important. A textbook is a constructed, organised text, selectively using particular means of discourse to produce its interpretative effect. Under analysis, it can throw light on the way in which social psychologists make sense of and interpret their discipline, not by paying attention straightforwardly to their formal and self-conscious claims, but by examining their mode of discourse in the social contexts which a textbook and its use encapsulates. While discourse is the subject-matter of social psychology, the discourse of social psychologists is both subject and meta-subject.

The discourse of the textbook is not 'caused' by its writer or by the subject-matter itself, but by the generalised attempt to present coherent, seamless accounts. This attempt may be peculiarly difficult in the case of textbooks. For students demand that these authorities facilitate as far as possible their access to and retention of that information which effectively will serve as a medium for advancing their social position. It is this demand, though not its motive, which is reflected in the preface to nearly every textbook. Textbooks are interesting texts, in a context of deconstruction, because their prefaces uniformly and often explicitly refer to difficulties of the author. Through their preface they thematise their problematical status; and thus, in principle, are readily open to deconstruction.

Disclaimers

At this point, several disclaimers need to be made. It should by now be clear that when, in what follows, examples of problems from textbooks are cited, there is no wish to 'criticise' the authors. We are only revealing ways in which they failed to carry out an impossible task; and even then we have no interest here in agency. We pay no attention to such aspects as the usefulness, quality, or accuracy of a certain textbook or of textbooks in general. Textbooks may be produced to make money for the writers and publishers; but that does not, as such, invalidate their claims to represent a part of a discipline. No more does a view of them as socialising agents or an imperialistic operation.

There are many ways in which one might examine the discourse of social psychology textbooks; of how they go about the attempt to produce an impression of generalised truth or reality behind (or in front of!) multiple and incoherent models and empirical studies. One might, for example, examine how they variously interpret identical sources or similar topics; and the variation might be analysed historically or culturally. But here we will simple-mindedly begin at the beginning of the textbook itself, and focus our reading on the preface, against a background of what the main text contains.

PREFACES

The dictionary defines 'preface', beyond its original liturgical meaning, as an introduction to a literary work, usually explaining its subject, purpose, scope, and method. Textbooks of social psychology would scarcely count as works of literature. (Is *The Social Animal* still the only example which one could perhaps imagine people wanting to read as a book, and not just as a textbook?) And their prefaces are better seen as justifying aspects of the main text, even though the justifications may often be couched as explanations. If a preface is read as explanation, it will strongly suggest to the reader what *should* be found in the main text, rather than encourage the reader to construct his or her own reading. It will appear to offer the definitive version of the writer's intentions, and thereby resist alternative interpretations. In the case of textbooks, a preface may even give quite detailed instructions on how to make sense of and assimilate its material.

Unlike the liturgical preface – a prelude to the central part of the Eucharist – a preface pretends to stand aloof from the main text. Its status as an introduction is frequently denied by the presence of another text which is labelled 'Introduction'. As a result the preface may be treated as quite peripheral, and be ignored. If it is read, it will probably be taken as a legitimate and authoritative commentary on the main text, rather than as being implicated in it. In a textbook, the author uses it as a means of distancing himself from and objectifying the reality of the account which follows.

At one level, prefaces are interesting as a rare form of discourse, one in which social psychologists interpret and justify a part of their own practice: in this case, making sense of social life for their students – even though one can also see their endeavour as one of making sense for themselves of social psychology. The preface is a particularly concentrated and explicit set of justifications, and one which is often couched in quite personal terms. At another level, the justifications should challenge the reader to look for the criticisms which they are implicitly fending off. But the student may be particularly unwilling to do this when preparing to read 'the textbook'; the student dare not have it undermined. Or again, a preface can be read in order to provide pointers as to how texts are constructed, both from the viewpoint of the self-conscious author, and in a more deconstructive manner. The preface seems to recognise and make explicit what would be necessary to produce a simple, coherent text, if that were ever possible.

Prefaces do not contain definitive statements about what they preface, but persuasive ones. They need to be 'accepted'. Precisely because of their justificatory and pedagogic goals, because of their self-conscious and concentrated enunciation of the coherence and reasonableness of what follows, they are a most useful analytic basis for deconstructing the plausibilities of the main text. They may conceal contradiction between themselves and what they preface; internal inconsistencies and incongruities; and a dichotomising tendency which ultimately points to the undesired incoherence and fragmentation of the main text. Each of these features reveals crucial resources of organisation used in the impossible task of producing a simple, coherent text.

On the surface the prefaces to social psychology textbooks may seem straightforward, perhaps rather boring, and certainly restrained, appeals for one to attend to their own rather than another competing book's message. The content is rather standardised, to the extent that one can readily produce a stereotyped version of it. It begins with a statement that social psychology is about everyday social life, and is of personal relevance to every student. The discipline is in a period of considerable growth and change, demanding the incorporation, perhaps in what is a revised edition of an earlier textbook, of much up-to-date material. One innovation frequently claimed is a greater attention to applications of social psychology. At the same time, it is argued, social psychology has scholarly, theoretical and classical bases which cannot properly be ignored, despite the complexity which they may sometimes introduce. To overcome the complexity, a number of special teaching aids are adopted – a logical organisation, a clear style, boxed inserts, liberal illustrations, summaries and glossaries. In nearly all cases, the preface ends with acknowledgments to other people for the help and advice which they gave to the author.

Despite this bland exterior, there are always internal struggles internally expressed. Worchel and Cooper make them very clear:

> there is a need for a text that respects the scientific integrity of social psychology but which escorts research findings beyond the laboratory and into the world. Further, the scope of such a text need not be so encyclopedic that it becomes boring to the reader nor should it be so incomplete that it gives a false or overly optimistic view of the field. Finally, the style of writing should not resort to formal journal jargon nor should it be so simplistic and chatty that the reader is being 'talked down' to.
>
> The format of the book is problem or topic oriented rather than theory oriented.
>
> We recognise the pitfalls that exist in writing a textbook that is relevant and interesting but which still maintains a high level of professionalism and scholarship . . . exciting but not equivocating, challenging but not cumbersome.
>
> *(Worchel and Cooper 1976: ix,x)*

The dichotomies which are spelled out here can be found, in varying combinations and variously expressed, in most of the prefaces. (Incidentally, the claim that laboratory research findings only need to be 'escorted' into the world beyond suggests an optimistic view as to their automatic relevance and application there.)

The Personal

One interesting contradiction in many prefaces is that between their standardisation of format and the personal and even emotional references which they often contain. Prefaces are usually written in the authorial first-person, and often refer to 'my' personal interest in the discipline and in writing a textbook. Raven and Rubin's preface begins:

> Footprints in the snow. This was my earliest conscious association with the intricacies of social interaction. As a young child in the Midwest, I recall going out early on a wintry day and seeing the footprints of those who had gone

24

out earlier. I found myself wondering about the unseen figures who had left their marks so vividly before me.

> *(Raven and Rubin 1976: vii)*.

This preface is in fact a dialogue between the two authors; and eventually they reflect in unison:

> How, though, do two separate individuals combine in working toward a joint product or goal? How do their individual characters merge into one in the process of communication?
>
> *(Ibid.: x)*

In Sampson's book, the preface reflexively refers to itself in an earlier, intriguing version.

> The preface to the previous edition opened with an interview purportedly between myself and an unnamed interviewer. Through probing questions, the interviewer wrested from me the truth behind that book and its writing. No comparable interview is included here.
>
> *(Sampson 1976: v)*

The contradiction between personal and formal is reproduced in the main texts. The textbooks show a remarkable uniformity both in content, and in the programmed injection at intervals of personal and human interest. But there is also a difference. While in the preface personal elements of the teaching and professional role come through, they are suppressed in the main text. There it is the voice of the researcher which is speaking, and research is a formal, impersonal activity. The splitting between researcher and teacher is already alluded to by Schneider in the preface:

> Working social psychologists have a number of ways of simplifying data, usually by inventing complex hypotheses or by derogating the competence of the researcher who produced results they do not like. The text writer cannot afford the luxury of either approach.
>
> *(Schneider 1976: vii)*

If a personal element is injected in the main text its reference is predominantly to aspects of student life and culture.

This text provides what has been missing: it presents *personal* social psychology. It will help amateur social psychologists better understand their own social behaviour. The book does cover traditional academic and applied social psychology, but the focus is on concepts and principles that will be useful in the daily lives of students.

(*Stang 1981: vii*)

This approach not only promotes a narcissism in the student, which most social psychologists are not willing to admit in themselves; but it also reinforces the impression, which in other contexts one might wish to dispel, that Social Psychology is too often only the social psychology of the university student. (Though in parentheses, I would say that it has to be, while we continue as a discipline to validate our identity predominantly within conventional academic institutions). Stang continues that 'in making it [social psychology] personal', his book uses new ways of presenting the subject: for example, drawing on classic and contemporary research, reorganising material to show conceptual rather than historical relations among ideas, and introducing some new material in the areas of research and theory. The suggestion that what are in fact quite common textbook devices play some part *in* making the discipline *personal* reveals the strain under which the preface's claim labours. How could those devices make social psychology 'personal'?

Although I have used the word 'personal', and that is the term which prefaces sometimes use in their frequent claims as to the relevance of social psychology, the student is rarely treated as a 'person' in the text, but as the occupant of a social role. It would take quite a re-interpretation of mainstream social psychology to give it a properly personal element. One of the more pressing concerns of a student, for example, might be the prospect of future employment. Stang's preface lays considerable emphasis on the applicability of social psychology to students' concerns. The book concludes with a two-page 'epilogue' on 'employment as a social psychologist'; but nowhere is this concern, or even the concept 'work', incorporated substantially in the main text. The author supplies references to his own research on the topic, but apparently could not allow his researcher's voice to speak clearly in the text. The book, like many others which tried to answer the 1970s call for 'relevance', in fact did remarkably little to the point.

26

Purely stylistic devices are made to answer. Simple language, short paragraphs, key concepts in bold type, cartoons, documentary photographs are all intended to create the impression that the content has some connection to the needs and interests of readers.

History

Another remarkable example of contradiction between the researcher's and teacher's voices occurs in the textbook of Gergen and Gergen (1981). Although the interesting ideas of Kenneth Gergen on the nature of social psychology are referred to in introductory chapters, nowhere subsequently are they allowed to influence the interpretation of the body of social psychology. Textbooks' wish to be seen to be giving the approved version of the discipline is very strong. In prefaces it is revealed in the practice of listing, sometimes quite effusively, long acknowledgments. (Middlebrook 1980, for example, devotes one page of a four-page preface to acknowledgments. Berkowitz (1980) also gives over one-quarter of his shorter preface to acknowledgments; though they are anonymous!) Any re-interpretations of the canon which are admitted to are generally justified in terms of apparently formalistic aims of achieving balance, logic and organisation, simplicity without simplification. But the inevitably interpretative (and thus re-interpretative) basis of any discourse is poignantly illustrated by the third sentence of the Gergen and Gergen preface:

> [Social psychology] is the discipline that focuses most sharply on people's thoughts about themselves and others, their passions and fears, their sense of right and wrong, their attempts to help and hinder each other, and their accomplishments and failures. In fact, no other field of psychology cuts common experience so close to the bone.
>
> (*Gergen and Gergen 1981: vi*)

Independently of the appropriateness of our purpose behind such a proposition, it is a radical interpretation of the contents of the main text.

A recurrent dichotomy in the prefaces is that between 'classical' and 'up-to-date' references, with associated remarks about the contemporary rapid changes and developments in social psychology. At a superficial level, this may serve as a justification for a new edition of the textbook, sometimes after as little as three years; as a claim to the lively quality of the subject; or as a promise to the student that she will not be burdened by what is out-of-date. More fundamentally, it is expressed in such a way as to conceal doubts about how to deal with the temporal dimension of the subject, particularly when convention demands the shackling of every empirical study to a particular point in time.

> I did not want to write a book that would be only topical or 'socially relevant'. The rapid changes of the last twenty years testify to the way interests alter, new social concerns develop, and old controversies fade away. What is topical at one time is old-fashioned soon afterwards. The really important matters of social psychology are its theoretical concepts.
>
> (*Berkowitz 1980: v*)

In the main texts themselves these doubts are not allayed, and largely because the genuinely historical dimension which would be necessary to do so is almost entirely absent. The unwillingness to distinguish properly between temporal and historical processes is well illustrated by the preface which begins:

> Whether or not one agrees with Gergen that social psychologists are capable only of studying historical, time-bound phenomena ... there can be little doubt that, historically, changes in the content of social psychology have occurred quite rapidly.
>
> (*Goldstein 1980: ix*)

The second 'historical' denotes only temporal change.

The same preface is interested to note the almost complete lack of overlap between the main topics found in social psychology textbooks of the 1950s and 1970s (even though at another moment it develops a strong argument that the discipline is not topic-oriented). But nevertheless, it says, the book will be looking for commonality and continuity in social psychology. And in preparation for that task the threat of Gergen's argument is shrugged off:

> Conceivably, as Gergen maintains, social psychology is

merely experimental history – social psychologists simply
explore in their laboratories topics that interest them as
private citizens of a particular culture at a particular time.

(Ibid.: x)

Yet the main text of this book is able finally to conclude (Goldstein
1980 p. 467) that Gergen's 'history' paper provides 'perhaps the
most important step' in a series of papers of the 1970s which raised
basic questions about what social psychologists were doing. In the
preface it is able to claim simultaneously as among its purposes an
emphasis on the historical relativism of knowledge and on studies
that have stood the test of time!

The readers

Goldstein's preface (though, in common with instances in one or
two other textbooks, it is not called a 'preface') is addressed 'To
The Instructor'. In a parallel preface 'To The Student', the
temporal aspect is given a rather different emphasis.

There is considerable emphasis on social psychology's past
and its future. This is largely because I believe social
psychology to be going through a transition phase wherein
new directions are being charted. But it is difficult to present
what now appears to be chaos in a meaningful way for
students. By focussing on the past it is easier, perhaps, to
make sense out of the present. So it is not my intention to
bring the reader up to date on all theory and research in
contemporary social psychology.

(Goldstein 1980: vii)

The *all* could never, of course, have been satisfied. The
exaggeration reveals a latent nervousness about having included
'classical studies' which 'seem hopelessly out of date'.

The fact that Goldstein includes two prefaces draws our
attention to a possible ambiguity in the target of the more usual
single preface. For example, one preface begins: '"What the world
needs most" is probably not another social psychology textbook'
(Seidenberg and Snadowsky 1976: ix) and ends with 'We hope that
teachers and students of social psychology will agree' (ibid.)

Students could only be said to agree or not if they had read the sentence. Yet the opening is surely not addressed to them?

The gentle preamble with which Gergen and Gergen begin is perhaps directed more at the student than the instructor:

> The course of our lives is powerfully influenced by our experiences with others – in private relationships, small groups, and the larger institutions of society. Social psychology is chiefly concerned with understanding the character of those relationships.
>
> (*Gergen and Gergen 1981*)

And so on. Its subsequent discussion of the form of the book can be read as addressed equally to student and instructor. However, the second half of the preface refers to the student obliquely as a third-party ('This book is intended for introductory courses in social psychology'); and includes one-and-a-half pages of acknowledgments, which are more likely to be intelligible (whether literally or as legitimation) to the fellow-professional than the student.

Generally, prefaces seem to be addressed to the researcher, if one judges by the 'sales-pitch' features which are frequently referred to (up-to-date treatment, balance, interesting and communicative format, etc.) and the lists of acknowledgments. For the hundreds of student readers who sit before each teacher, the preface may indeed be intended to be apart from the text. For the preface's thematising of the problematic status of social psychology should presumably be passed over by the first-year student. In an unusually frank example, Schneider begins the preface:

> Surely there are disciplines which better lend themselves to comprehensive treatment in text form than social psychology does. Social psychology is a discipline which has lost touch with its intellectual roots and which, in the hard battle to establish a respectable identity, succeeded primarily in becoming fragmented and concrete in both theory and application. Social psychology has no widely accepted methodologies, no generalizations of major importance, and no models which integrate even a large minority of research

findings. As every teacher of social psychology has learned, it is hard to give the beginning social psychology course a rigorous integrity, an intellectual cement, which makes it more than a loose collection of ideas.

(*Schneider 1976: v*)

The main text begins more resolutely:

What is social psychology? Social psychology can be defined as the study of how people organize, evaluate, and respond to their social experience.

(*Ibid.: 2*)

CONCLUDING

Textbooks are an important part of the body of discourse of social psychology, continuous with its other media. They can tell us 'what social psychology is'; but they necessarily offer re-interpretations, or *re*presentations, of the discipline. One of the things which they can tell us about social psychology derives from how the telling is done. Each *re*presentation has its own purposes and its own devices to achieve them. A universal purpose is to produce a plausible text – approved, clear, organised, and persuasive. In the case of a textbook this may be seen as a natural function; but it does also serve to enhance the acceptability, prestige and power of the discipline. The devices of any text are revealed most acutely through its contradictions. Their general interest in the case of textbooks is that they often derive from a clash between the voices of teacher and researcher, instigated by the incompatibility between what are accepted as students' learning needs (clarity, logical organisation, relevance, and so on) and the manner in which that material is produced through research (complex, discontinuous, specialised). The teacher's voice can most readily be heard in a condensed, confused, rhetorical, and revelatory form in the preface to textbooks, where it makes impossible claims for having achieved what it recognises as the necessary elements for a plausible text.

What might one *do* about this state of affairs? Do as researchers and teachers – because the separation of these roles is one of the roots of the problem. In research, we might place a greater emphasis on exploring and elucidating the points of contradiction

31

which emerge when we try to teach social psychology, treating them as a necessary programme for the next stage of the discipline. In teaching, in writing and using textbooks, we might be more open about the contradictions instead of glossing them over; enable students actively to work them through, rather than passively and uncritically assimilate them. The pity of it is that most students whom I have asked do not seem to want such an approach! In research-and-teaching, we might reflect on the extent to which we may be assuming that we are teaching future researchers; and on the possibility that without this assumption the product of much research may be unteachable.

Chapter Two

CRISIS WHAT CRISIS?

DISCOURSES AND NARRATIVES OF THE 'SOCIAL' IN SOCIAL PSYCHOLOGY

Corinne Squire

Social psychologists have been telling themselves, and anyone else who will listen, that their field is in crisis, since the 1950s. The antecedents of the problem can be traced much further back, to the discipline's nineteenth-century psychological and sociological precursors (Jaspers 1983). But the fact that social psychologists go on researching and writing in spite of this persistent difficulty, suggests that the discipline may be enabled, as well as limited, by its crisis. This chapter explores the problems and possibilities raised by the different narratives of crisis which operate in social psychological texts. First, though, the chapter looks more generally at the nature of the crisis in social psychology, and the different discourses, or structures of power and knowledge, which articulate this crisis.

Today, social psychologists usually accept that their attempts to understand human behaviour and experience scientifically generate serious and permanent difficulties with, for example, the objective assessment of subjectively significant events, and with the separation of psychological from social influences on subjectivity. This tendency shows up clearly in textbooks, the medium through which knowledge of social psychology is most broadly disseminated – especially in their introductory chapters (see Stringer, Chapter 1, in this volume). Brown, who in 1965 put social psychology alongside the physical sciences, now admits 'that social psychology is a less objective discipline than physics' (1986: xiii). Social psychologists still tend, however, to give simple, stable accounts of the discipline's crisis. Once they have explained it, they do not feel obliged to ask, '*what* crisis', again. Instead they suggest that, within its limits, social psychology should go on trying to develop scientifically, as it always has. Brown claims that social psychology makes a vital experimental-scientific contribution to the 'unchanging agenda of basic questions' (1986: xiii). Even Aronson, one of the most critical textbook writers, admits to the 'secret belief that social psychologists are in a unique position to have a profound and beneficial impact on all our lives' (1988: xi). This chapter tries to formulate social psychology's crisis in a less homogeneous and rose-tinted way.

DISCOURSES OF SOCIAL PSYCHOLOGICAL CRISIS

Social psychology's crisis is, in part, a manifestation of general problems within psychology. Canguilhem (1980) describes psychology as a discipline set up to solve the problems other disciplines encounter with subjectivity, by taking subjectivity as its object. The problematic status of this object, defined largely by its exclusion from other sciences, combined with the unreliability of psychology's methods, and the complex, incomplete and non-predictive nature of psychological theories, cast doubt on psychology's scientificity. The discipline's close association with biology mitigates these difficulties, providing it with a concept of a unitary, consistent subject, and with some parasitic scientific validity.

Psychology is also interested in the subject as a social being. It has contributed to twentieth-century western discourses of social phenomena such as the family, education, work, social conflict, crime, and mental disorder (Henriques *et al.* 1984; Riley 1983; Rose 1985). But it centres on an ultimately biological subject, and biological theories remain most powerful in it. Sometimes, biological explanations are offered for phenomena, like gender-specific play and excessive drinking, which it would be much simpler to account for socially. More generally, social factors are reduced to modifying influences on a biological foundation, and are treated as if they all belong to the same category. Psychologists are continually trying to improve this situation by becoming more socially aware, but are continually unable to do so. And so psychology's crisis is a crisis of its relations with the social world. This crisis of the 'social' emerges with particular force and persistence in social psychology, where the objects of investigation are social behaviour and experience, and where the methods are close to those of sociology. One sign of this is that social psychological discussion of feminism is widespread in comparison to that in other psychological fields. But conventional social psychology's dominant, social-cognitivist approach leads it, too, to relate all social differences to the same, ultimately biological cognitive processes, and to see these differences' categorisation and even their hierarchisation as inevitable (Condor 1986a, 1986b).

The mainstream discourse

Social psychology's crisis of the 'social' takes different forms. In the mainstream discourse it is formulated in a reformist way, in appeals for the revision and extension of existing objects, methods and theories. These appeals let the conventional discourse display its vitality, and cater to its need to demonstrate its social relevance, without endangering its specifically psychological character. The reforms' negative, disruptive effects are outweighed by the good new ideas they import from outside. And they too subscribe to social psychology's dominant cognitivism, and its underlying biological rationales. For these reasons, social psychologists working on fashionable topics, like attribution and social representation, are often keen to study topics of social concern, such as gender differences. But here, as elsewhere in the traditional discourse, the cognitive interpretation of psychological gender differences denies their specificity, and makes them seem unavoidable.

The alternative discourse

Social psychology's crisis is articulated more openly in a second discourse, which sets itself up against the conventional and reformist discourse, as an alternative to it. This 'alternative' discourse does not just demand a socially wider realm of study and explanation. It also insists on a method which departs from natural-scientific standards of objectivity, and which is not restricted to experiments. Such a move is specially important for a discipline like social psychology, which, in claiming to be a science, makes method its priority.

The alternative social psychological discourse addresses low-prestige subject areas outside the mainstream, like women's experiences, and leisure activities. And it tries to use ways of getting knowledge which are associated with these areas, like personal accounts and sociological analysis. I have called this 'alternative' social psychology, both because it presents definite alternatives to the mainstream discourse, and because its most obvious examples showed, after social psychology's usual cultural lag, an affinity with 'alternative' social and political movements of the 1960s. The book to which this book's own title refers, *Reconstructing Social Psychology* (Armistead 1974), is an obvious case. It questions the methodological and philosophical assumptions of traditional empirical social psychology, takes an interested but critical approach to third-force, phenomenological and ethnomethodological psychology, and tries, often within a Marxist framework, to find ways to think about human interaction and agency in the context of its social heterogeneity and complexity.

The alternative discourse of crisis is, nevertheless, tied closely to mainstream social psychology. Its 'alternatives' are attempts to enumerate all that the conventional discourse leaves out, and so it is indirectly defined by that discourse. As a result, it, too, tends to homogenise social relations. Harré's call for a social psychology of the real world, 'out in the streets, at home, in shops and cafés and lecture rooms where people really interact' (in Armistead 1974: 250), for instance, implicitly equates very different environments, across a range bounded by the experiences of academia. The alternative discourse also often replicates humanist psychology's interest in self-actualisation, and the cultural insularity of this 'middle-class leisure activity' (in Armistead 1974: 326). These limitations develop because the alternative discourse, despite its interests in the social construction of subjectivity, centres, like the mainstream discourse, on a concept of a socially modified but ultimately biological individual subject.

The commentary discourse

A third discourse of social psychological crisis exists, alongside the other two. Current, self-conscious versions of this discourse challenge the mainstream's dominant cognitivism by addressing the structure and contents of subjects' collective representations of the social world, rather than their individual cognitions of it; or by exploring mainstream social psychology's own concepts, and their historical and social determinants; or by adopting some combination of the two (e.g. Billig 1982, 1987; Henriques *et al.* 1984; Parker 1989; Potter and Wetherell 1987; Shotter 1986b). These initiatives are influenced by structuralist and post-structuralist concerns with signification's uncertain meanings, authority, and materiality, and by social psychology's own history of treating language as an index of the social relations which it neglects. Such initiatives also frequently express a commitment to reflexivity.

The third discourse of social psychological crisis occurs more widely, however, in implicit, unconscious versions. It emerges wherever social psychologists explore the structural ambiguities of the traditional discourse, rather than reforming it or producing an alternative to it. Such a discourse is often less clearly oppositional, more obviously involved with the difficulties it describes, and hence more modest, than the 'alternative' discourse. It seems to take a step backwards from it: a step marked in this book by a concern with *de*construction, rather than *re*construction. But this concern is really a step sideways, into commentary, rather than critique. This commentary discourse of social psychology does not ignore the boundaries of the mainstream discipline, as the alternative discourse does; but it questions them, and develops connections with fields close to them, like sociology, linguistics, and philosophy. Such moves are important in a discipline so preoccupied with its autonomy, yet so vaguely and controversially defined.

The commentary discourse is close to the kind of philosophical and literary critical work called deconstruction. Like deconstruction, social psychological commentary looks as if it could generate endless random readings of text – in this case, the 'texts' of behaviour and experience. But as with deconstruction, social psychological commentaries concentrate on particular, symptomatic details. This selectivity gives them a definite direction. And so they have an affirmative, as well as a sceptical effect (Derrida 1976, 1988).

No social psychological text fits exactly into the reformist, alternative or commentary discourses of crisis described above. But the rest of this chapter tries to operate broadly within the last of them, in order to give an account of the narratives which characterise each discourse, and of how these narratives' patterns of omission, contradiction, and elision can produce a kind of deconstructive commentary within all three discourses.

NARRATIVES AND SOCIAL PSYCHOLOGY

A narrative is the story of a series of events, usually in chronological order, involving descriptions of the people and other circumstances involved. Why is this a useful object of analysis? Narrative is, first of all, a form of signification, and so many interests of recent, language-oriented versions of the commentary discourse can be examined through it. Second, studying different narrative forms is a good way of questioning social psychology's shaky but fiercely-defended boundaries. So far, when social psychologists have addressed narrative, they have concentrated on its logical story-telling structures. The specificities of narrative genres, which are studied predominantly in non-psychological, literary work, have been ignored. Rhetorical forms (see Billig, Chapter 3, in this volume) with their extrapsychological affiliations, in this case with linguistics and philosophy as well as literary criticism, have been similarly neglected. If social psychologists are going to continue working on language, they will have to start looking at such nonpsychological bodies of knowledge. This is especially helpful with narratives, whose familiarity and accessibility present a particularly clear challenge to social psychology's esotericism. Third, and most importantly, specific narrative forms resemble specific approaches to social psychology in important ways. Many twentieth-century western fiction narratives have, like social psychology, been interested in individual subjectivity, and in the conflicts between this subjectivity, and the social relations in which it is embedded. This interest is expressed differently in different narrative forms. Comparisons between these forms, and different forms of social psychological narrative, produce interesting readings of social psychology's crisis.

I am going to describe three narratives of social psychological crisis: the detective story, the autobiography, and the science fiction story. These are not the only narrative forms which can be identified within social psychology. I have chosen them because of their marked relationships to particular social psychological discourses, and because a lot of work has been done on them outside psychology, in literary criticism. Much of this work resists mainstream literary theory, often from a feminist perspective; and within social psychology, too, feminist interests are becoming an increasingly frequent mode of resistance to the mainstream discipline. The special popularity and straightforwardness of these narratives is, finally, a good antidote to social psychology's theoretical isolation.

The detective narrative

The detective story is a widely-read and increasingly self-critical and self-conscious form of fiction narrative (e.g. Craig and Cadogan 1981; James 1986; Mann 1981). By setting up a problem, an unresolved crime, and resolving it, step by step, it crystallises narrative's interest in logical completeness, or closure. It also expresses a kind of social psychological concern with subjectivity, through what P. D. James (1986) describes as its recapitulation of the morality play. Like a morality play, the detective story is concerned with events to which it attributes definite meanings, rather than with inner experiences or multiple meanings. But the detective story's quest for knowledge follows events which concern the self, rather than the social body. This quest is pursued most importantly through the central figure, the detective, who furthers the narrative by discovering missing knowledge. This figure is an outsider, an enemy of criminals and, more broadly, of any moral order which permits or produces them.

Texts in the conventional social psychological discourse resemble detective stories in a number of ways. Like them, they begin with a problem, and try to investigate and resolve it logically. Introduction, method, results and discussion, strung together in this order, generate a chronological, continuous, closed narrative. Mainstream texts often display elements of the thriller's driven, concise style, especially where the topic of study has popular as well as psychological currency. Haney and Zimbardo's writing on the Stanford prison experiment is an obvious example. Bypassing any introductory theoretical review, it plunges into an account of method, delivered at thriller-level pace and force: 'The quiet of a summer morning in Palo Alto, California was shattered by a screeching squad car siren as police swept through the city, picking up college students in a mass arrest' (Haney and Zimbardo 1976:

226). This style increases the immediacy of the experimental hypothesis. It also intensifies the reformist crisis of the 'social' which is implicated in conventional social psychological research. Haney and Zimbardo's experiment was concerned not just with whether the prison role-play would work, but with the strength of social, 'situational' influences on behaviour; and the detective-story style makes both issues seem more urgent.

More general structural features of detective narratives also work within conventional social psychological texts to express their reformist discourse of crisis. Like detective stories, such texts discover knowledge about the individual subject through events, or behaviours, rather than through less certain experiences or meanings. And they, too, are preoccupied with the morality of these events. For although an experiment seems to be pursuing facts, it is committed more to the scientific process than to the facts themselves, just as a detective story is committed to pursuing justice, at the expense of confusing or extenuating aspects of the evidence. Social psychological texts often use their moral scientific authority to bid for a wide explanatory range, finding, not just scientific knowledge, but solutions to social dilemmas, in their results. The clearest examples are US texts from the 1950s, which used the moral status of experimental method to extend their experiments' conclusions on conformity, obedience, and prejudice from the laboratory, to 'society' as a whole. While such broad extrapolations are rare now, mainstream social psychological texts continue to use the moral clout of psychological science to claim a wider social expertise.

Social psychological narratives usually differ from detective stories in writing the investigator out, stating that 'an experiment was performed', for instance, rather than that 'X performed' or 'I performed' an experiment. But the authority of the absent investigator lies behind every passive textual construction. It is he or she who decides hypotheses and methods, and draws conclusions from results. The investigation tries to increase scientific order and truth at the expense of the chaos and errors in the field. In so doing, s/he becomes like the detective, the moral reformer guiding the narrative.

The detective story narrative, then, helps articulate the reformist crisis of the 'social' in the conventional discourse. It is possible to understand more of the structure of this crisis by looking at the crises in detective narratives. Like all narratives, detective stories are inconsistent and incomplete. Questions remain at the end, about clues missed as well as found, about the interpretation of facts, and about the failings as well as the successes of the investigator. These uncertainties arise from the ambiguous morality of the investigator, who struggles against criminality, yet is often complicit with the criminals scapegoated by the dominant moral order. The investigator is outside this order, but is also necessarily a part of it, reforming it by his or her opposition to its worst excesses. Often these uncertainties generate a continual moral debate within the story. This does not always create, as James (1986) suggests, a self-absorbed melancholy; often it also gives rise to a sort of mourning (Parkes 1972), involving grief, resentment, and anger at dominant discourses of justice, but also a tentative exploration of possible alternative justice systems. Such a mourning process works as a deconstruction of or commentary on the dominant storyline.

Social psychology's detective-type narratives generate similar internal commentaries. They, too, are contradictory and illogical. Methods and results constitute an inner, procedural narrative, bracketed by the theoretical outer narrative of the introduction and discussion. The text often anticipates or repeats itself. The introductory hypothesis may predict the conclusion, for example. Some narrative strands may conflict, or may not be tied up. Elements of the results may be ignored in the discussion, and mismatches between the hypothesis and its methodological operationalisation are common. As in the detective story, these ambiguities arise from a perpetual moral anxiety – in this case, about the investigation's balance between scientific and social validity, and about the investigator responsible for this balance. In another version of deconstructive mourning, the morality of science is bewailed, railed against, and continually modified and reformulated. In detective stories, the clearest example of such a process is when the investigator agonises over his or her place in the dubious justice system which the narrative explores, and speculates on other courses of action that could have been taken. This is paralleled in Milgram's (1963) and Zimbardo's (1973) exhaustive and defensive commentaries on their own ethics.

The autobiographical narrative

The second form of narrative whose relation to social psychological texts I want to examine, is that of autobiography. Autobiographical writing has often been seen as an inferior sort of literature, limited in scope, and characteristic of writers' first books, of one-book writers, and of writers who write the same book again and again. But twentieth-century western literature's concern with subjectivity often brings it close to autobiography. Structurally, this link has resulted in less logical and more psychological lines of narrative, incorporating associations, repetitions and elisions that represent conscious and unconscious psychic processes. In terms of content, the western literary mainstream has started to notice, and sometimes to include, the autobiographical voices of black people, white working-class people, and white middle-class women.

Autobiographical writing is rare in conventional social psychological texts, where its distance from objectivity, and its inability to support wide-ranging, predictive theories, tend to make it an index of failure. Even here, some autobiographical elements intrude, in opaque comments about the psychologist's role, and in fragments of qualitative data about individual subjects. But social psychologists working within the alternative discourse use their own and their subjects' autobiographical narratives more explicitly, as a way of challenging what they see as narrow empiricism and restrictive obsessions with objectivity in the conventional discourse. Harré and Secord's (1972) emphasis on self-reports, and *Reconstructing Social Psychology*'s (Armistead 1974) interest in phenomenological, ethnomethodological, and symbolic interactionist approaches, are good examples. These autobiographically-oriented narratives also allow alternative social psychology to express aspects of subjectivity which the conventional discourse's narrative structures exclude, and to increase the representation of neglected subjects. Armistead, for instance, begins *Reconstructing Social Psychology* with a chatty coming-of-age story about his difficult experiences as a psychology student and academic, which is miles from textbook introductions' standardised treatment of students' lives (see Stringer, Chapter 1, in this volume). Work on social identity, social representations, and interpretive repertoires, frequently includes quotations from individual subjects' speech or writing about their experiences. This use of autobiographical data supports the work's interest in how subjects from specific social groups, especially groups which social psychology has neglected, structure their representations of themselves and of the social relations which affect them.

Autobiographical narratives generate tensions and crises of their own (e.g. De Man 1979; Marcus 1987; Steedman 1986). They are alternatives to conventionally objective narratives, but as such, they also retain an intimate relationship with them. They often present themselves as complete or at least completely truthful accounts, for instance, as if to mimic the objectivity of conventional texts, and claim their power. 'I know this from personal experience' can sound as authoritative as 'the evidence shows this'; and a few quotations presented, in the common conference phrase, 'to give you a feel of the material', are often forced to bear the weight of a complex theory. But autobiography never sets forth experiences absolutely fully or accurately. It always expands, condenses, or displaces them. And so it oscillates between being a definitive account, and tracing out the endless uncertainties and contradictions of an individual life. Autobiographies also have to work on the unsupportable assumptions that the significations they deploy have single, direct relationships to experience and reality; and that the story of one subject's life can represent the lives of other subjects.

Similar self-deconstructing elements of commentary emerge within autobiographical social psychological narratives. Armistead's (1974) confessional words, for example, do not erase his power as an author, or his discursive power as a psychological professional. And so his confession has double meaning, affirming conventions, as well as opposing them. In contemporary, language-orientated research, quotations from subjects' own accounts often give a more complex and valuable picture than the surrounding text, and despite disclaimers, this endows them with the status of incontrovertible evidence.

Science fiction narrative

I want to look now at a third form of narrative within social psychology, the form in which elements of deconstructive commentary emerge most clearly. This is science fiction. Like the detective story, science fiction has recently received some serious critical attention (e.g. Green and Lefanu 1985; Parrinder 1980). Like both detective stories and autobiographies, it has acquired a particular twentieth-century significance as a literary way of exploring subjectivity. Even the most technologically obsessed examples of the genre relate the changed circumstances they describe, implicitly or explicitly, to their concepts of the human subject. For however rigorous science fiction aims to be in its own terms, and however many connections it alleges with scientific knowledge, it is not a science, but fiction, and this encourages it to be much more interested in subjectivity than scientific texts usually are.

Science fiction's departures from consensual knowledge about reality involve infractions of conventional narrative logic. Often, in common with much western twentieth-century writing on unconventional subjects – like a lot of early Marxist fiction, for instance – it has tried to redeem its radicalism by being conservative about narrative structure; by insisting on internal consistency, for instance. Contemporary science fiction, particularly feminist science fiction, is more stylistically adventurous. But the persuasive effect of any science fiction story depends on it maintaining strong connections with traditional narrative, and the realities it represents: connections which distinguish it from both fantasies and utopias. It ends up too far from conventional representations of reality to be taken seriously as an alternative to them, but also close enough to these representations in some ways, to be co-opted into them. This ambivalence provides a powerful means of commenting on existing narratives and reality.

Science fiction's ambivalence is a kind of speculation (Derrida 1987), a qualified, uncertain exploration beyond the conclusions derived from evidence. Psychologists have started to explore the psychological significance of such narratives (Ridgway and Benjamin 1987), but they have not addressed the science fiction aspects of psychology itself. Traditional social psychology is, in any case, opposed to science-fiction speculations. It wants to tell stories about a wholly real world, while science fiction bridges metonymically the imaginary and the real. But science-fictional speculations generate the new hypotheses, models and theories which sustain social psychology as a discipline. The mainstream discourse's denial of such speculations leaves processes like hypothesis formation in the realm of mystery, or reduces them to deduction.

Science fiction narratives are more explicitly speculative than detective stories or autobiographies, and so they articulate social psychology's crisis of the 'social' in a more consistently deconstructive way. In social psychology, they take over where detective story and autobiographical narratives leave off, and move further outside the discipline's conventional borders. They explore roles for the psychologist other than that of the detective, for instance, or introduce a speculative twist to autobiography by sketching different interpretations of the same life events. Recent work within the commentary discourse of social psychological crises develops more cautious, involuted speculations. Billig (1987), for instance, examines the rhetorical structure of psychology and its material, and leaves this new, 'antiquarian' psychological project open and unresolved.

The majority of science fiction narratives in social psychology, however, are less self-conscious and coherent. They appear briefly, alongside conventional, detective-story narratives, in texts that belong predominantly to the dominant, reformist social psychological discourse. The relative abundance and familiarity of these fragments of unconscious science fiction narrative make them the most interesting cases. A forceful example is Bem's account of gender schema theory, which, half-way through, takes what she calls a 'highly speculative' (1983: 609) turn, and starts to plot parental strategies for teaching children that sex differences, but not gender differences, are important; and for giving them alternative, subversive, sexism schemata, to inoculate them against the wider gender-schematic world. Bem sees her work as preliminary, not definitive; yet, with deliberate boldness, she wonders how such practices could be adopted more generally, and pictures the gender-aschematic future which might result. And so the paper manages to be, as she later described it, both a 'feminist utopia', and an example of 'theory-building and logical inference in an empirical science' (1984: 198, 197).

A social psychology which is really 'social' cannot be simply or solely scientific. Social psychologists might better understand and work with the crisis which this contradiction provokes, if they wrote more science fiction. A social psychological narrative would then be more like those which the science fiction writer Joanna Russ describes herself as producing: a story that can seem ridiculous, and may be derided and ignored, but that tells itself persistently to everyone, inside and outside the discipline, until, suddenly, it appears 'quaint and old-fashioned' (1985: 213). Its time has passed, and, for a different reason, it is, again, ignored.

Chapter Three

RHETORIC OF SOCIAL PSYCHOLOGY

Michael Billig

Any essay which takes as its topic 'the rhetoric of social psychology' immediately sounds like a critical challenge. The reader might reasonably expect social psychology to be attacked, as the rhetorical tricks of social psychologists are ruthlessly exposed. No doubt those social psychologists, who spend much of their professional lives conducting and teaching about experiments, will interpret this essay as an attack, and possibly they will be correct. However, the terms of the attack must be clarified. At the outset it needs to be said that the present essay does not seek to expose rhetorical tricks nor to accuse experimentalists of dishonestly manipulating language. In order to avoid misunderstanding on this score, it is important to specify what is meant by 'rhetoric', and most importantly what is not meant by the term. If this is not done, then the experimentalists might read more into the criticism than is implied, and, worse still from the point of the critic, the nature of a rhetorical analysis, and indeed of rhetoric itself, may be misunderstood.

RHETORIC AND SOCIAL PSYCHOLOGY

The word 'rhetoric' is often used as a pejorative term. To call a piece of discourse 'mere rhetoric' is to dismiss it, with the implication that the discourse contains no substance. Thus, one politician might label the speech of a rival as being 'rhetoric', and in so doing gives the impression that only empty phrases have been uttered by the rival, in contrast with one's own substantial political efforts. In this context, the accusation of being 'merely rhetorical' can carry with it a moral implication. The 'rhetorical' politician is

47

one who is deliberately using fine phrases as a camouflage, whether it be to hide incompetence, inactivity, or venality. For instance, the speech, which is accused of being 'rhetorical', might be thought to contain the sort of uplifting phrases, which might lull the audience in to thinking that the politician is actually doing something about the issues, rather than merely speaking eloquently about them. In this case, not only is the speech accused of being merely words, but the mere words are considered dishonest, for they give the impression that more than words are involved.

If the word 'rhetoric' is used in this way, then calling experimental social psychology 'rhetorical' is most certainly a strong accusation, and one that would justifiably anger experimentalists. In essence it would be alleged that social psychological writing is empty of real content, and, moreover, that social psychologists specifically choose their language to hide this poverty of content. Some critics have claimed that social psychology is 'rhetorical' in this sense. For instance, Rom Harré (1981) uses the word in this way, when he reproduces a lengthy example of social psychological writing, which is full of impressive sounding, technical jargon. Harré demystifies the jargon, in order to claim that the writer is really saying something quite banal. Not only is the writing devoid of any genuine significance, but the writer has deliberately chosen a form of expression which conceals this emptiness. Harré calls this sort of writing 'rhetorical' and he suggests that experimental social psychologists commonly write in this way. Because this writing is devoid of interesting ideas, but is clothed in the uniform of dense, scientific verbiage, it is, according to Harré, merely rhetoric. Once the rhetoric has been stripped way, nothing much remains. In consequence, a rhetorical analysis of social psychology, in this sense, would be a process of exposure. The aim would be to substitute a social psychology, which was flawed by being rhetorical, by one which was essentially free from rhetoric.

Harré's analysis assumes that 'rhetoric' is something to be avoided, for rhetoric is equated with empty phrase-making or the adornment of language, which can get in the way of the communication of meaning. Harré's rhetorician is like Plato's: a clever but morally suspect person who juggle with words to make poor ideas appear impressive. However, there is another sense to the word 'rhetoric' and in this sense a rhetorical analysis has a somewhat wider, and less accusatory, role than in Harré's sense. The term rhetoric need not be used in a derogatory manner. In fact, until the twentieth century, 'rhetoric' specifically occupied a central, and much venerated, place in western education. Every well educated person was expected to have studied the discipline known by that name, reading with respect the writings on rhetoric by Aristotle, Cicero, and Quintilian. These rhetorical writings were certainly not to be dismissed as being devoid of content.

The rhetorical classics were held to contain the essentials for instructing the arts of good speaking and good writing. In other words, rhetoric was the discipline of good communication. According to this conception of 'rhetoric', acts of communication are, and should be, rhetorical. The aim is not to reduce the rhetorical elements from communication. The accusation against experimental social psychological writing is not that it is *merely* rhetorical, but that it is *insufficiently* rhetorical, in the sense that it overlooks the essentially rhetorical aspects of communication. It will be suggested that social psychology expresses a philosophy which opposes and seeks to transcend rhetoric. By espousing such a position, social psychologists then tend to overlook the inherently rhetorical nature of the topics which they investigate as well as the rhetorical nature of the enterprise of social psychology itself.

Aristotle at the start of his *Rhetorica* defined rhetoric as being the study of the available means of persuasion (1355b). To be sure, this included the less reputable tricks which a speaker might use to impress an audience, and it would embrace the use of scientific jargon, which is designed to make readers think that the author is an incredibly clever expert. However, Aristotle dealt with far more than the stratagems by which a superficial idea can be presented as a profound one. He discussed the basic ways of arguing, to be employed by anyone wishing to convince an audience. For example, he noted that ordinary speech was different from formal logic. Normally, people do not fill their discourse with logical syllogisms, which deduce single conclusions from two separate premises. Instead, they use forms of reasoning, which Aristotle called 'enthymemic'. Although Aristotle seemed a bit confused about what constituted the basic character of an enthymeme, he suggested that it involved the assertion of a conclusion and a justification.

The study of rhetoric was a reflexive study, for the rhetorical authors, when they wrote their textbooks or delivered their lectures on rhetoric, were themselves using rhetoric. Aristotle's *Rhetorica*, based upon the afternoon seminars given to his advanced students, was itself intended to be a piece of persuasive communication. Its own mode of argument was enthymemic, as opposed to syllogistic. Similarly, Harré's debunking of the 'merely rhetorical' nature of social psychological writing was itself a piece of writing designed to persuade an audience and thereby was itself rhetorical. The present essay is, on this account, rhetorical. In short, the wider conception of rhetoric does not view rhetoric as something shameful, to be avoided by all speakers and writers. In fact, the idea of advocating the use of language as communication in a way which escapes rhetoric is seen as self-defeating, just as it would be to utter 'this is not an utterance'.

In recent years there has been an intellectual revival in the traditions of rhetorical scholarship. Habermas (1987) has discussed the deconstructionist and post-structuralist movements in modern philosophy in terms of an attempt to establish the primacy of rhetoric over logic. These modernist movements, or perhaps more accurately post-modernist movements, do not downgrade rhetorical communication as an illegitimate form of discourse, for they accept the wider conception of rhetoric itself. This sort of modernism, or post-modernism, specifically sets its face against any attempt to transcend rhetoric by seeking a higher realm of discourse, in which truths will have an absolute status, impossible in ordinary discourse. For example, post-modernists do not suggest that formal logic or mathematics can supply a higher realm of philosophical truth than can natural language. Nor is there the belief that scientific methodology can provide an escape from the reflexivity of rhetorical language. By contrast, science itself is seen as an intrinsically rhetorical, or persuasive, activity, and, consequently, a rhetorical analysis of science is not so much an exposé, but an analysis which looks at the way that scientists argue and discuss their scientific cases (Leff 1987; Rorty 1987; for examples relating to psychology, see Bazarman 1987; Potter 1988; Potter and McKinlay 1987).

The modern approach to rhetoric stresses the enthymemic aspects of rhetoric, rather than seeing rhetoric as a means of providing elegant adornment to essentially non-rhetorical discourse. Consequently, reasoned discourse is held to be rhetorical. Perelman and Olbrechts-Tyteca (1971), who have done much to lay the basis for 'the new rhetoric', have stressed the key role of justification and criticism in rhetorical communication. In persuasive communication, speakers and writers attempt to present their discourse as reasonable by giving justifications for their position and by countering objections with criticisms. In short, they produce reasoned arguments and rhetoric involves the production of argumentative discourse, which in a literal sense is justified and reasonable. Habermas (1984) develops the point by suggesting that any theory of rational communication must embody a theory of argumentation.

As far as social psychology is concerned, there are a number of implications from this link between rhetoric and argumentation. Billig (1987) has suggested that the processes of thinking are modelled upon those of argumentation: when we think we conduct internal arguments, which would not be possible were there not public arguments between people. In consequence, a number of cognitive phenomena, which psychologists have traditionally treated as individual processes, can be seen to possess argumentative aspects. Attitudes represent a case in point. They are not to be viewed primarily as personal schemata for organising information around a stimulus topic, nor as expressions of individual affect. As Lalljee *et al.* (1984) suggest, attitudes are communicative acts. Yet they are communicative with a rhetorical, or argumentative dimension, for they are rhetorical stances taken in matters of public controversy (Billig 1988a and 1988b; Billig *et al.* 1988). As such, justifications and criticisms are very much intrinsic to attitudes. When one expresses an attitude *in favour* of a particular position, one is expected not only to justify that position enthymemically, but one is also criticising the counter-attitude. For instance, a central part of expressing an attitude in opposition to capital punishment is opposing critically the arguments of the counter-position, which advocates the death penalty. In other words, attitudes are held in a general context of public controversy, which argumentatively pits stance and counter-stance, justification and criticism against each other.

There is an implication here about how to understand reasoned discourse. It is tempting for psychologists to approach the problem of meaning in terms of information processing or affective state:

the meaning of an attitude or belief is to be based upon the function that it serves for organising the individual's stimulus world, or upon a hypothesised inner motivational state. By contrast, the rhetorical position suggests that an argumentative meaning must be sought for expressions of attitude. To understand the attitude, one must place it alongside the counter-attitude; and to understand a justification, one must search for the possible or actual criticisms which the speaker is seeking to deflect. In this respect, a rhetorical analysis explores the meaning of a piece of discourse by locating that discourse within its context of controversy, for the meaning of the discourse is contained in its rhetorical relation to the counter-discourses.

All this is relevant for any rhetorical analysis of social psychology itself, for it sets up the basic question to be asked by any such rhetorical analysis. When faced by the textbooks and the journals of social psychology, with their specialised vocabularies and their descriptions of the strange rituals of experimentation, one might ask 'what is the meaning of all this activity?' The answer is not to be found merely by examining the motives, laudable or otherwise, of the practitioners of social psychology; nor is it to be discovered by looking at the stylistic qualities to be found in their discourse. Instead, the argumentative context of social psychology must be sought. In consequence, the fundamental rhetorical question is 'what is this social psychological discourse arguing against?'

SOCIAL PSYCHOLOGY AND COMMON SENSE

A short, and deliberately over-simplified, answer is that contemporary social psychology, considered as a single activity, constitutes an argument against common sense. The experiments, in which college sophomores are lied to and then have a choice between alternatively strange reactions, are not to be dismissed as meaningless. Nor, because their reports are composed in a singularly graceless language, which often expresses a myopic vision of the world, should they be considered as lacking any philosophy, or argumentative purpose. The experiments are justified by a wider argument, and in turn they are cited as the rhetorical justifications for that argument. At the basis of that argument is the contention that ordinary common sense is unsatisfactory and that social psychologists must labour hard to correct its imperfections, or, better still, to replace it by a new form of knowledge. Experiments are producing the statistically significant data which will provide the elements for the new, improved, uncommon sense.

The topics of social psychology are those which are covered by common sense. Students studying the discipline are introduced to issues, about which they already have opinions, such as, for example: How do people make good impressions an each other? Why do people get angrily violent? Do people always do what they say they will do? To all these social psychological questions, it is possible to give ordinary non-specialist answers, which are quite reasonable but owe none of their reasonableness to the technical journals. Ordinary people answering the broad questions, which professional social psychologists have addressed, can draw upon their own experiences and, most importantly, upon the collective experiences contained within common sense. They have a store of collectively shared lay theories, or what are sometimes called social representations (Jodelet 1984; Moscovici 1984a; Moscovici 1984b; Moscovici 1987; for criticisms of the notion of social representations, see, *inter alia*, Potter and Litton 1985; Potter and Wetherell 1987; McKinlay and Potter 1987).

The situation is quite different from most other academic disciplines. The ordinary non-specialist is not expected to have lay opinions about the structural form of neutrons, protozoa, or *A Midsummer Night's Dream*. In few other disciplines do teachers feel the need to warn first year students against answering examination questions on the basis of common sense: candidates, if faced by the question 'Why do people fall in love?', should put aside their previous knowledge and should concentrate upon newly acquired information about experiments. Students are not warned against common sense because social psychologists are claiming to have discovered dark continents of hidden psychic forces. For example, psychoanalysts often addressed common sense issues, but claimed that the common sense answers were unsatisfactory, because in ordinary life people were unaware of the operations of the unconscious. It has always been a part of psychoanalytic theory, not merely to claim the existence of a hidden psychic force, which explains psychological reality, but also to explain why that force has remained hidden.

However, social psychologists do not criticise common sense

because the latter has ignored the vital substrate of psychic reality. In fact, the argument against common sense is not based upon an alleged empirical finding. It is a philosophical argument, which would still be made, regardless of whether the experimental results fall one side or the other of the conventional boundary dividing the significant result from the non-significant one. The argument is that common sense is inherently suspect, because it is unscientific. This argument was clearly expressed, for example, in Fritz Heider's *Psychology of Interpersonal Relations* (1958), which advocated a 'naïve' or 'common sense' psychology . However, the naïve psychology which Heider advocated was not one which would respect ordinary common sense. It was naïve in that it took ordinary common sense, or naïve perceptions, as its subject matter. Heider proposed that social psychologists should examine how ordinary people make sense of their world. However, this examination was not itself to be naïve, but sought to transcend the naivety of its subject matter.

This desire to transcend the naivety of common sense is expressed in the introductory chapters of most textbooks in social psychology. For instance, it can be seen in a book by two modern cognitive social psychologists, who have attempted to bring Heider's influential psychology up-to-date. Fiske and Taylor (1984) write on the first page of *Social Cognition* that research on social cognition can be conducted by asking people how they make sense of others. However, the information collected is not merely to be left to speak for itself. It must be tested for accuracy. A great deal of cognitive social psychological research has been devoted to showing how inaccurate naïve perceivers are in the way that they form their expectations about the world (i.e. Hamilton and Trolier 1986; Nisbett and Ross 1980; Tversky and Kahneman 1980). Kelley's work on attribution theory assumes that ordinary perceivers assign causes to events using strategies, which are crude versions of the more sophisticated analyses of variance techniques used by professional social psychologists (Kelley 1972; Kelley and Michela 1980). This sort of work contains an argument against common sense, for the biases and inaccuracies of naïve perceivers are compared unfavourably with the rationality of the scientific expert. Yet common sense is not merely to be dismissed because it might be wrong. Even if correct, it cannot be accepted unmodified. Fiske and Taylor state: 'if people are right, one can build formal theories by making their insights scientific, by pulling together patterns across many people's intuitions' (Fiske and Taylor 1984: 1). In other words, right or wrong, common sense is to be transcended by a new form of knowledge. At best it can provide a preliminary step to a scientific reconstruction. At worst, it is an erroneous obstruction. Either way, common sense is unsatisfactory as it stands.

One reason why common sense is held to be unsatisfactory is that it contains so many contradictions. This view is often expressed in the textbooks, which feel the need to express a justification for the whole subject. A frequent argument is to suggest that common sense is confused, because it contains contrary maxims. For instance, social psychology textbooks often point to the contradiction between 'absence makes the heart grow fonder' and 'out of sight out of mind' (see Billig 1987: 205 ff. for details). It is not suggested that experimentation will reveal one maxim to be completely correct and the other incorrect. Both have elements of truth, but the existence of contrary, but equally reasonable, truths is held to be unsatisfactory. Something must be done to sort out this state of affairs. Therefore, it is claimed that detailed experimentation will tell us the limits of the truths of contrary maxims; they will specify the situations when the one is right and the situations when the other is. Thus science will clear up the confusions of common sense and allow 'unfounded speculation' to be replaced by 'orderly and precise experimentation' (Baron, Byrne, and Griffit 1974: 2).

There is a further point to note about the social psychological critique of common sense. It is based on the notion that truth must be unitary and agreed upon. It contains what Nelson, Megill, and McCloskey (1987: 11)have called 'the vision of a single, certain, natural and rational order'. The vision contains an implicit critique against rhetoric, which accepts that there can, and indeed must, be open-ended contrary truths (Perelman 1979; Rorty 1987; Billig 1987). It has been suggested that the contrary elements of common sense, far from being an impediment to ordinary life, actually are necessary for ordinary thought (Billig *et al.* 1988). Because common sense contains contrary elements people can argue, using common sense, and, indeed, they can think by arguing with themselves. In consequence, it is the contradictions of common sense which permit the existence of what Moscovici

(1983) has called 'the thinking society' (see Billig, in press, for an elaboration of this argument). By contrast, the contradictions of common sense are presented by scientific social psychologists as a challenge and an obstacle. The social psycho- logical aim of clearing up the contradictions of common sense is tantamount to a wish for the end of argumentation. Matters of con- troversy, which can be argued about, and for which justifications can be given on both sides, will be finally settled by a unitary, agreed scientific truth.

SCIENCE IN ACTION

In practice the scientific activity of social psychologists has not succeeded in clearing up the messy confusions of common sense. The dream of producing clear psychological principles each neatly tied to different sorts of situation has not been realised. Instead, an intricate and sprawling subject has been created, whose own internal theoretical structure is every bit as contradictory as common sense. This can be illustrated briefly by considering one of the major trends in social psychological research during the 1960s and 1970s, which went under the general, and rather misleading, heading of 'risky-shift' research (for comparatively recent reviews of this research tradition, see Doise and Moscovici 1984; Fraser and Foster 1982).

A vast amount of experimental research was provoked by a commonsensical question: do groups of people tend to make riskier or more cautious decisions than do solitary individuals? Common sense maxims and observations suggested that answers could be given either way. However, social psychologists decided that the question needed answering definitively with experimental evidence. Therefore, an experimental paradigm was constructed, in which groups and individuals discussed and made decisions about hypothetical risk-taking situations. Initial results suggested that groups were riskier than individuals (i.e. Wallach, Kogan, and Bem 1962). Various explanations were formulated to suggest why groups should show this propensity to risk-taking (Brown 1965). However, the simple social psychological law, linking enhanced risk-taking to group situations, did not remain intact for long. Soon experimental evidence was produced to show that sometimes groups could be more cautious than individuals, and, thus, there was a cautious-shift, to match the risky-shift (Fraser, Gouge, and Billig 1971). Explanations and psychological principles were formulated to explain why groups could be more risky, less risky and just the same as individuals.

Later, it was suggested that the shifts had nothing to do with risk or caution, but that there was a general principle that groups become more extreme than individuals: they polarise individual tendencies, whether towards conservatism or towards risk (Moscovici and Zavalloni 1969). Just as the original risky-shift phenomenon provoked numerous experiments, so too did the phenomenon of polarisation. And just as this research gave rise to a process which was the reverse of the original process, so too did the polarisation research: depolarisation was announced. And again it became a matter of discovering the situations to which the process or its opposite applied. As Fraser and Foster have written:

> Now that sufficient evidence has been accumulated to support the polarization hypothesis, greater attention can be given to the fact that it may occur only in particular conditions and that other conditions may produce depolarization instead.
>
> *(Fraser and Foster 1982: 482)*

By the time of depolarisation, however, the popularity of the risky shift area of research has declined. When there was a chance that a clear psychological principle might be discovered, the area attracted considerable interest and research effort. The result has been a proliferation of findings, so that the reviews of the research now creak under the weight of accumulated experimental evidence, contrary psychological principles and claims about special circumstances. Far from anything having been made more orderly, the result is greater complexity and diminishing theoretical interest. Nor have any of the basic questions been resolved, except that complexity, based on contrary principles, has been found where social psychology, but not necessarily common sense, seemed to have expected simplicity. And because the whole area by now lost any neat theoretical shape, the sharp experimentalists have moved on to other issues.

The pattern is not one, which is peculiar to the area of group decision-making, but has been found many times in the recent history of social psychology. A seemingly simple psychological principle occasions a burst of research activity, which then in its turn produces the discovery of the reverse principle. Research on the reinforcing qualities of rewards has been countered by research on intrinsic justification, in which rewards lessen the chance of behaviour being repeated; research about attitudes giving rise to behaviour has been followed by studies showing the reverse process, as behaviour is shown to produce attitudes; studies revealing people to avoid inconsistent information are followed by those in which people seek out such information; studies showing people having a propensity to explain events in terms of personal, rather than situational, qualities are then countered by studies revealing an opposing propensity. In each case, a simple theory, or psychological principle, is confronted by the opposite theory, or principle. And, in each case, both principles have their respective empirical justifications and, rhetorically speaking, are quite reasonable.

In point of fact, the above description is far too simplified, for it only mentions very broad psychological principles. On a detailed level, minor psychological principles find themselves qualified by their opposites. The issue, then, is not to prove whether either principle is wholly correct, but to search for the situations which are relevant to either. For example, researchers might conduct studies to demonstrate when either polarisation or depolarisation will occur. The researcher, having conducted an experiment, will then claim that a particular principle is relevant to this sort of situation. In making this claim, the researcher is stating another principle: i.e. in situations, containing characteristic X, one will find depolarisation. The researcher will not leave matters there, but will offer a reason, or more typically a new technical term, to say why X gives rise to depolarisation. This, on a very detailed level, will be another psychological principle, and will be vulnerable to qualification from an opposite principle. As likely as not, an ingenious experimenter will design a study, whose results predictably contradict the principle, and suggest an opposing principle to explain why sometimes polarisation occurs in some situations bearing the characteristic X. In its turn, this new principle will be qualified by further experimentation. This process is potentially infinite, for there is an infinity of different situations to which the opposing principles can be applied.

The net result is a growing complexity of social psychological research. Moreover, areas of research, like the risky shift, are not abandoned by researchers because the problems have been solved. In fact, few of the problems are solved. Instead the number of problems becomes multiplied and their range becomes increasingly restricted. And as the interesting common sense problem becomes fragmented into these potentially infinite chippings, so suddenly a fresh problem takes the attention. A new social psychological breakthrough will be announced. Then, the process from the simple, easily comprehended idea, to diverse and contradictory qualifications will be repeated. The net result is that the more comprehensive textbooks become ever more complex and their writers claim that this complexity is the real discovery of social psychology.

The social psychological theories and findings do not form an orderly picture, but there is a sprawling mass of conflicting principles and research findings. No simple laws are permitted to stand on their own, but each law provokes an equally reasonable reaction. In this respect, the uncommon sense of social psychology resembles the more ordinary common sense, which it seeks to replace. 'Shift-to-risk' and 'shift-to-conservatism', 'group polarisation' and 'group depolarisation' indicate pairs of principles, just like the maxims of common sense: 'absence makes the heart grow fonder' and 'out of sight out of mind', 'many hands make light work' and 'too many cooks spoil the broth', 'nothing ventured nothing gained' and 'look before you leap', etc. Nor have the infinitude of social situations been so classified that to each can be unarguably affixed the relevant psychological principle.

The maxims of common sense provide the basis for arguments in ordinary life, or, to use the jargon of classical rhetoric, they are the argumentative *common-places*, simply because they are generally held to be reasonable and conflict with each other (Billig 1987; Billig 1988c; Billig *et al.* 1988). If common sense, then, has an argumentative structure, in that it contains reasonable but conflicting elements, then so does social psychology. One might say, that social psychology, in common with common sense, possesses an argumentative structure. Social psychologists, rather than abolishing argumentation in their discipline, are caught up in an argumentative context, as each experiment, and its justificatory principle, argues against the counter principle. As a result, the argument against common sense possesses the structure of ever increasing internal arguments. No end is in sight as social psychologists are unwillingly caught up in their rhetorical activities of argumentation. In short, for all their zeal, they have not succeeded in planting the orderly Eden, whose sense of harmonious agreement would install tranquillity upon the ruins of the rhetorical Babel.

Chapter Four

THE RHETORIC OF PSEUDOSCIENCE

Celia Kitzinger

Pseudoscience is would-be 'science' that fails to live up to the lofty ideals of True Science – and there's a lot of it about. Entire disciplines and areas of study have been described as 'pseudo-science', including astrology (Furfey 1971: 204), the IQ controversy (Blum 1978), Skinnerian psychology (Machan 1974), bonding theory (Arney 1982), research on the paranormal (Hines 1988), and the whole of social psychology itself, often 'seen as a trivial pseudo-science that expends a great deal of effort describing or proving what we already know' (Furnham 1983). The label 'pseudoscience' is commonly believed to have a powerful discrediting effect: it is generally thought that research findings which are successfully attacked as pseudoscientific lose their legitimacy as privileged knowledge, and fear of this label is such that we recently witnessed 'the unusual sight of the many UK universities anxious *not* to be given the half million pounds of the Koestler bequest to establish a chair of parapsychology, lest they be tarred with the brush of giving house room to pseudo-science' (Wallis 1985).

Over the past few decades, many radical, feminist and humanistic writers have attacked the 'pseudoscientific' nature of the psychological theories used to legitimate oppressive practices. Studies of race and IQ have been dismissed as 'pseudoscientific racism' (Fryer 1987); studies purporting to demonstrate women's emotional volatility are 'pseudoscientific' (Steinem 1983: 185), and Eysenck's work on personality constitutes yet another example of 'pseudoscience' (Ingleby 1974: 316). The proposed new entry to the American Psychiatric Association's Diagnostic and Statistical Manual, 'self-defeating personality', is intended to describe the

61

person who deliberately chooses mistreatment, failure and humiliation; it has been criticised as a diagnosis likely to be used particularly against women victims of domestic violence and attacked as being 'without any adequate scientific basis' (Franklin 1987). It is, some say, 'pseudoscience' which allegedly demonstrates the hereditability of IQ, the moral inferiority of women and the pathology of homosexuals: it is pseudoscience that proves trade unionism to be against nature, or which relates juvenile delinquency to maternal employment outside the home. Pseudoscience is bad science, false science, erroneous science, science marred by fundamental flaws, science that is only pretending to be scientific, pop science, ethnoscience, scientism, science harnessed to political causes, ideology masquerading under the name of science. In summary, racist, sexist, heterosexist and class biased research is often described by its opponents as 'pseudoscientific': at worst, like Cyril Burt's work on IQ, it is deliberately fraudulent; more usually it is merely influenced by the personal convictions of the researcher or the social stereotypes of the culture, and marked by experimental bias, inadequate sampling techniques, lack of control groups, conclusions that are unwarranted by the data, and by a failure of objectivity.

When an author attempts to persuade readers that a particular piece of research is pseudoscientific and that its alleged results cannot, therefore, be taken seriously, that author is engaged in what I call 'the rhetoric of pseudoscience'. Rhetoric, in this sense, is language designed to persuade and seduce (see Billig's discussion, Chapter 3, in this volume): it may be flowery and eloquent or succinct and straightforward; it may be dishonestly self-serving or offered in good faith; it may take the form of poetry or of mathematical formulae; it may be truthful or dishonest, empty of real meaning or rich with ideas – what all rhetoric has in common is an attempt to persuade. The rhetoric of pseudoscience constitutes an attempt to persuade the reader that certain alleged findings should not be believed. For example:

> Despite the neutral position they attempted to assume, most of the scientists believed Blacks to be inferior to whites. When the evidence appeared to contradict these beliefs, they sought to rationalise it away.
>
> (Jones 1973)

Post natal depression is not a 'scientific' term but an ideological one. It mystifies the real social and medical factors that lead to mothers' unhappiness.

(*Oakley 1979*)

Many psychiatrists, by searching for the 'causes' of gayness and then inventing 'cures' reinforce the myth that homosexuals are sick and deviant. (Actually there are psychological studies which show gays to have personalities which are, on the average, at least as well, and perhaps better, integrated and more flexible than those of non-gays).

(*Goodman et al. 1983: 18*)

In these examples, the writers argue that what appears to be supported by science is in fact based only on social beliefs, ideology and myth: evidence which contradicts these myths and stereotypes has been mystified or rationalised away. True science would describe the nature of oppression and demonstrate the equality (or even superiority) of the oppressed.

The rhetoric of pseudoscience is very attractive to many people because it appears to offer a legitimate and intelligible language with which to discredit unpalatable or oppressive research findings. It is sometimes suggested that if only we can demonstrate that a given assertion lacks scientific authority, we can remove its credibility: it will be demoted from fact to fallacy or from truth to hypothesis. As a result, a great deal of feminist social psychology has been devoted to pointing out the pseudoscientific nature of allegedly 'objective' research saturated with male perspectives and values. Such critiques have led many feminists to advocate a stricter adherence to True Science and empiricist methodologies, and to demand that researchers pay more attention to the biasing effects of personal values, build into their research designs increasing numbers of variables (including gender), employ more rigorous sampling procedures and so on (see Harding 1986). 'It is not the scientific method *per se* that we criticise,' says the Brighton Women and Science Group (1980: 4), 'but the distortion of that method in the service of particular ideologies.'

But while some feminists have tried to replace pseudoscience with True Science, other feminists have begun to question the whole nature of science itself, rendering problematic the concept of objective knowledge and the special status of scientific methodologies in pursuing it: this means that the distinction between pseudo- and true science is erased as True Science loses the special claim to represent incontestable knowledge that otherwise serves as its distinguishing characteristic. My discussion of the rhetoric of pseudoscience arises out of the latter position. The argument of this chapter is that radical researchers should eschew altogether the rhetoric of pseudoscience. I offer three overlapping reasons in support of this argument. First, contrary to many people's expectations, demonstrating that a piece of research is pseudoscientific does *not* seem to work as a method of discrediting it: consequently, there is no point in employing the rhetoric of pseudoscience as it does not achieve our aim. Second, I will show how the rhetoric of pseudoscience is institutionalised within psychology and constitutes part of the ritual of academic psychological writing, such that, in using the rhetoric of pseudoscience, we are participating in the production of normal science, rather than presenting a challenge to it. Third, and most importantly, I will show that when we use the rhetoric of pseudoscience to dismiss the research of our ideological or political opponents, any short-term victory we may (possibly) achieve is gained only at the cost of a much more damaging concession – a concession that positivist–empiricist science does indeed have privileged access to true knowledge: in so doing we reinforce and legitimate the power of social science. Finally, I will illustrate these points with reference to the research on lesbianism and male homosexuality, and argue that it is counterproductive for radical psychologists to use arguments which rely on the concept of pseudoscience. Instead of perpetuating the pseudo/true science dichotomy in our own work, we need to deconstruct this traditional distinction. It is not pseudoscience but science itself which we should challenge.

First, on a purely pragmatic level, there are serious doubts about the effectiveness of the rhetoric of pseudoscience as a method of dismissing research findings. The professional psychological literature is full of unsubstantiated claims presented as verified fact and alleged 'findings' which have been dismissed as pseudo-scientific by many well-known and respected psychologists: 'inconsistency, lack of scientific proof, and obvious elimination of critical data are no obstacles to the acceptance of a paradigm or a method' (Lévy-Leboyer 1988). Consequently, even if radicals were able to demonstrate, unequivocally, that a particular model, theory, test or methodology is fundamentally pseudoscientific, there are no guarantees that such evidence will lead to it being expunged from the scientific canon. If the grosser examples of racism and sexism have disappeared from psychology it is more likely to be because they became socially and politically unacceptable than because they have been scientifically disproved. Several reviewers have illustrated the prevalence of pseudoscience in the core textbooks and journals of the social scientific disciplines. One researcher quotes a range of introductory psychology textbooks which claim that women are capable of making finer visual colour discriminations than men, a common belief in western cultures, but a statement for which there is apparently no empirical evidence; the textbooks, nonetheless, 'report this as fact citing either no references or tangential references which don't in fact support their claim' (Reynolds 1966). Another candidate for the label of 'pseudoscience' (also frequently quoted in introductory textbooks) is the Hawthorne data, reanalysis of which has shown 'a vast discrepancy between evidence and conclusions', such that one researcher felt compelled to contemplate 'the gnawing possibility that, if anyone were to take the trouble, the same results might obtain to the reanalysis of the data basic to all of our classic empirical monographs' (Deutscher 1968). This seems not unlikely as, on reanalysis by other researchers, the data published in professional psychology journals is frequently found to involve 'gross errors' (e.g. Wolins 1962), and several psychologists have suggested that work known to be flawed will nonetheless be published as long as it is 'interesting' (e.g. Davis 1971). The well-known Asch effect (a demonstration of social conformity), also typically presented in psychology textbooks as a basic universal demonstration of the way people are, is another alleged example of 'pseudoscience': it was found to be unreplicable in America just twenty years later, and the sole British study in existence found that on only one out of 396 trials did a subject join the erroneous majority (Perrin and Spencer 1980). Until at least forty years after its invention, research projects continued to use the discredited Bogardus social distance scale (a fact described as 'a shocking condemnation of our professional craft' [Lastrucci 1970]), and journals still accept and publish studies of authoritarianism resting on an invalid F scale, studies of 'human relations' resting on the invalid Hawthorne scale, and opinion and attitude research which has been rigorously criticised for decades (Deutscher 1968). Far from being relegated to the dustbin, 'pseudoscience' is incorporated into and forms a fundamental part of psychology today. The claim that, historically, science develops through a process of rejecting pseudoscience and building on truly scientific and empirically sound research has been described as 'a distortion of the historical record so extreme as to approach caricature' (Farley and Geison 1974).

This widespread retention of pseudoscience is partly due to the fact that if all of it *were* to be expunged there would be precious little psychology left. The idealised norms and practices of True Science are so lofty, its standards so elevated, that the pedestrian offerings of actual scientists rarely or never achieve them. Each person's 'science' is someone else's 'pseudoscience'. Which samples of 'pseudoscience' are retained and which rejected depends on the personal preferences of individual psychologists and on the requirements of psychology as an institution. On an individual level, pseudoscience is research whose findings you dislike. It is common to find that people are far less critical of research logic and methodology when the conclusions are ones with which they are in agreement. In one study, 75 reviewers from a respected academic journal – *Journal of Applied Behavior Analysis* – were sent identical manuscripts on a controversial topic in behaviour modification, some with results favourable to behaviour modification, the others with the curves and data tables reversed so that the conclusions challenged behaviour modification. When reviewers read manuscripts in which the data supported their own perspective they rated its methodology as 'adequate' or 'excellent' and recommended that it be published; when the same procedures yielded results that challenged their own perspective, the method was rated as 'inadequate' and the reviewers recommended rejection of the manuscript (Mahoney 1977). The prevalence of pseudoscience is, then, partly a consequence of disagreement amongst social scientists as to the desirable outcome of research, so that each side in any controversy is especially sensitive to the methodological shortcomings of its rivals. In fact much of the research widely believed to be 'pseudoscience' is at the very least equal to its 'scientific' successor in terms of positivist methodology: the work of phrenologists was 'often technically extremely proficient and could not be obviously distinguished as methodologically inferior to that of their opponents' (Wallis 1985), while 'the best of modern parapsychology comprises some of the most rigorously controlled and methodologically sophisticated work in the sciences' (Collins and Pinch 1979: 243-4).

On a social level, the scientific status of research seems to be of less concern to psychology as an institution than is its ideological and political function, and if 'pseudoscience' serves a useful ideological function it is retained – perhaps in an adapted or disguised form. The survival of the MMPI despite the 'awesome empirical case against it' is attributed by Rogers (1980) as due to its useful function in reifying the 'psychiatrist as master' ideology. A similar case can be made for the Kohlbergian cognitive developmental model of morality which has been around for more than a quarter of a century; each critical onslaught is met with minor modifications to the scoring manual and the model retained because it serves the useful purpose of reifying and supporting the liberal ideology of Western democracy. In summary, if certain methods, tests or results serve the vested interests of social science as an institution, then no amount of criticism of their 'pseudoscientific' status will expunge them. Instead of allowing ourselves to be deflected into arguments about scientific evidence, validity, reliability and methodological adequacy, radicals would do better to attack those vested interests directly. Instead of engaging in a doomed attempt to reconstruct 'pseudoscience' for our own purposes, we should be deconstructing the pseudoscience/true science dichotomy and exposing the reliance of True Science on the ideas, ideologies, and material interests of those who author it.

Second, contrary to the claims sometimes made, radical researchers using the rhetoric of pseudoscience are doing nothing new, nothing radical, nothing that cannot be readily incorporated into institutionalised experimental psychology. Radicals sometimes claim that by exposing the pseudoscientific errors of oppressive research they are 'beating psychology at its own game': in exposing its biases, and drawing attention to its patent shortcomings and failings, they are undermining the established power of science. Even some sociologists of science have claimed that 'most practising scientists regard the existence of error as a threat to the enterprise of science' (Gilbert and Mulkay 1982). This is simply not the case. Pseudoscience is *not* a threat, or even an embarrassment, to the advocates of true science; on the contrary, it is an essential part of the institutionalised support structure of science itself.

Psychology actively encourages its disciples to be alert for pseudoscience, and to be sceptical of the claims of any research to 'truly scientific' status: one of the venerated norms of True Science is 'organised scepticism' (Merton 1968). Science is represented as a self-correcting institution. No one scientist can simply decide to be 'objective' – rather objectivity is the product of a scientific community which monitors and assesses the work of its members: 'objectivity is a matter of the continuous collective correction of each individual sociologists' work by others' (Banks 1979). The unveiling of pseudoscience is thus constructed as an essential part of the progress of True Science. In this way, radicals who expose the research of their colleagues as pseudoscientific are conforming precisely to the rules of scientific endeavour and, in arguing that other people are not playing by the rules, they necessarily reinforce the validity of those rules. In that sense, we cannot 'beat psychology at its own game'. Psychology as an institution is not deeply concerned about which of a rather limited range of possible theories 'wins' – whether the cognitive developmentalists beat the social learning theorists, or the behaviouristic approach defeats the humanistic approach. What matters is that the game should go on. The game of science is constructed as an intellectual battleground where you grapple with opposing theories or results according to the accepted rules and rituals of science as it depends upon controversy and disagreement about a small range of strictly circumscribed issues: rival claims and counterclaims of 'pseudoscientific' activity sustain science as an institution. Socialisation into the scientific community is a process of learning how to be critical about other people's science, how to evaluate theories according to the accepted rules, how to locate holes in the existing literature so that you can confidently end a literature review with the suggestion that 'more research needs to be done . . . .', and hence obtain a research grant, a Ph. D., a fellowship, or another publication. As the first chapters of Ph.D. theses and the introductory sections of research papers illustrate, scientists are required ruthlessly to expose and subject to detailed analysis the pseudoscience of their disciplines as a suitable curtain-raiser for their own superior 'truly scientific' research. One cynic offers this advice to ambitious scientists in search of status and prestige:

> Be prepared to point out glaring deficiencies of other studies competitive with your own .... Slash or at least slightly wound the competition in introductions or literature review sections of papers [...] and make it clear that the 'others' are interlopers and usurpers, deficient in data, naïve in conclusions and sterile in concepts.
>
> (*Sinderman 1982: 16*)

In sum, there is no need to turn to radicals, or to the writings of a sceptical public, in order to find vivid and detailed documentation of the failings of science. The most vicious attacks on pseudoscience, the most conscientious discussions of its errors, the most prolonged complaints about its pervasiveness come from mainstream social scientists themselves. Denunciation of the opposition as 'pseudoscientific' is nothing new; in fact, it constitutes part of the accepted formula for writing academic papers. When we engage in the rhetoric of pseudoscience, far from contributing to the radical deconstruction of psychology, we are participating in the production of normal positivist–empiricist science. Rather than attacking 'pseudoscience' for failing to be True Science, we should be deconstructing True Science itself.

The third and most important reason why radicals should avoid the rhetoric of pseudoscience is because it reaffirms the idealised norms of positivist–empiricist (True) science. Pseudoscience is used to sell true science in the way that Brand X is used to sell New Improved Wonder Washing Powder: pseudoscience leaves dirty rings around the collar – True Science washes whiter. In his book *Winning the Games Scientists Play*, Sinderman (1982: 198) describes the 'relish with which the scientific community exposes phonies'. Deliberately fraudulent science is particularly useful to the scientific community because it allows the presentation of such activities not as intrinsic to science but as alien contaminations. Fraudulent scientists are scapegoated so that the purity of the scientific community can be preserved, presenting it as a society of dedicated searchers after truth, harbouring only the occasional 'false prophet' (Kohn 1986) or 'betrayer of truth' (Broad and Wade 1983). As one critic points out, 'the revelation that Burt faked his data serves to exempt the rest of science from social criticism, as if the problem were a few racist apples in the barrel, or "ideology" polluting an otherwise neutral science' (Levidow 1987: 43). (The Register of Chartered Psychologists, introduced in the United Kingdom in 1988, also serves to create the necessary framework for future distinctions between *bona fide* 'real psychologists', whose names appear on the Charter, and unscrupulous charlatans masquerading as psychologists, the 'pseudopsychologists'.)

Most pseudoscience, however, is described not as deliberately fraudulent, but as simply bearing witness to human failure adequately to serve the hard master of empirical science. Defenders of true science describe pseudoscience as a testament to human struggle towards the high ideals we set ourselves. In Karl Popper's words: 'Admittedly, science suffers from our human fallibility, like every other human enterprise [...] But we *learn* from our mistakes: scientists turn our fallibility into objectively testable *conjectural knowledge*' (Popper 1988). As the following examples illustrate, even our errors can be put to good use: 'no experiment is ever a complete failure. It can always be used as a bad example' (Carson's Consolation 1978):

> Even though the monograph has little scientific merit, it is of didactic value and illustrates many of the errors that can enter into case studies.
>
> (*Rachman 1978*)

> One of the more important purposes [of this volume] is to train the reader to be a skeptical and discerning consumer of past, current and future literature on mental health and homosexuality. To this end, a number of otherwise seriously flawed studies may be put to use as illustrations of poor technique or methodological problems.
>
> (*Gonsiorek 1982*)

The accusation of 'pseudoscience' thus affords the scientist the opportunity to restate and reinforce the norms of scientific methodology, so flagrantly breached by the pseudoscientists. The implication is that if only the correct scientific procedures are followed, then truth (or at least knowledge increasingly approximate to reality) will be revealed.

Compared with the physical sciences, the social sciences have little in the way of incontestable truths or concrete knowledge: 'the difference between what sociologists know and what everybody else knows is practically nil. This certainly isn't the state of affairs in the real sciences such as physics' (Mazure 1968). But our literature reviews, while lamenting the poor quality of the past research are typically confident that future work will bring significant improvement: 'surely almost all the good work and brilliant innovations in social psychology', say the authors of one textbook, 'are yet to come' (Rosenblatt and Miller 1972: 72). The story of scientific progress is told as ever onward and upward toward enlightenment. The 'up the mountain' research saga (Rorty 1980) depicts the apparent progress of social science from the dark ages of conformity to the dictates of social convention and religious prejudice, forward into the brave new world of scientific rigour and objectivity. The history of the notion of 'masturbatory insanity' is often told in this way (Hare 1962); so too are the histories of research on blacks and women, which progress from the early depiction of blacks and women as inferior beings, through a focus on them as being the innocent victims of prejudice, to the now common portrayal of racism and sexism as part of pathological personality patterns. The allegorical meaning of these histories is clear: past research findings symbolise human error, ignorance and taboo, current research findings represent the application of reason, logic and rationality, and psychology itself symbolises the triumphant emergence of scientific objectivity, out of a sea of bias, prejudice, and ideology.

Just as the heretic can only be defined in relation to a body of faith from which she or he dissents, so too pseudoscience is dependent on a concept of true science as objective, disinterested, uncontaminated by ideologies and free of the taint of prejudice. In complaining that a particular piece of (pseudo) science merely reproduces cultural stereotypes, we imply that true science is (or can be, or should be) able to transcend these contaminating influences, that science is privileged knowledge which, despite its alleged deficiencies in this particular instance can and should be divorced from ordinary everyday conceptualisations of the world. The rhetoric of pseudoscience thus functions as a jeremiad – a

71

rhetorical form devoted to bringing good out of evil: out of the pseudoscience of the past, out of the pseudoscientific moralising and politicising of the present, a new truly scientific psychology is waiting to be born.

My central argument, then, is that when radicals use the rhetoric of pseudoscience we uphold and reinforce the positivist–empiricist model of science as a privileged form of knowledge distinct from commonsense versions of reality and free from political influences. Let me illustrate this argument with specific reference to one particular area of research which has attracted accusations of pseudoscience in epic proportions – the research on lesbianism and male homosexuality. The following discussion is drawn from the more detailed review of this literature in Kitzinger (1987).

Despite more than fifteen years of 'gay affirmative' research from radical social scientists concerned to counter the traditional social scientific image of lesbians and gay men as sick and perverted, the pathological model is still considered respectable by some researchers (e.g. Kronemeyer 1980; Moberly 1983). In the last two or three years this model has appeared to gain popularity in scientific writing – not because more evidence has appeared to support it, but because of the increasingly repressive political climate, and the moral panic about AIDS. From the early 1970s until recently, however, there was a marked shift away from the 'pathological' model of homosexuality towards a 'lifestyle' model, which presented homosexuality as a normal sexual orientation or choice of lifestyles. This model, too, gained popularity not because of scientific evidence supporting it, but because of the rise of the Gay and resurgence of the Women's Liberation Movements in the late 1960s. Each competing theory arises out of its particular political and social context. It is this dependence of social science on its cultural context and political implications that is obscured by the rhetoric of pseudosciences. In place of explicit political discussion, both sides claim that their model represents true science and that of their opponents, pseudoscience. In so doing, both sides reinforce the notion of science as a privileged form of objective knowledge.

Lifestyle researchers typically recount a story of research on homosexuality which relies on the 'up the mountain' saga. Once upon a time, the story goes, researchers thought that homosexuals were sick and perverted; this is because they were blinded by religious prejudice and trapped by the social conventions of their time. Now we are more sophisticated and objective up-to-date research demonstrates that lesbians and gay men are just as normal, just as healthy, and just as valuable members of a pluralistic society as are heterosexual people. The story tells of the heroic triumph of True Science over pseudoscience. But an alternative way of telling this same story draws on explicitly political language. In 1974 the American Psychiatric Association removed homosexuality from the category of pathological illness. This reclassification did not result from an exhaustive review of the scientific literature, but was decided by members' votes: 'truth' was established by numerical majority. When this decision was made there was a small and tentative body of research literature purporting to demonstrate the mental health of lesbians and gay men, but it was vastly outweighed by the writings of the pathological school: certainly, as the 'pathologists' pointed out at the time, it would have been hard to argue, solely on the basis of this pre-1974 research, that homosexuality is *not* pathological. The decision to depathologise homosexuality seems, then, to have been taken not as a result of scientific enquiry, but rather to have been influenced by the changing social climate and, in particular, by the disruption of APA meetings by Gay Liberation activists for several years previously (a fact never mentioned in the professional literature). It was not the effectiveness of the rhetoric of pseudoscience, but rather overt political protest and large-scale social change that resulted in the (temporary) demise of the pathological model. When lifestyle researchers choose to attribute it instead to the inexorable progress of science, they present an image of science as striving towards objective truth, and obscure the role of political and ideological factors in determining that 'truth'. They also reinforce the notion that the rhetoric of pseudoscience, on its own, is effective in bringing about scientific (and, sometimes, sociopolitical) change.

Just as the lifestyle researchers accuse the pathologists of producing pseudoscientific research which depends on religious taboos and social stereotypes, so too proponents of the pathological model accuse the lifestyle researchers of engaging in pseudoscientific attempts to defend and justify their own deviant sexualities, or of succumbing to Gay Lib propaganda and sexual liberationist ideology. The argument between the two factions then becomes constructed in terms of who has the best evidence and the most objective methods – who is doing the 'most scientific' research. In this debate the social function of beliefs about homosexuality is obscured. Potentially interesting discussion of the ideological and political uses of various constructions of homosexuality is submerged beneath a welter of discussion about sampling methodologies and testing procedures. Homosexuality and its political context is replaced, as the topic of debate, by an arid and repetitive argument about which side is doing the best science.

Both sides, then, accuse the other of pseudoscientific reliance on 'centuries old prejudice' (Birke 1980: 108), 'stereotypes' (Browning 1984), 'popular concepts' (De Cecco and Shively 1984) and 'public opinion' (Gonsiorek 1981). One researcher dismisses the theories of another with the statement: 'One might expect that sort of uninformed flap from Germaine Greer, but not from a scientist' (Karlen 1972). True science, it is implied, is free of the biasing social influences of prejudice, taken-for-granted notions and political ideology. Thus pseudoscience reinforces the image of science as the only legitimate purveyor of valid knowledge. Moreover, the prevalence of pseudoscience is used to justify the need for continuing social scientific research in this area. Lengthy reviews of past research describing the 'sorry state of the literature' and the 'extraordinary inadequacy of the research findings' end with a plea for 'solid empirical research on homosexuality' (Suppe 1981). One researcher first complains – in a rash of alliteration – that the 'sickness theory of homosexuality is shabby, shoddy, slipshod, slovenly, sleazy, and just-plain-bad science' and then goes on to exalt the scientific method claiming that 'the person who could give a good course in science [to psychiatrists] . . . would be a major benefactor of mankind' (Kameny 1971). 'It is only with the rubble of bad theories that we shall be able to build better ones', argue Bentler and Abramson (1981). Given that one could equally well argue that a research area so conspicuously lacking in 'truly scientific' findings should be abandoned forthwith, this rhetorical use of pseudoscience can be seen as a selective account of scientific development designed expressly to enhance the image of science. In sum, the recent work of radical researchers on homosexuality is politically counter-productive. Employing the rhetoric of pseudoscience in their anxiety to dismiss the 'pathological' model, they serve a useful function for social science by upholding and reinforcing its institutionalised norms. Their research constitutes an impressively coherent public-relations job on behalf of positivist–empiricist social science.

I have argued in this chapter that when we rely on the rhetoric of pseudoscience to criticise oppressive scientific findings, we are reinforcing scientific norms. Accusations of pseudoscience contain the criticisms within the boundary limits of the positivist–empiricist paradigm. We often resort to the rhetoric of pseudoscience in order to make ourselves intelligible to the opposition: in using it we play by the rules of a game they understand. But in attempting to adhere to those rules, in attempting to speak in legitimate and intelligible ways, we reproduce the very positivist–empiricist discourse we want to challenge. As long as we limit our criticisms to those intelligible within positivist–empiricist science, we are subject to what John Shotter (1986a) has called a 'condition of entrapment': there is no way of demonstrating the invalidity of positivist–empiricism – its very functioning is designed to prevent this. Instead of allowing ourselves to be deflected into arguments about scientific evidence and methodological technique, and thus participating in the production of normal science, we need to take an imaginative leap beyond the boundary walls of the positivist paradigm. Only if we can rise to the challenges of post-positivism can we begin to deconstruct social psychology's oppressive structure and create practical alternatives which will offer real opportunities for radical social and political change.

Chapter Five

'I GOTTA USE WORDS WHEN I TALK TO YOU':
DECONSTRUCTING THE THEORY OF COMMUNICATION

Antony Easthope

The human species is not only a political but a talking animal. From very early in our evolutionary history we have used signs, both physical and verbal, as a way of taking part in the human community. And today through the mass media our lives are even more saturated by a world of signs, signs spoken and written but now increasingly visual in the form of photography, cinema, poster advertising, television. A theory of the sign as communication is fundamental to conventional social psychology. Yet, as I shall argue, the conventional theory is one-sided and inadequate because it assumes that living in a community of signs is simply a matter of communication. In fact communication is only one special and particular effect within the whole range of what it means to be human, to be a signifying animal, to be able to function in discourse.

THE CONVENTIONAL THEORY

Shannon and Weaver define communication as 'all the procedures by which one mind may affect another' (1949: 3) and diagram it as a thick black line or 'Message' passing from an 'Information Source' via a 'Transmitter' and a 'Receiver' to its 'Destination', the only possible break in the line being envisaged as a 'Noise Source' (ibid.: 7). This is the model of communication discussed by Deaux and Wrightsman (1984). Reproducing Shannon and Weaver's diagram because it 'has had a tremendous influence on the study of communication' (p. 108), Deaux and Wrightsman illustrate it with a drawing of a Message coming out of one male head and transmitted via a mouth and an ear to its

76

Destination, another male head. Similarly, Roman Jakobson, in a widely influential article (Jakobson 1960), asserts that in communication 'The *addresser* sends a *message* to the *addressee* (see Figure 5.1).

Figure 5.1

Context
Message

Addresser ——————————————————————— Addressee

Contact
Code

Context, message, contact and *code* are all seen as subordinate and exterior to what is central: communication as a direct connection between two individual minds or subjects, *addresser* and *addressee*, standing there at each end of an unbroken line.

This, the dominant conception of communication, does consider other issues and questions – about the linear directionality of the model, the dependence of communication on a shared social system and a context, how messages are encoded and decoded, the nature of the *contact* – questions in fact about the *process* of communication. But these questions are relegated to a marginal position while the possibility of direct transmission is given priority.

A sign may be defined as 'something which stands to somebody for something' (Peirce, cited in Hawkes 1977: 126), and, as suggested already, a sign may be verbal, written, visual, or any other form of sign system. Here I shall concentrate on the linguistic sign rather than signs in the visual field (though the implications of the argument hold there also, Lapsley and Westlake 1987). The crucial assumption in the dominant model of the sign as communication is that the sign is by nature transparent, however much it is subject to noise and external interference or to the dangers of polysemy (multiple meaning). I shall demonstrate that the sign is not by nature transparent to meaning and that transparency (and so communication) can never be more than a contingent effect conditional upon a specific application of a particular form of discourse.

77

SIGNIFIER AND SIGNIFIED

We are so familiar with the linguistic sign or word that we overlook its strange and arbitrary nature. However, Ferdinand de Saussure (1974), the founder of modern linguistics, follows a tradition reaching back to the rhetoricians of the ancient world (who discriminated between *significans* and *significandum*) by analysing the 'word' as consisting of two components: the signifier and the signified. The signified is the concept or meaning of a word and the signifier is the shaped *sound* necessary to give existence to a meaning. When the two – signifier and signified – are brought together they then and only then make up the sign, the completed word. But the two orders – the shaped sound of the signifier, meaning in the signified – are by nature separate and different.

Linguistics distinguishes between phonetic, syntactic and semantic levels in language, the first pertaining to sound, the second to grammar and sentence structure, the third to systems of meaning. Out of all the sounds possible for the human voice, a specific language selects out and organises a limited number as the *phonemes* of that language, the smallest units systematised within it. In modern English the sound /l/ is opposed to the sound /r/ and this allows us to say 'law' rather than 'raw'. (Japanese, however, does not make this distinction and so cannot draw on it to make up words). Phonemes are characterised not 'by their own positive quality' – they are simply 'opposing, relative and negative entities' (Saussure 1974: 119). As subsequent work has indicated, the kinds of phonemic oppositions in all the known languages in the world 'amount to twelve oppositions, out of which each language makes its own selection' (Jakobson and Halle 1956: 29). Single phonemes strung together syntagmatically in time can be combined to make up morphemes, the smallest units of the signifier to which meaning can be attached in a language (thus in English /cat/ is a morpheme, as is /s/ since it can be drawn on to change the singular /cat/ to the plural /cats/).

The distinction between signifier and signified has two implications, both of the first importance: (1) the system or order of the signifier, based as it is in the negative oppositions constituting the phoneme, has an autonomous and systematic reality of its own. This is both physical and material (the shaped sounds of a language are not merely physical but are precisely shaped, derive from an internal organisation which is identical whether the sound is represented physically by a tape-recording or by writing or on a compact disc); (2) because it is self-defining and autonomous, in this way signifiers do not have any *natural or necessary relation to any signified or meaning*. In Modern English the sound we write down as 'mare' or 'mayor' has been agreed to mean 'female horse' or 'municipal leader'. But an almost identical sound in the French language is used to give the meanings 'mother' and 'sea' (in which case the sound is written down as either *mère* or *mer*). Though the relation between signifier and signified is by nature arbitrary, signifiers come to be linked up with particular signifieds through the conventions of a given language.

The distinction between signifier and signified is both onto-logical and epistemological for it indicates different orders within reality and poses the problem of how we can live with them and know them. Yet the distinction is very close to common sense. Almost everyone now has had the experience of visiting a country and not being able to speak its language. The feelings of alien-ation and anxiety this usually causes arise from the fact that every-one else is confidently 'jabbering' away because they know the convention of that language allowing them to pass from signifier to signified, while the visitor can only hear the signifiers. Or again the case of an infant and so-called 'language-acquisition' is rele-vant. A baby is not born with access to any signifieds or meanings – for the very good reason that these vary from language to lang-uage and a baby arrives with the potential to speak *any* language in the world (and indeed others which have not yet come into existence). The infant (Latin: *infans*, not speaking) encounters a human world which excludes them and in which he or she has to begin by picking out the particular phonemes and so the signifiers of that language. This the infant does during the very early babbling period, between about 6 and 9 months, simply by playing with and practising the sounds well before he or she, at about a year and a half, lines up signifier with signified to produce its first word and so qualify as a child (de Villiers and de Villiers 1979).

Fundamental though it is to understanding how discourse operates, the signifier/signified distinction is misunderstood and misrepresented by proponents of the theory of language as communication. Thus, in his *Introduction to Communication Studies* (1982), Fiske erroneously identifies the signifier as 'a physical object' and claims that 'the signifier is the sign's image as we perceive it – the marks on the paper or the sounds in the air' (p. 47). In fact, the signifier in language is a material not simply physical reality; and far from having a secondary and derivative existence dependent on the sign as 'the sign's image', the signifier is one side of the sign (the other being the signified) constituted by the autonomous and independent order of phonemic organisation in a given language. Similarly, Deaux and Wrightsman (1984), after noting that in its 'elements' and 'at the most basic level' a language consists of phonemes, immediately rule these outside the concern of a theory of communication: 'Although these concepts are basic to linguistic analysis, our own concern really lies at the level of *semantic analysis* – what is the meaning transmitted' (1984: 110–11). They therefore proceed on the assumption of an *already* completed sign, the word, in which signifier and signified have *already* been brought into relation.

This is no accident. Those who equate communication with the nature of language *must* misrecognise the signifier/signified distinction because that distinction devastates communication theory. It is assumed that 'the addresser sends a message to the addressee', that a message is transmitted or conveyed all but directly from one head to another in very much the same way oil might be carried by road from (say) Aberdeen to Manchester. Someone (the addresser) puts oil in a tanker at Aberdeen and someone else (the addressee) pumps almost all of it out again in Manchester; and the tanker is merely a passive vehicle perfectly adapted for transporting oil.

But language does not work like that. Barring telepathy (in which a meaning or signified might be passed directly and silently from one head to another), the only means by which one subject can have access to another is by means of the signifier and you simply cannot put a signified *into* a signifier. Whereas an oil tanker as a vehicle or means of transport is perfectly adapted for carrying oil, the relation between signified and signifier is by nature arbitrary and they have no necessary correspondence. More than this, the order of the signifier conforms in the first place not to the needs of the signified but to its own autonomous and self-defining organisation. The signifier is not a transparent means of communication through which the signified may be passed as light waves pass through a pane of glass.

Nevertheless, the signifier *can* be treated as a mere passive vehicle for the signified, as transparent to meaning, as external to the process of discourse. The error of conventional communication theory is to take part for whole, to equate *one* partial effect of the signifying process with its general nature. Communication, meanings passed from one subject to another, does of course take place but it is one contingent effect of discourse which occurs under special conditions. One condition for the seeming transparency of the signifier and the communication effect is a certain definition or positioning of the subject. For discourse can appear to be a transparent means of communication if the subject as addresser or addressee is able to ignore or overlook the signifier.

TRANSPARENCY AND THE SUBJECT

Subject and object always come into existence together in a reciprocal process. As regards discourse, the signified is an object for an addresser or addressee as its subject (Lacan 1977). The signifier is the means of representation by which the object and the subject are positioned in relation to each other. It is a condition for the communication effect to take place that the signified be treated as a self-sufficient and unproduced – this happens if the signifier is treated as weightless and invisible, as it is when considered merely as a passive vehicle for transporting meaning. Reciprocally, however, if the signified as object is presented as autonomous and self-sufficient, the subject equally will be so presented – it will be positioned as an unproduced I dominating the signified as its object: meaning and the I will appear together as simply *there* (Easthope 1988). This is precisely the conception of the subject assumed in the diagrams and by the model of the communication theory, the subject as unconditioned source or point of origin of meaning. On this basis it can be argued that the subject presumed by the communication model – and by communication theories within social psychology – is the supposedly unproduced, transcendent subject whose history marks it out unmistakably as the bourgeois subject (Henriques *et al.* 1984).

This difficult area can be approached and perhaps better illustrated in terms of the concept of the unconscious. Unless it is

81

innate, the I has to be developed (Freud 1914). A necessary condition for this development and for its continuation is that the signifier be disavowed or overlooked, as it is for example by most adults with their unreflecting assumption that words are words, completed signs in which signifier and signifier are *already* united, and so words can be strung together fluently and without much conscious effort. How different it is for very young children, constantly struggling to find ways by which signified can seem to master signifier (Freud 1920) while constantly seduced by the desire to play with the signifier, treating words as things in verbal nonsense, rhymes, jests, silly sayings, and puns. From this pleasureable play the adult I must hold itself back unless it can find a legitimate adult mode for such play in the form of adult jokes, jokes with a point (Freud 1905).

Besides childhood and jokes, in both of which the signifier is not treated as weightlessly transparent and not overlooked, another vivid example of the actual material existence of the signifier is provided by so-called 'Freudian slips'. These happen all the time though we generally contrive to ignore them: the man on the television game show who says 'tarts' when he means to say 'darts', the schoolgirl who writes in an essay that 'An octopus has eight testicles'. Or there is poor old George (Bush) who to an audience in Southern Idaho on 6 May 1988 described his relationship with Ronald Reagan by saying 'we've had triumphs, we've made mistakes, we've had sex' – then explained he meant 'setbacks' and that he felt like 'the javelin competitor who won the toss and elected to receive' (a remark which explained just what kind of sex with Ronald Reagan he consciously did not want to have). In each of these instances the signifier reasserts itself, as it were, appearing from underneath the signified and so available to express a meaning supposed to remain unconscious. To conceive the subject only in relation to the signified and deny the force of the signifier is to assume the I as masterful and self-sufficient, exactly the form of subject presupposed by conventional social psychology and by communication theory.

COMMUNICATION FROM ABSENT SUBJECTS

Negatively, the signifier/signified distinction renders the communication model untenable because the reality of the signifier shatters the transparency assumed by the communication model. Now, more positively, I want to examine some ways in which the signifier always intervenes actively in making meanings possible. One way to begin is by noting how the communication model privileges speech and personal presence – it almost always prefers the example of two living subjects in contemporary communication with each other, either face to face in conversation or on the telephone. Yet an area of human signmaking essential for the persistence of culture consists of messages handed down from one generation to another, a process facilitated by the invention of writing. If we consider *inscriptions* – old manuscripts, documents, printed books, letters, epitaphs on tombstones, every linguistic means by which the past communicates with the present – the materiality of the signifier and its effects is revealed. Inscriptions are messages communicated to an addressee from an addresser who is radically absent, often in fact dead.

Attacking the speech act theory set out in Austin's *How to Do Things With Words* (1962) in the essay 'Signature Event Context' (1982a), Derrida takes writing as an example of communication. Thus, to write a message presupposes that communication can still function in the absence of the addressee – 'one writes in order to communicate something to those who are absent' (p. 313). Equally, writing presupposes a function in the absence of the addresser. (I can read a text even if I am not the original addresser, for example I can read today a sonnet by Shakespeare, an addresser who has been completely absent since his death in 1616). Writing is 'a kind of machine' and 'is not exhausted in the present of its inscription' (pp. 316, 317). Signifiers materially present in any utterance, enable speech to be written down, inscribed and so preserved as writing.

Therefore, *a text can always be cited*. Within the social convention of a particular language a text can always be read by others for whom it was not 'originally' intended. In fact a written text – a Shakespeare sonnet, a football report in yesterday's newspaper – can never appear as it was 'originally' intended and is always cited with a difference. That difference arises from the present context in which it is read and reproduced. Though always dependent on a context of reading, meaning always exceeds any original intention the addresser intended to communicate. This does not entail that communication is impossible but it does follow that a text always and necessarily gives rise to meanings different from any 'originally' intended (and any supposedly 'original' intention itself can never be more than a retrospective construction). Because of the necessary non-correspondence of signifier and signified any reader of a text produces from its signifiers signified meanings beyond any the addresser aimed to transmit via that text. Communication, meaning as completed sign, the signifier read as transparent to signified, can never be more than one privileged and partial account of the process of signification.

AN EXAMPLE: THE *SUN*

Because signified meaning can only be communicated to others by means of the system of the signifier, the meaning read out of an utterance, act of communications or text, is always both the same and *different* from anything any addresser tries to put into it:

> YOU BASTARD! 'Plane bomb' girl screams at Arab lover. The pregnant girl who was turned into a human bomb to blow up a Jumbo jet glared at her ex-lover across a court yesterday and screamed: 'You bastard',

> (*SUN, 8 October 1986, p.5, headlines and first sentence*)

'The addresser sends a message to the addressee': this brief text has been chosen to demonstrate how inadequate would be analysis according to any conventional notion of communicating a message. In the first place, although the text and subsequent story derive from factual information (as factual as any report of proceedings in a British court of law may be) its intended meaning is less a message than an occasion for entertainment.

The story is by-lined 'James Lewthwaite', who probably but not certainly was the journalist present at the Old Bailey on 7 October 1986. But the story, with the addition of headlines written by a sub-editor as well as photographs, is the result of a collective rather than individual process. It conforms closely to the genre of popular newspaper writing and its 'author' therefore is the *Sun* newspaper. It is best regarded then as an act of communication within a social institution, an act of exchange between the *Sun* as a capitalist institution producing as commodities texts for pleasurable consumption by the purchaser and reader. The nub of the argument is that because what it produces are texts it is only through a procedure of enforced reduction that this brief text can be equated with communication between producer and consumer, addresser and addressee. Because with texts there is an intervention of the signifier whatever the social intention to communicate, the reader is constituted as active in producing meaning from the text. Some of the meanings produced may well be consistent with the presumed intention of the text as commodity and others not. But this consistency alone is not enough to guarantee the communication model.

In the first instance at the level of the signifier the text is made up from within the phonemic organisation of Modern English, depending on such oppositions as /p/ and /b/ to enable distinctions between /Plane bomb/ and (say) /Blane pom/. The syntactic system of English makes possible the elaborated syntax of the first sentence, with 'the pregnant girl' as subject, 'glared at' and 'screamed' as main verbs in a co-ordinate structure, 'her ex-lover' and the quoted phrase as objects ('who was turned . . . . ' is the antecedent and verb for a subordinate clause). At every point this sentence sustains a coherent syntagmatic chain by denying entry to other possible terms, for example, 'hysterical', 'furious', 'betrayed', 'heavily', etc. as substitutes for 'pregnant', 'lady', 'woman', 'feminist', 'person', etc. as possible substitutes for 'girl'. Thus the meaning intended is contingent upon an active *suppression* of other possible meanings which would 'make sense'.

At the lexical level of words there is a further act of suppression by the intended reader, the reader of communication. Certain signifieds have to be actively discarded, such as the meaning that 'turned into' means 'underwent total bodily transformation' familiar from such utterances as 'The handsome frog turned into a chauvinist prince', or the idea that 'blow up' means 'to breathe into until inflated'. The reader must actively discard such meanings, relegating them to the unconscious, for the intended act of communication to take place (it follows from the nature of the signifier plus the semantic system that such meanings are *necessarily* present in excess of anything envisaged by the theory of communication).

Thus, although the syntagmatic chain acts to close down any such excess or rather contain it in ways consistent with the *Sun's*

85

intended communication, such closure is temporary, provisional and ultimately impossible. Any term can be taken with any other term as the text is read to produce meanings, cited in contexts beyond any definable as the 'original' context, the 'original' communication between addresser and addressee.

Briefly, there are three such contexts. One is that in which the text may be cited in the theoretical framework of historical materialism in which case it can be read as an instance of social ideology (in concentrating upon the legal and moral actions of individuals the text background, a political meaning implicit in the fact that the Palestinian Hindawi could be seen as acting as hero in the colonial struggle against Israel – the aircraft belonged to El Al), and also in terms of an ideology of gender (the relation between the man and the woman can be used as traditionally phallocentric – she is the betrayed lover, a photograph of her is captioned 'Ann Murphy . . . sobs', while he is the sexually exploitative male 'who has it all and doesn't get caught'). A second, derived from Edward Said's *Orientalism* (1985), would emphasise the presentation of the self and its cultural other (thus the woman, represents self and home, and is described by the judge as 'a simple Irish girl', while Nezar Hindawi, his photograph captioned as ' . . . denies plot', can be read as reproducing the stereotype of a foreign other, the untrustworthy and unscrupulous Arab).

A third context, drawing on psychoanalysis, would construe the text in terms of different points of identification offered to but not necessarily taken up by masculine and feminine readers, the woman as daughter and point for masochistic empathy ('Tears trickled down Ann's face . . . . ') vindicated by the father figure of Mr Justice Mars-Jones, and Hindawi as the sadistic male. A psychoanalytic reading would also construe the text in terms of a traditional if illegitimate patriarchal phantasy regarding unanticipated pregnancy – and this would seek substantiation in the way the text, somewhat anomalously, insists on the target aircraft as a *Jumbo* jet (since the pregnant woman was inside this plane, exploding that could be read as equivalent to detonating the enormous stomach of an elephant).

Each of these readings would seek to justify itself from different readings of the text, readings to which the text undoubtedly lends itself. Each would in fact be a citation, one which far exceeds anything envisaged by an account of the text as communication. To these a fourth context for citation must be added, in conclusion: the text was read as an example, cited in the context of an argument, which proposed that conventional communication theory in social psychology was reductive and inadequate.

Part Two

POWER AND SCIENCE

The texts examined so far are located in practices; the next five chapters situate social psychology in sets of practices in which psychologists enjoy power and their subjects are at the sharp end. For social psychology as a laboratory-experimental discipline with roots in America at the beginning of this century, the 'subjects' are these individuals manipulated by experts who attempt to extract data from them. Ian Parker sketches out the links between social psychology and scientific management, and then goes on to show how the 'subject' does not fare much better in the alternative forms of social psychology that emerged at the end of the 1960s. There is in both the orthodoxy and popular critiques a dangerous notion of abstraction at work. In order to deconstruct the power of the discourses that make up social psychology we have to go further and look at the surrounding culture, including the recent 'post-modern' changes in western culture which have made deconstruction so popular. Crucial discourses are those that allowed modern individual subjectivity to come into being as a body observed and regulated by psychology as part of government. Nikolas Rose carefully traces the ways in which these discourses enmesh its subjects in regimes of power. Taking Foucault as a guide, it is possible to produce a 'genealogy' of psychology which shows it produces certain types of truth.

Deconstruction facilitates a continual unravelling, and (like genealogy) it does not pose a critique from another 'true' standpoint. This is unnerving, and Edward Sampson makes it clear in his chapter that there is a point at which the undoing of concepts, discourses and practices may have to stop. His use of Foucault is taken forward to raise questions about what changes might be occurring in western culture after modernity has run its course, and extended to allow for an alternative progressive vision of 'embedded individuality'. John Bowers is more pessimistic, and the links between power, science, and the discourses which make up cognitive psychology (and cognitive social psychology) are starkly elaborated in an overview of abstraction from the Turing test to the Strategic Defense Initiative. Here again is a powerful example of the way texts, and the discourses that inform them, produce 'truth' – this time permitting us to see the intimate and necessary links between cognitivism and militarism.

These academic deconstructive, and associated genealogical, studies of power are subversive. The problem that faces a social psychologist doing research, engaged in the practices we are arraigning, however, has not been addressed. How can subjects resist? Kum-Kum Bhavnani's chapter brings the deconstruction of power into direct contact with the political issues, and shows how her practice as a researcher can empower those who are usually used and then forgotten. An opposition that urgently needs deconstructing (all the more so as it is an opposition that post-structuralism often encourages) is that between the silence social psychology routinely imposes on its subjects and the giving of a voice to them. While pluralists may be satisfied with letting everyone have their say, it is clear not only that this is insufficient but also that this solution is at times downright unhelpful. In order to deconstruct power, there must be an understanding of the overall political context that distributes it.

Chapter Six

THE ABSTRACTION AND REPRESENTATION OF SOCIAL PSYCHOLOGY

Ian Parker

We need to understand what social psychology is, the way it operates to produce a certain knowledge, and the way that it reproduces certain relations between people in western culture, in order to deconstruct it. That task of understanding and unravelling involves some attention as to how it arose; what were the conditions which enabled an experimental analysis of human behaviour to come about? I want to show in this chapter that if we pursue this question we will also be able to appreciate the significance of the 'crisis' which struck the discipline in the late 1960s and early 1970s, and see why the alternatives that were put forward by radicals then failed to accomplish the much vaunted revolution in the discipline. Some (e.g. Harré and Secord 1972) argued at the time that this revolution would be restricted to 'paradigms', while others, including a number of the contributors to the Armistead (1974) collection, went further to implicate the wider society. The crucial question now is; how can we avoid simply rehearsing once again those crisis critiques, and set in train a dynamic which will actually *change* the discipline?

After sketching out the main contours of the early history in social psychology, I will go on to look at what we might mean by ideology and power so that the descriptions we give help us to deconstruct them. Ideology and power can only be grasped when we put a critical distance between ourselves and the discipline. This will lead us to taking seriously new post-crisis developments inside social psychology, and the culture of deconstruction that has emerged outside it. The conditions which led to the crisis exploding, and throwing into question the theoretical and methodological presuppositions of social psychology, were primarily political and cultural – the dissent in the discipline owed something to the upheavals of 1968. This much was pointed out by Moscovici (1972), and I will return to his ideas below. A point I want to stress throughout this chapter is that a dynamic and enduring deconstruction of social psychology also has to be informed by politics.

THE DISCIPLINE . . .

If we glance back to the beginning of the century in America where experimental social psychology began, we see economic and political upheavals profoundly affecting academic life. The economic changes, the developing organisation of labour, and the violent company responses made for a series of conflicts within which any account of social behaviour has to be situated. It would not be going too far to say that the tensions in American society *constituted* social psychology. One crucial change in American life, which has been well documented in the critical histories of the relationship between intelligence testing and eugenics (e.g. Kamin 1974), was a massive rise in population. The increase in the indigenous (white settler) population, and in southern and eastern European communities through immigration, was accompanied by a rise in xenophobia. It is tempting to see this racist response as confined to extremist groups, but it was not. Racism helped structure the way psychology and social psychology treated non-whites. Alongside this, there was a massive concentration of the forces of production which absorbed these people into new factories and industrial plants. There was work for newcomers, but the 'problem' which immediately became apparent to the employers was that these people were not acquainted with the discipline of factory life.

Control

The 'solution' to this problem was Taylorism. Taylor's (1911) programme for the 'scientific management' of workers was used to 'predict and control' the new workforce, and thus required the examination and calculation of human work. Here, in a replay, a century later, of Foucault's (1977) descriptions of surveillance in European prisons, was the penetration of the gaze of the factory managers into the smallest of the workers' movements. Not only did this facilitate the exploitation of labour, but it also resulted in the draining away of the expertise of each individual. The worker was 'de-skilled' and left to carry out simple task-routines. There are conceptual links here with the way cognitive psychology treats its 'subjects' (Shotter 1987).

A critical account of activity at work should include some attention to such de-skilling and to the experience of alienation which arises when others control the labour process. Instead, in 'scientific management' we had, for technical and commercial purposes, the *abstraction* of behaviour from a meaningful whole and the *re-presentation* of that behaviour in the worksheets and ledgers of the managers. Behaviour was broken up and reconstituted. You might think that while individualist cognitive psychology could happily ignore the social context of action, *social* psychology would have reflected on the position of power it holds over its subjects. It did not.

For social psychologists at that time, factory work exemplified human behaviour. Many of the early studies on social facilitation had the workshop as the setting or pretext for the laboratory experiment. In the process, social psychologists imagined that they were able to bridge the gulf between pure and applied research in psychology. This breaking up of human action – social action – also solved for social psychologists the problem of how to deal with the spectre of mass activity which was, they read in Le Bon's (1896) lurid descriptions, haunting Europe. The laboratory-experimental framework enabled them to break up collective action into components that would be meaningless to people engaged in it, but meaningful (in a bizarre way) to social psychologists steeped in descriptions of such processes as 'social facilitation'. The enterprise of social psychology became that of abstracting behaviour from its meaningful context and re-presenting it.

Fragmentation

These events are important, for the past is not just like another place. What happened then conditions, limits and creates, what happens now. We live out the effects, live as heirs to that state of things when social psychology was a kind of 'laboratory for the manufacture of souls' in which experience is individualised and

93

quantified (Carter 1985: 214). The ideological effects of the crowd theories, as of other popular theories, live on, and later developments in the social psychology of collective action reproduce the politics of the early Le Bon inspired accounts. The effects also live on in the way individual activity is deliberately fragmented in social psychology.

There is a dual, double and dialectically connected, consequence of the breaking up of social action. The two aspects of this twin effect are these. First, the individual subjects are torn from social context, and collective action is depicted as abnormal or deviant. It is no surprise, then, to find that social psychology joined the *Journal of Abnormal Psychology* in 1921, and with its 'sister science' attempted to track down pathologies. Second, and crucially, the individual subject was 'protected' against collective phenomena. Part of the function of social psychology was to defend the ideal rational autonomous citizen from the horrors of the crowd or group mind. Sometimes the defence against the collective mind was developed by way of a refusal to accept that such a thing existed, but so much energy was spent on such denials that the phenomenon was continually re-produced as an absent presence. This double effect of the 'deconstruction' of social action in the service of oppression means that a radical social psychology will not succeed in deconstructing the discipline by simply reintroducing meaning. Social psychology as a set of theories and practices, of texts and discourses, succeeded in tearing apart the individual and the social in such a way as to ensure that the two halves when joined again in academic work do not make up the original whole.

The upshot of my account so far is that a cultural and economic crisis constituted social psychology, so that the concepts it employed and the methodology it adopted ensured its isolation from analysis of properly social behaviour. The First World War ensured the isolation of the now dominant American strand of social psychology from European theory, and G. Stanley Hall's comments immediately after the war capture a feeling for the experimental and national climate (as well as for what gender our discipline is): 'As we have put more psychology into this war than any other nation, and as we have more laboratories and more men than all the others we should henceforth lead the world in Psychology.... Hence the future of the world depends in a peculiar sense upon American psychologists' (Hall 1919). These optimistic sentiments also inspired psychologists concerned with 'social' behaviour, and fuelled their activities, until critics broke through in the early 1970s and asserted the importance of personal meanings.

. . . AND THE CRISIS

Paradoxically, the crisis some fifteen years ago, and the arrival of 'new social psychologies' (Harré and Secord 1972; Shotter 1975), reinforced the very isolation of individuals from social life that they intended to overcome. The account gatherers of the supposed 'new paradigm' imported material from microsociology (Garfinkel 1967; Goffman 1971; Mead 1934) and they tried to use this to capture the meaning of action. The key mistake they made was to attribute that meaning to individuals using the dubious touchstone of 'common sense'. Unfortunately it was not good enough calling for people to be treated as if they were human beings (Harré and Secord 1972) when the dominant image of the human being was the traditional individual of liberal western political thought (see Shotter, Chapter 11, in this volume). The crisis literature, such as the Armistead (1974) book, contains many powerful political arguments against social psychology, but the most influential strand of thinking on the radical fringes in the following years was to be a generous commonsensical image of our 'selves' as potentially autonomous undivided beings (in post-structuralist parlance what we would call 'unitary subjects'). It is difficult to step back from that image of ourselves when it is rooted in the common sense of an academic discipline and its circumambient culture. However, we *must* do so if we want to deconstruct its ideology and its power.

The phenomena of ideology and power were sometimes acknowledged by the critics (with laboratory-experimental social psychology portrayed as the villain of the piece), but new social psychologists generally laboured under the illusion that if the laboratory shackles were removed good common sense would gush out from the free subjects. What were missing from the critiques were two points. The first was to do with the hold of power and ideology in social psychology, and the second concerned the external forces which social psychology supports.

The power of ideology

First then, ideology and power cannot simply be wished away. To be aware of them does not automatically solve the problems they pose for social psychologists, for these phenomena form as well as constrain human action. Power, as Foucault (1980) pointed out, is not only repressive; it is also productive. The relations it reproduces then require justification through an ideological 'social reality' that all the participants should adhere to. During the crisis, Moscovici published a review of the state of the discipline. There he argued that social psychology should be the study of 'everything that pertains to *ideology* and to *communication*' (Moscovici 1972: 55). We need to reassert this point now, and insist that included within that 'everything' should be social psychology itself; what is the influence of ideology in social psychology, and what is the significance of its power?

For an adequate answer to these questions the link between ideology and power is the key, and in order to forge that link we have to uncouple ideology and 'communication'. They are not the same thing. The everyday commonsensical meaning of communication that Moscovici appeals to is that of the transfer of information from one person to the other(s). Communication is not actually like that at all, and can be deconstructed (as Easthope shows in Chapter 5, in this volume), but if we follow Moscovici for a moment and accept the traditional picture, we will find that a consequence is, that when we run ideology and communication together, we lose a sense of the particularity of ideology. Ideology certainly 'communicates' something, but its power is to do with what (individual or collective) actions are enabled or inhibited by it. Ideology sets the framework for the continuation of, *and* resistance to, power (Billig *et al*, 1988). The struggle against it is a struggle to recognise contradictions and to try to move beyond them. In deconstructionist terms, the struggle involves the positing of new terms, new practices, which disrupt the present concepts.

So, for example, our 'subjects' are generally viewed as active when alone and aberrant when allied with others. But in the face of economic changes and attempts to research such phenomena as unemployment in the real world, subjects out of work are depicted as passive when out of company (or companies). A case in point is Bhavnani's descriptions of the social psychologists role in the study of social representations of politics (in Chapter 10, in this volume). As one of the recently proposed solutions to the confusions in social psychology, the concept of 'social representations' repays some attention. Moscovici's (1984a) development of the theory of social representations has actually run together ideology and communication in exactly the way I have been warning against, and ideologies are all too often treated as if they were just systems of ideas, which they are not.

The ideology of power

The role that social psychologists play in the oppression (or empowerment) of its 'subjects' raises the second point that was missing from many of the crisis critiques of social psychology. This was a recognition that social psychology's part in the production of disciplined 'subjects' used to being individualised and observed was actually very minor. Social psychology is a mere thread in the webs of modern culture. In order to understand the ideological function of social psychology, and the limited power it does enjoy, we have to be able to strike some critical distance not only from particular mistakes in the field, but also from modern culture as a whole. There are two ways we can do this:

A spatial metaphor

The first is to strike a critical distance by thinking in spatial terms. This may mean turning to the struggles of women, or of black people or of other oppressed groups, as reference points to engage with what social psychological knowledge does, and who it excludes. This means going further than simply allowing the oppressed to speak. It means dragging political examples into academic forums (e.g. Reicher 1988), and employing a political vocabulary to reflect on how social psychology shuts them out. For example, to talk of sexism and racism is to name, to constitute as a recognisable problem. The words chosen, and the discourse within which those words operate, identifies an ideological process. In these cases, the criteria for affixing the label 'ideology' are essentially glosses on the political support we give to the groups that social psychology, as a matter of course, traditionally disempowers.

It is true that I am appealing to a variety of common sense in this case as a stepping stone to taking ideology seriously. The difference I want to mark from the new social psychologies is that it is an *oppositional*, a deliberately and transparently fragmented, common sense which arises from experiences of oppression rather than from within the dominant culture. At the same time, we should beware of objectifying experience, and of using ideology as a noun, for that will mislead us into imagining it is a fixed thing. Borges (1985), among others, has suggested that there need be no nouns, and in this case he is right. We have to be able to think, as Borges did, 'otherwise' to support our practical objections to the cultural power social psychology enjoys. We also have to leave some space for the analysis economists give of the material interests that underpin that cultural power.

A temporal metaphor

The other way to produce a critical distance from ideology and power inside and outside social psychology is to think of it in temporal terms. Historical shifts can be described and used to legitimise new ideas and to discredit old ones if a notion of 'progress' is proposed (e.g. Billig 1976), or the supposed changes can be used to support traditional notions dressed up as radical signs of the times. I want to use the rest of the chapter to tease out the implications of a historical shift we appear to be undergoing into a culture of deconstruction, and I will do this by following Moscovici ten years on from his argument that we should study ideology and communication, to a claim he makes which attempts to solve all our crisis and paradigm problems by establishing social representations as a proper field of study for social psychology.

POST-CRISIS, AND THE POSTMODERN CONDITION

Moscovici claims that we are moving into a 'new era' of representations. He says: 'Just as painting has returned from abstract art to representational art, psychology has reverted from behaviour to consciousness' (Moscovici 1982: 117). Equivalences are being drawn here between abstraction and behaviourism on the one hand (and we are invited in his rhetoric to see both of these negatively), and some variety of realism and mentalism on the other. It is this second link (which Moscovici applauds) which causes problems. Among the problems is the ease with which 'communication' can be slotted into the pair of terms cited by him as the solution, and the corresponding way in which 'ideology' (used as a pejorative term in this case, in contrast to Moscovici's earlier usage) would be associated with abstraction and behaviourism, and thus seen as fortunately fading into the past.

I do not have the space to pursue these connections here, and they run counter to the pessimistic picture of the present Moscovici (1984a) paints elsewhere (Parker 1987). It is helpful, though, to attend to such inconsistencies, for contradictions are characteristic of ideology and, when we find them, they are the points where we can start deconstructing it. The suspicion that ideology is being relegated to the past in Moscovici's statement arises not out of other things that *he* says, but from the way that a corresponding historical shift has been described in contemporary cultural and literary theory. This theory locates the emergence of deconstruction at the close of modernism and in the move into a 'postmodern' condition (Lyotard 1984).

We have to take these theories seriously for two reasons. First, because talk of 'ideology' and 'power' in collections like this one is uneasily jostling for space with talk of rhetoric (Billig 1987), discourse (Potter and Wetherell 1987) and social representations (Farr and Moscovici 1984). Some of this material is very useful, some not so immediately radical. This means we have to hold firm to *political* criticisms of the discipline, and be aware that an optimistic delusion that ideology was a 'thing' whose power has come to an end would seriously blunt our criticisms of the ways those approaches are used in traditional (ideological) ways. Second, because the cultural changes are being discussed in other disciplines, it is a useful interdisciplinary tactic for us to make these links. (Incidentally, if it was *just* a tactic, then this would be in keeping with the way that the theories are usually used in postmodern social science; Parker 1990). The shift in culture is a shift to a state of things in which deconstruction is continually at work, continually undermining the cluster of old modern beliefs in the power of individual rationality, truth and underlying meaning, necessary historical progression and scientific social reconstruction.

Pastiche . . . .

In architecture the postmodern culture of deconstruction is found in the whimsical eggcup designs at TV AM or in the technicist pastiche of the Lloyds building and Pompidou centre. In music in the lyrics of 'Half Man Half Biscuit', or the ostensibly repetitive chants of Laurie Anderson or Philip Glass. In film in the surreal but pointless *Zed and Two Noughts* or *True Stories*. In literature we could find it exemplified in the self-consciously textual Italo Calvino or Umberto Eco. In television it could be Dallas or Dynasty. In philosophy we might find it in the critical readings of Derrida of libidinal deconstructions of Deleuze. In psychoanalysis it exists in the non-rationalist writings of Lacan or Kristeva. In sociology it appears in the dizzying rhetoric of Baudrillard or Castoriadis, and in microsociology in the descriptions of the grasping and losing of meaning given by Garfinkel. Coming closer to home now, we find the unravelling of truth claims and reflexivity in discourse analysis and studies of rhetoric.

The sense the idea of postmodernism makes for radicals is twofold. First, it serves a function in the distance it marks from the culture of 'modernity' of which our discipline is a component. Modern social psychology attempted to discover the truth about behaviour, safeguarded the autonomy of the 'subject' in whom that truth was thought to reside and constructed an elaborate series of scientific mechanisms to observe and control social action (Parker 1989). Its ideological power, which we are now in a position to reflect upon, lies in its ability to carry out this programme of observation unquestioned by all bar the occasional maverick. Its cultural power derived from its *identity* with a modern culture which is characterised both by a concern with the regulation of behaviour and, paradoxically, with the attribution of responsibility, and of consciousness, to individual subjects (Foucault 1979a).

Second, the idea of postmodernism allows us to see the context for the contradictory modern project of wrenching units of behaviour, action or experience from one another and then pretending to give a representation of what the object of study is presumed to be. We have an abstraction of action from its whole and a re-presentation of it. Scientific management and social psychology, then, are just two of the apparatuses of this process of abstraction and representation. We now have to recognise the cultural specificity of all the concepts we employ, including that of representation. To 'represent' appeared in English in the fourteenth century with two overlapping and contradictory senses: to make present to the mind, *and* to stand for something that is not present. To abstract the key elements of something may or may not serve to represent that thing (Williams 1976). The concept itself is contradictory, and so it is not possible to clearly represent it. The category poses a problem rather than a solution.

If we return now to Moscovici's statement about the promise of the new era of representations, we should read him as a *modern* social psychologist who simply switches focus from behaviour to consciousness or from abstraction to representation with *none* of these terms marking a real critical break with the discipline. He remains in modernity. While this helps deconstruct Moscovici's claim, we should also be aware of the negative side of uncritically falling in the company of postmodernism, and this is because the new times can come packaged with post-capitalism and post-marxism (or, worse, with post-feminism and the end of ideology). We could risk buying something which will rot away our critical work on ideology and power the moment we put it to work.

. . . *or politics?*

There are, however, at least three positive reasons for adopting the idea. The first is that the phenomenon has already been correlated with economic changes – the growing service sector, information technology and microelectronics (Jameson 1984). Postmodernism may reflect not 'post' but merely late capitalism; and it *is* vital that we hold on to some notion, however 'modern' that may be, that real material interests influence culture (Mandel 1978). The second positive reason is that the deconstruction of a deconstruction is not such a bad thing. It is useful as a tactical procedure, and there will always come a point when we will want it to unravel itself so we can move on from ideas to practices. The third reason for adopting it is that it opens the discipline of social psychology up spatially to developments in other academic fields and to the voices of the oppressed outside the academic world. It also pushes us temporally beyond each seemingly radical alternative social psychology which threatens to capture and immobilise opposition within the subject.

We cannot do the job of connecting each and every action to material economic changes because the connections are not that direct. We are, after all, only social psychologists. However, we *can* open up the contradictory meanings of social psychology's discourse and practice and thereby reveal its nature as a social construction. This is a necessary step to revealing its power. Every social and social-scientific construct is fragile, and this sometimes makes deconstruction seem easy. It is easy to get caught in the temptations of being 'post' and just leaving it at that, but by using political spatial and temporal reference points we can keep our critical distance from the re-emerging modern social psychologies (such as the theory of social representations) as well as the newer postmodern approaches (such as discourse analysis).

To say we are post-something is to mean that we are after it, dislodging and replacing it. We should be after modern social psychology in this sense. However, we are also after it in another sense. We need to be close behind it, continually chasing it to track down its ideological, and power effects. This is what motivates the deconstruction of social psychology. So we are behind and beyond it. I have tried to show that in order to stay in both positions at once we have to ensure that deconstruction is accompanied by a historical analysis of ideology and a political awareness of the power relations which hold disciplines together. We have to know what it is we are after.

Chapter Seven

PSYCHOLOGY AS A 'SOCIAL' SCIENCE

Nikolas Rose

To many of its critics, psychology is an 'anti-social' science, focusing on the properties of individuals abstracted from social relations, reducing social issues to interpersonal ones, servicing an unequal society. But suppose we were to reverse our perspective, to view psychology as a profoundly *social* science. The sub-discipline of 'social psychology' would be located within a broader web of relations that connect even the most 'individualistic' aspects of psychology into a social field. It is not only that truth is a constitutively social phenomenon: like any other body of knowledge staking its claims in the commonwealth of science, the truths of psychology become such only as the outcome of a complex process of construction and persuasion undertaken within a social arena. It is also that the birth of psychology as a distinct discipline, its vocation and destiny, is inextricably bound to the emergence of the 'social' as a territory of our thought and our reality.

GOVERNING SOCIAL LIFE

No doubt all humans are 'social' animals. But the social territory is an historical achievement, a shifting and uncertain terrain that began to consolidate in western societies in the nineteenth century (see Deleuze, in Donzelot 1979). It is the terrain implied by such terms as social security, social welfare, social workers and social services. The social is a matrix of deliberation and action, the object of certain types of knowledge, the location of certain types of predicaments, the realm traced out by certain types of apparatus and the target of certain types of programme and ambition.

Psychology as a discipline – a heterogeneous assemblage of problems, methods, approaches and objects – was born in this social domain in the nineteenth century and its subsequent vicissitudes are inseparable from it. And psychology, as a way of knowing, speaking, calculating, has played a constitutive part in the formation of the social. As the human soul became the object of a positive science, human subjectivity and intersubjectivity became possible targets of government.

Government, in the sense in which I use it, is not a matter of the minutiae of political intrigue or the complex relations between politicians, civil servants, bureaucrats, pressure groups, and so on. But nor should it be understood in terms of 'the State', an omnipotent and omniscient entity extending its control from the centre throughout the social body. It refers, rather, to 'the ensemble formed by the institutions, procedures, analyses and reflections, the calculations and tactics that allow the exercise of this very specific albeit complex form of power, which has as its target population' (Foucault, 1979b: 20).

Government is a combination of *political rationality* and *social technology*. It is a way of construing the proper ends and means of political authority: the objects to which rule should be addressed; the scope of political authority, the legitimate methods it may use. And it is a way of seeking to operationalise such ambitions, devising techniques and constructing devices to act upon the lives and conduct of subjects, to shape them in desired ways (Foucault 1979a, 1979b, 1981: Miller and Rose 1988).

Governmentality, as Michel Foucault has termed it, became an operable programme in eighteenth-century Europe. Previously the tasks of Princes and rulers had largely been limited to the maintenance and augmentation of the power of the state through accumulation of wealth, raising of armies and the exercise of sovereignty by the promulgation of laws and decrees. Now population became the object *par excellence* of political rule. The strength of the state came to be associated with the good order and correct disposition of the persons, goods and forces within its territory. And the exercise of political power came to depend upon procedures of rational calculation and planning, upon experts who could develop methods to act upon individuals and populations, not just to avert evil, but also to promote good.

This distinctive combination was termed, in the eighteenth

century, the 'science of police' (Pasquino 1978; Oestreich 1982; Schumpeter 1954). The three dimensions of police mark out the space within which the discipline of psychology was to be born. There were the objectives of police, which concerned not just the minimisation of lawbreaking and other harms, but simultaneous augmentation of the coffers of the State and the wealth of the population, the maximization of public tranquillity and the qualities of individuals. This went hand in hand with the elaboration of procedures for the collection of information on the realm to be governed, on all the capacities and resources that comprised the population of a territory. And this was linked to the invention of techniques for the administration of the population, in the form of regulations governing the good order, education, habits and security of persons in various towns and regions.

The three dimensions of police constitute a kind of diagram of government as it would take shape over the next two centuries. Government entails ways of thinking about the population, ways of rendering it the object of political discourse and political calculation. It requires ways of knowing the population, instituting a vast enterprise of enquiry into its state and condition. And it demands the bringing into being of the mechanisms which can enable those in authority to act upon the lives and conducts of subjects. Government thus opened a space in which the psychological sciences would come to play a key role. For these sciences are intrinsically tied to programmes which, in order to govern subjects, have found that they need to know them.

THE KNOWLEDGE OF GOVERNMENT

Government depends upon knowledge. Not simply the knowledge of statecraft which had been the subject of innumerable books of advice to princes. But a positive knowledge of the domain to be governed, a way of rendering it into thought, so that it can be analysed, evaluated, its ills diagnosed and remedies prescribed. Such 'representation' has two aspects: the articulation of languages to *describe* the object of government and the invention of devices to *inscribe* it. On each of these dimensions, psychology will play a key role.

The languages of government do not merely mystify domination or legitimate power: they make new sectors of reality thinkable and practicable. Only through language can the ends of government be formulated, by portraying their object as an intelligible field with identifiable limits within which certain characteristics are linked in systematic manner. Whether it be a question of governing a population, an economy, an enterprise, a family or oneself, the domains in question are realised, brought into existence, through the languages that 're-present' them, and the calculations, techniques, and apparatuses which these languages make conceivable (Braudel 1985; Forquet 1980; Miller and O'Leary 1987, and forthcoming; Rose 1988; Miller and Rose forthcoming; Tribe 1976).

The vocabularies of the psychological sciences have made two distinct but related contributions to social powers over the last century. First, they provided the terms which enabled human subjectivity to be translated into the new languages of government of schools, prisons, factories, the labour market and the economy. Second, they constituted subjectivity and intersubjectivity as themselves possible objects for rational management, in providing the languages for speaking of intelligence, development, mental hygiene, adjustment and maladjustment, family relations, group dynamics and the like. They made it possible to think of achieving desired objectives – contentment, productivity, sanity, intellectual ability – through the systematic government of the psychological domain (Rose 1989).

The succession of vocabularies in which psychology has been articulated since the nineteenth century is affiliated to a sequence of *problematisations*. The schoolroom, the slum, the court, the army, the factory, the family each constituted *surfaces of emergence* upon which problems would take shape – racial degeneration, intellectual decline, juvenile delinquency, shell shock, industrial inefficiency, childhood maladjustment – that psychology would make its own (see Foucault 1972). In and around these sites, psychology would find its subjects, scrutinise and study them, seek to reform or cure them, and, in the process, elaborate theories of mental pathology and norms of behaviour and thought. A psychological knowledge of normality did not precede these concerns with abnormality; quite the reverse. It was in terms of problems of pathology, identifying them and managing them, that psychology would begin to elaborate its theories of psychological normality (Rose 1985). And psychology, in turn, fed back into social and political thought, the diversity of its languages making it a fertile resource for transforming, in many different ways, the problematisations of human existence, and opening up new domains for thought and action.

One example must suffice. In the twenties and thirties, the vocabulary of mental hygiene defined the terms for the government of subjectivity. This language reconstrued phenomena from crime to industrial accidents as symptoms of mental disturbances originating in minor troubles of childhood that themselves arose from disturbances in the emotional economy of the family. A new gaze was directed at family life and children's behaviour, structured in psychological terms: fears, early experiences, anxieties, attitudes, relationships, conflicts, feelings of persecutions, wishes, desires, phantasies and guilt. The language of mental hygiene made it possible to conceptualise a range of new institutions such as child guidance clinics, which were to be at the fulcrum of a comprehensive system for the inspection and treatment of all those pathologies now described as 'maladjustment'. It made it possible to reconceptualise existing institutions, from the courtroom to the factory, in terms of mental hygiene, seeing problems within them in terms of poor mental hygiene and defining a future for them in terms of their potential for promoting health, contentment and efficiency. The new language was disseminated to family members through the broadcasts and popular writings of psychologists and experts on child development, who came to experience and interpret their domestic and conjugal affairs in new ways. Mental hygiene was both a 'public' and a 'private' value: it linked social tranquillity and institutional efficiency with personal contentment. And psychological languages of this type acted as crucial go-betweens, linking subjective and intersubjective existence into governmental programmes (Rose 1989).

Such associations between governmental ambitions, organisational demands, scientific knowledge, professional expertise and individual aspirations are fundamental to the political organisation of liberal democracies. It is not only that regulation extends way beyond the control of the pathological persons and conditions and embraces, as its preferred mode of operation, the production of normality itself. Crucially, regulation does not take the form of the extension of direct State scrutiny and control into all the petty details of social, institutional and personal life. Political authorities 'act at a distance' upon the aims and aspirations of individuals, families and organisations. Such action at a distance is made possible by the dissemination of vocabularies for understanding and interpreting one's life and one's actions, vocabularies that are authoritative because they derive from the rational discourses of science not the arbitrary values of politics. It depends upon the accreditation of experts, who are accorded powers to prescribe ways of acting in the light of truth not political interest. And it operates, not through coercion but through persuasion, not through the fear produced by threats but through the tensions generated in the discrepancy between how life is and how much better one thinks it could be.

INSCRIBING SUBJECTIVITY

For a domain to be governable, one not only needs the language to render it into thought, one also needs the information to assess its condition (Rose 1988; Latour 1986a; see Lynch and Woolgar 1988). Information establishes a relay between authorities and events and persons at a distance from them. It enables the features of the domain accorded pertinence – types of goods and labour, ages of persons, prevalence of disease, rates of birth or death – to be represented in a calculable form in the place where decisions are to be made about them – the manager's office, the war room, the case conference, the ministry for economic affairs, and other such *centres of calculation*. Projects for the government of social life were dependent upon the invention of devices for the inscription of subjectivity.

Statistics – literally the science of state – was originally the project to transcribe the attributes of the population into a form where they could enter into the calculations of rulers (Cullen 1975; Hacking 1986). The projects of police and government in the eighteenth century inspired a huge labour of enquiry. Inspectors were sent out and information gathered from throughout the realm on the numbers of persons, their wealth and forms of habitation and trade, their births, illnesses and deaths. From this avalanche of figures, transported and communicated from all corners of the land, tables were compiled, charts drawn up, rates calculated, trends noted, averages compared, changes over time discovered. Those in authority – in the executive, in the civil service, in the professions, philanthropists, social critics, and social planners – pored over these figures, sought to interpret their meanings and divine their implications.

The transformation of the population into numbers which could be utilised in political and administrative debates and calculations was extended into a statisticalisation of the morals and pathologies of the population. The statistical societies in Britain compiled charts and tables of domestic arrangements, types of employment, diet, and degrees of poverty and want (Abrams 1968). Moral topographies of the population were constructed, mapping pauperism, delinquency, crime, and insanity across space and time and drawing all sorts of conclusions about changing rates of pathology, their causes and the measures needed to ameliorate them (Jones and Williamson 1979, Rose 1979).

These, however, were superficial measures of subjectivity, relying upon counting cases of evident pathological conduct. Psychology would stake its claim to be an effective social discipline on its capacity to individualise subjects in a more fundamental manner. Michel Foucault argued that all the sciences which have the prefix psy- or psycho- have their roots in a transformed relationship between social power and the human body, in which regulatory systems sought to codify, calculate, supervise, and maximise the levels of functioning of individuals (Foucault 1977). In this 'reversal of the political axis of individualisation', the kinds of detailed attention which had previously been focused only upon the privileged – royalty, nobility, the wealthy, the artist – now came to be directed upon the infamous – the criminal, the lunatic, the pervert, the schoolchild.

The power of psychology lay in its promise to provide inscription devices that would individualise such troublesome subjects, rendering the human soul into thought in the form of calculable traces. Its contribution lay in the invention of diagnostic categories, evaluations, assessments, and tests that constructed the subjective in a form in which it could be represented in classifications, in figures and quotients. The psychological test was the first such device. Codification, mathematisation, and standardisation make the test a mini-laboratory for the inscription of difference, enabling the realisation of almost any psychological scheme for differentiating individuals in a brief time, in a

manageable space and at the will of the expert (Rose 1988). Tests
and examination combine power, truth and subjectification: they
render individuals into knowledge as objects of a hierarchical and
normative gaze, making it possible to qualify, to classify, and to
punish (Foucault 1977: 184–5). Hence the ritual of the test, in all
its forms and varieties, has become central to our modern
techniques for governing human individuality, evaluating
potential recruits to the army, providing 'vocational guidance',
assessing maladjusted children – indeed in all the practices where
decisions are to be made by authorities about the destiny of
subjects.

The translation of the individual into the domain of knowledge
makes it possible to govern subjectivity according to norms
claiming the status of science, by professionals grounding their
authority in an esoteric but objective knowledge. In the school,
factory, prison and army, psychologists were to become experts on
the rational utilisation of the human factor. Psychology began to
claim a capacity not merely to individualise, and classify, but also
to advise upon all facets of institutional life, to increase efficiency
and satisfaction, productivity and contentment.

It was here that the social psychologies were to be instated,
playing a key role in rendering interpersonal relations thinkable
and inscribable (Rose 1989). Persons, it appeared, were not
automata; they acted in terms of a subjective world of meanings
and values, in short, of 'attitudes'. The concept of attitude went
hand in hand with a method for inscribing it. The 'attitude survey'
became a key device for charting the subjective world, enabling it
to be turned into numbers and utilised in formulating arguments
and strategies for the company, the political party, the military –
indeed anywhere where individuals were to be governed through
their consent. This psychological gaze was to be directed at the
nation as a whole through such devices as public opinion surveys.
The social psychology of opinions and attitudes presented itself as
a continuous relay between authorities and citizens. Government
needed to be undertaken in the light of a knowledge of the
subjective states of citizens and needed to act upon that subjective
state, if citizens were freely to discharge their social obligations.
Though its capacity to inscribe and translate subjectivity,
psychology was to become no less than a science of democracy.

TECHNOLOGIES OF SUBJECTIVITY

It is thus no accident that psychology – as a language, a set of norms, a body of values, an assortment of techniques, a plethora of experts – plays such a significant role in technologies of government within liberal democracies. Such societies do not exercise power through the domination of subjects, coercing them into action by more or less explicit threats or inducements offered by the central powers (Miller 1987). On the contrary, they establish a necessary distance between the legal and penal powers of the state and the activities of individuals. Government is achieved through educating citizens, in their professional roles and in their personal lives – in the languages by which they interpret their experiences, the norms by which they should evaluate them, the techniques by which they should seek to improve them. It is exercised through assemblages of diverse forces – laws, buildings, professions, techniques, commodities, public representations, centres of calculation, and types of judgement – bound into those more or less stable associations of persons, things, devices, and forms of knowledge which we refer to as education, psychiatry, management, family life.

'The State' is neither the origin nor puppet master of all these programmes of government. Innovations in government have usually been made, not in response to grand threats to the State, but in the attempt to manage local, petty, and even marginal problems. Programmes for enhancing or changing the ways in which authorities should think about or deal with this or that trouble have sometimes issued from the central political apparatus, but more characteristically they have been formulated by lawyers, psychiatrists, criminologists, feminists, social workers, bosses, workers, parents. Effecting these programmes has sometimes involved legislation, and sometimes entailed setting up new branches of the political apparatus, but it has also been the work of dispersed professional groups or social organisations. Innovations have been sporadic, often involving the ad hoc utilisation, combination and extension of existing explanatory frameworks and techniques. Some have come to nothing, failed or been abandoned or outflanked. Others have flourished, spread to other locales and problems, established themselves as lasting procedures of thought and action. In the apparatuses and

111

relations that have solidified, the very realities of State, politics, and society have been radically transformed.

Psychology is not merely a space in which outside forces have been played out, or a tool to be used by pre-given classes or interest groups. To the extent that various of its theories have been more or less successful in enrolling allies in their support, in producing calculable transformations in the social world, in linking themselves into stable social networks, they have established new possibilities for action and control. In establishing and consolidating such networks, in forcing others to move along particular channels of thinking and acting, psychologists have participated in the fabrication of contemporary reality. It is not merely that new ways have been introduced for construing the entities and relations that exist in the world. It is also, as we have seen, that new associations have been established between a variety of agents, each of whose powers may be enhanced to the extent that they can 'translate' the arguments or artifacts in question so that they may function to advantage in relation to their particular concerns or ambitions (see Latour 1984, 1986b; Callon 1986; Law 1986, 1987). Technologies of government, that is to say, take the form of loose assemblages linking diverse agents through a series of relays through which the objectives and aspirations of those at one point – Departments of State, Expert Committees, professionals, managers – can be translated into the calculations and actions of those distant from them in space and time – health visitors, teachers, workers, parents and citizens.

Psychology has become basic to such associations. It provides the languages to establish translatability between politicians, lawyers, managers, bureaucrats, professionals, businessmen, and each of us. It establishes the norms and techniques that can be applied in so many different contexts. And its expertise, grounded not in political partiality but in a claim to truth, allows for an indirect relationship to be established between the ambitions of governmental programmes for mental health, law and order, industrial efficiency, marital harmony, childhood adjustment and the like, and the hopes, wishes and anxieties of individuals and families. Convinced that we should construe our lives in psychological terms of adjustment, fulfillment, good relationships, self-actualisation and so forth, we have tied ourselves 'voluntarily' to the knowledge that experts have of these matters, and to their promises to assist us in the personal quests for happiness that we 'freely' undertake.

THE SOUL OF THE CITIZEN

Psychology, then, has been bound up with the entry of the soul of the citizen into the sphere of government (Gordon 1987; Rose 1989). The apparently 'public' issue of rationalities of government is fundamentally linked to the apparently 'private' question of how we should behave, how we should regulate our own conduct, how we should judge our behaviour and that of others. This link has not been a merely 'external' one, in which government has sought to manipulate otherwise 'free' individuals. It has been an 'internal' one, in which our very constitution as 'free' individuals has been the objective and consequence of regulatory programmes and techniques (Foucault 1982).

As early as doctrines of police, an explicit relationship was established between government of a territory and government of oneself. The individual was to be taught 'to control his own life by mastering his emotions and to subordinate himself politically without resistance' (Oestreich 1982: 164). This entailed a training in the minute arts of self-scrutiny, self-evaluation, and self-regulation ranging from the control of the body, speech, and movement in school, through the mental drill inculcated in school and university, to the Puritan practices of self-inspection and obedience to divine reason. Only to the extent that such self-regulatory practices were installed in subjects did it become possible to dismantle the mass of detailed prescriptions and prohibitions concerning the minutiae of conduct, maintaining them only in limited and specialised institutions: penitentiaries, workhouses, schools, reformatories, and factories. Through such practices of the self, individuals were to be subjected not by an alien gaze but through a reflexive hermeneutics.

The concept of subjection may suggest that persons are entrapped in devices whose ends they do not share. Of course, there is an important sense in which this was and is the case in social machines such as prisons, the army, the factory, the school and even the family. But even in the nineteenth-century prison, the aim of the isolation, the daily delivery of moral injunctions from the pulpit, and the reading of the bible was to provoke self-reflection on the part of the inmate. The rationale was to transform the individual not merely through mindless inculcation of habits of obedience, but through the evoking of conscience and the wish to make amends. In the classroom, the factory, and the asylum ward, the moral order of the child, the labourer or the lunatic was to be restructured such that the individual would take into him or herself the constant judgement of skill, punctuality, comportment, language, and conduct which were embodied in the organisation and norms of the institution.

Thus these apparatuses did not seek to *crush* subjectivity but to produce individuals who attributed a certain kind of subjectivity to themselves, and who evaluated and reformed themselves according to its norms. This should not be viewed in terms of ideology but analysed as *technologies of the self* 'which permit individuals to effect by their own means or with the help or others a number of operations on their own bodies and souls, thoughts, conduct and way of being, so as to transform themselves in order to attain a certain state of happiness, purity, wisdom, perfection or immortality' (Foucault 1988: 14).

If psychology has played a key role in the technologies of the self that produce the modern subject, this has not been merely through its individualistic, adaptive and behaviourist branches. For in contemporary rationalities and technologies of government, the citizen is construed and addressed as a subject actively engaged in thinking, wanting, feeling, and doing, interacting with others in terms of these psychological forces and being affected by the relations which others have with them. It is upon these social and dynamic relations that government seeks to act. In the family, the factory, and the expanding systems of counselling and therapy, the vocabularies of mental hygiene, group relations and psychodynamics are translated into techniques of self-inspection and self-rectification. These techniques are taught by teachers, managers, health visitors, social workers, and doctors. Through the pronouncement of experts in print, on television, in radio phone-in's, they are woven into the fabric of our everyday experience, our aspirations and dissatisfactions. Through our attachment to such technologies of the self, we are governed by our active engagement in the search for a form of existence that is at once personally fulfilling and socially beneficial.

Within contemporary political rationalities and technologies of government, the freedom of subjects is more than merely an ideology. Subjects are *obliged* to be 'free', to construe their existence as the outcome of choices that they make amongst a plurality of alternatives (Meyer 1986). Family life, parenting, even work itself, are no longer to be constraints upon freedom and autonomy: they are to be essential elements in the path to self fulfilment. Styles of living are to be assembled by choice amongst a plurality of alternatives, each of which is to be legitimated in terms of a personal choice. The modern self is impelled to make life meaningful through the search for happiness and self-realisation in his or her individual biography: the ethics of subjectivity are inextricably locked into the procedures of power.

The modern citizen is thus not dominated or repressed by power, but subjectified, educated and solicited into a loose and flexible alliance between personal interpretations and ambitions and institutionally or socially valued ways of living. The languages and techniques of psychology provide vital relays between contemporary government and the ethical technologies by which modern individuals come to govern their own lives. They are increasingly purveyed, not by univocal moralistic interventions of social agencies but through multiple voices of humanistic and concerned professionals, whose expert advice on the arts of existence is disseminated by the mass media. These may be polyvocal but they offer us solutions to the same problem – that of living our lives according to a norm of autonomy. Their values and procedures free techniques of self-regulation from their disciplinary and moralistic residues, emphasising that work on the self and its relations to others is in the interests of personal development and must be an individual commitment. They provide a language of self-interpretation, a set of criteria for self-evaluation and a technology for self-rectification that render existence into thought as a profoundly psychological affair and make our self-government a matter of our choice and our freedom. And for those selves unable to conform to the obligations of the free subject, unable to choose or anguished by the choices they have made, dynamic and social therapies offer technologies of reformation consonant with the same political principles, institutional demands, and personal ideals. They are mainly supplied by free choice in the market. They are legitimated in terms of their truth rather than their morality. And they

115

promise to restore the subject to autonomy and freedom. Government of the modern soul thus takes effect through the construction of a web of technologies for fabricating and maintaining the self-government of the citizen (Miller and Rose forthcoming).

GENEALOGIES OF THE SUBJECT

In the complex of powers over subjectivity entailed in modern apparatuses of regulation, 'the social' has inscribed itself in the very interior of our soul. We are governed through the delicate and minute infiltration of the dreams of authorities and the enthusiasms of expertise into our realities, our desires and our visions of freedom. To write the genealogy of psychology in such terms is not, however, to subject it to a critique. Genealogy seeks not to reveal falsity but to describe the constitution of truths. It does not ask 'why?' but 'how?'. It does not simply reverse hierarchies – pure vs. applied; soul vs. body, ethics vs. administration; social vs. personal – but fragments them. It attends to the 'marginal' and shows its centrality, to the pathological as the condition for normality, to that considered inessential to show how, through it, the essential has been fabricated. And if the genealogy of psychology brings into focus the parts that orthodoxy considers impure and shameful, it does so not to denounce but to diagnose, as a necessary preliminary to the prescription of antidotes.

Chapter Eight

SOCIAL PSYCHOLOGY AND SOCIAL CONTROL

Edward E. Sampson

The American Psychological Association states that one of the primary rationales for the science and profession of psychology is its role in promoting human welfare. It is apparent that this justification for the whole field of psychology applies with equal if not greater vigour to the subfield of social psychology, much of whose history has been written on behalf of serving the interests and benefits of society (e.g. McGrath 1980).

While the precise meaning of human welfare is nowhere stated, it is reasonable to suggest that any view of human welfare must rest on certain assumptions about the nature of personhood. When we deconstruct the prevailing conception of personhood (see Sampson 1983b, 1985), its political side is revealed. The dominant western understanding of personhood is based in great measure on a liberal individualist framework; the latter turns out to be rather inconsistent with the professed goal of attaining human welfare (e.g. see Cahoone 1988; MacIntyre 1984, 1988; Sampson 1977, 1983a, 1985, 1988; Sandel 1982). It is my intention to examine this contradiction and suggest an alternative view which is more in concert with the professed goals of genuine human welfare.

DECONSTRUCTING PERSONHOOD

Heelas and Lock's (1981) extensive review of the cultural dimensions of personhood helps us begin our deconstructive task. They suggest that all cultures differentiate between self and nonself and between the degree to which the self is 'in control' (i.e. autonomous) or 'under control' (i.e. subjected to external control). Cultures vary significantly in their manner of locating persons along these dimensions and thus in their very conception of the person. The currently preferred western form emphasises firm self–other boundaries and argues for a relation of personal mastery and control over self and the environment.

Social psychology's understanding of human welfare mirrors this cultural view of personhood. We cherish persons who stand out from the group, who chart their own course, who are the masters of their own fate (e.g. Weisz, Rothbaum, and Blackburn 1984). Our terms of esteem highlight such concepts as independence and autonomy while devaluing being 'under control' rather than 'in control'. We would be hard pressed to find instances in current social psychological work that argued, for example, that human welfare could best be achieved by blurring self–other boundaries or by valuing conformity to others.

The conformity tradition in the American version of social psychology, for example, stands as clear testimony to the manner by which we both understand personhood and cherish independence (e.g. see Moscovici 1976 for an alternative view). We pay lip service to interdependence, but invariably insist that the parties to this interdependence must first clearly and firmly define themselves independently (e.g. see Lykes 1985). I previously referred to this version of personhood by the term self-contained individualism (Sampson 1977, 1985, 1988). This describes a character whose clear boundaries separate self from other, and who is thereby able to function independently.

Although this view of the person seems to highlight personal autonomy, it is my intention that this cultural and social psychological understanding is actually a part of the mechanisms of societal control that have been effectively masked under the guise of individuation. Space limitations prevent me from providing a detailed historical examination of the evolution of this current formulation of personhood; it should be apparent, however, that the view I am espousing here is consistent with the position represented by the Frankfurt school (e.g. Adorno 1967, 1973; Horkheimer and Adorno 1972; Marcuse 1964, 1966); and is also congruent with several more recent critiques of the liberal individualist tradition (e.g. Cahoone 1988; MacIntyre 1984, 1988; Sandel 1982).

In order to deconstruct the prevailing conception of the person and so reveal its political underside, we need to move backwards somewhat in time to examine the context within which the modern science of psychology emerged. This was the period, roughly during the seventeenth and eighteenth centuries, when the traditional order of society yielded to the modern period, and in which the process of *individualisation* appeared, both creating the modern concept of the individual (i.e. its self-contained formulation) and with it, a different regime of societal control.

Individualisation and control

In psychology, the concept, individuation, emphasises a developmental process whereby the presumably undifferentiated and thoroughly merged infant separates from significant others to stand apart as an individual, distinct and separate from the world (e.g. Mahler, Pine, and Bergman 1975). Individualisation refers to a parallel social and historical process (see Foucault 1977, 1979a; also Dreyfus and Rabinow 1982). Historically, the creation of this free standing, detached individual, brought along with it the need for systems to examine and learn about this newly created social being. Free standing individuals, cast adrift from the traditional forms of behavioural management had to be managed by means of the knowledge that could be discovered about them. A new regime of societal control emerged based on knowledge that would provide the power to manage this new social character.

It is neither surprising nor coincidental that a discipline such as psychology began to develop within this context. Designed to fathom the deep secrets of the individual and chart the course of individuals behaviour, psychology's roots lay in the arena of societal management and control. Given these roots, we might rightly wonder about psychology's actual role in promoting human welfare.

REGIMES OF POWER AND TYPES OF PERSONHOOD

To speak of regimes of social power is to suggest that different societies and different historical epochs emphasise different modalities for managing people and integrating them into the social and moral order. Each regime both presupposes and helps create a different conception of personhood. Weber (see Gerth and Mills 1946) and Foucault (1977, 1979a) have provided us some important insights about the shift in the dominant regime of social power between the traditional and the modern western world. Each account permits us to infer a different kind of essential personhood required for that regime to operate effectively.

Weber's conception of traditional rule emphasised the role of group loyalties as the basis for achieving control over the populace. This traditional regime both created and required persons defined by their embeddedness in networks where self interpenetrated other selves. In other words, for an appeal to collective bonds to work effectively, persons had to be defined in and by their connections with others: they could not be free-standing entities.

Such individualisation had the effect of fragmenting (Tuan 1982) this embedded quality and created the disembodied nomad, the self-contained individual. Appeals to collective loyalties are less persuasive when persons are defined primarily by their separateness from others: where, for example, yielding to the group is seen to be a loss of personal autonomy rather than a mark of esteem.

The regime of social control suitable for free-standing nomads had to be based on different kinds of appeal. Weber referred to this modern form of rule as rational-legal, stressing its impersonal and universal qualities. Rules were to be applied equally to all persons and were based on principles presumed to be universal, free from the taint of any particular point of view. Thus the bureaucratic form of social organisation was born and with it the process of rationalisation.

Rationalised appeals do not stress collective bonds and loyalties which require an embedded or constitutive conception of the person (e.g. see MacIntyre 1984, 1988; Sampson 1988; Sandel 1982). Rationalised appeals are based upon impersonal rules applied with indifference to everyone. Rationalised rules presuppose the existence of self-contained individuals even as such a system helps to create and to sustain this kind of personhood.

Shifting objects of surveillance

Foucault's version of the transition from traditional to modern society and the consequent change in the regime of social power revolves around the concept of surveillance. We learn that in the traditional regime, power emphasised public spectacles designed to affirm the power of the monarch to exercise his authority over the people. These public displays helped to cement the social bond by giving the onlookers a sense of sharing the same community-wide experience and simultaneously directly revealed the monarch's power over people's very bodies: that is, the power to spare or take life.

With the creation of the self-contained individual, the object of visibility and surveillance was transformed. In traditional society, the only person possessing genuine individuality was the monarch. The new order saw individuality transferred from the monarch to the now individuated person. Surveillance thereby acquired a new meaning. No longer was the surveillance of the ruler by the people the dominant form; rather, surveillance of the people by the ruling state emerged to become central to the modern world. Documenting all facets of individual life became a modern fixation. Anonymity shifted: the once anonymous masses became objects of careful documentation and scrutiny; the ruling bureaucracy became the anonymous figure of modern society.

KNOWLEDGE AND POWER

Foucault's analysis provides us with a basis for understanding how knowledge about the individual plays a key role in processes of societal control. In the first place, surveillance demands gathering and filing extensive knowledge about the public. Testing and assessing individuals and evaluating public opinion, for example, are especially important as ways of gathering and storing information essential for societal management. In the second place, however, lest it appear that the only role for knowledge in social control involves discovering what already exists within individuals, a possibly more significant role involves the actual constitution of realities about persons. Once again, the social and behavioural sciences are central in this endeavour. To discover something about the individual in this latter instance has the meaning so aptly described by Snell (1982) in examining the discovery of the mind by the Greeks. This was not a discovery like the explorers discovery of America, but involved the conceptual constitution of a kind of mind: in effect, knowledge created a social reality.

One of the key roles played by the social sciences in the modern regime of power based on knowledge, thereby, involves constituting social realities, which in their design help to further the societal regime of management. This argument has been developed more fully by Deleuze and Guattari (1983), for example, who have argued that one of the functions of Freudian psychology has been less to discover inner secrets of the human psyche than to furnish the individual with inner secrets that play a part in justifying certain kinds of social practices designed to manage those secret impulses.

In like manner, social psychologists have provided their own set of internal personal qualities – attitudes, beliefs, values, personality types such as authoritarianism, external vs. internal locus of control, cognitively simple or complex persons, and so forth – which are helpfully understood as discoveries that constitute the shape of personal reality. Kitzinger's (1987) examination of the social construction of lesbianism is based on much this same kind of argument. This position is also similar to the framework of ethnomethodology (e.g. Garfinkel 1967), which examines how certain social practices constitute particular realities rather than assuming that these realities exist independently of those practices.

LIBERATING SOCIAL PSYCHOLOGY

To this point I have argued that both the creation of the self-contained individual and the constitution of particular qualities presumed to describe that individual must be seen within the context of the larger social process of modernism with its particular regime of societal control. In this view, therefore, the social and behavioural sciences, including social psychology, emerged within a context that required their kinds of service in order to assure improved forms of management over the newly created social character, the self-contained individual. What is clear from this perspective is the actual role that the social and behavioural sciences, including social psychology, play in constituting the realities of everyday life, which in turn, play a part in the modern regime of social control.

What then are the possibilities for developing a social psychology that is non-denominating in its social role? Two issues need to be addressed. First, we must establish a basis for human welfare that does not rest on the welfare of the self-contained individual. In other words, we must mount a challenge to the liberal individualist conception of the person, seeing both its internal contradictions and its inability to deliver on the promises of human wellbeing that it makes. Second, we must develop an alternative social psychology that flows from this revised view of the person. Both tasks are deconstructive insofar as they require undoing the currently dominant frameworks of understanding.

Welfare beyond self-contained individualism

Although the arguments are complex, I can summarise the conclusion of the positions I previously developed (Sampson 1977, 1983a, 1983b, 1985, 1988). In brief, my position is that there is an inherent contradiction between human welfare on the one hand and self-contained individualism on the other. In saying this, I am aligning myself with such current writers as Sandel (1982) who has persuasively argued that Rawls (1971) theory of justice is incoherent given its current conception of the individual; and with MacIntyre (1984, 1988), who has similarly suggested the virtual impossibility of achieving the liberal individualist project without so radically revising its understanding of the individual that the project no longer hangs together. In brief, an alternative to the self-contained individual, based on a more embedded and constitutive framework, is required for human welfare to be achieved.

Types of individualism

Self-contained individualism is a special breed of individualism, not its only form (see Sampson 1988). The hopes for contributing to human welfare require that we go beyond our current conception of individualism, moving towards a formulation that was not designed under the auspices of improved societal management. The idea that there are varieties of individualism forms the centrepiece of several other's works: for example, the writings of Gilligan (1982) and Lykes (1985) within the western feminist tradition; Miller (1984) and Shweder and Bourne (1982) have provided cross-cultural representation of a viable alternative. Lykes, for example, defines a kind of 'social individuality' with its emphasis on self-in-relationship. An individualism that derives from this kind of connectedness not only differs from self-contained individualism, but also introduces an alternative principle on which to found the social order.

To be an individual by virtue of one's connections and inter-connections, introduces a constitutive view of the person that I believe can more adequately include the possibility of human welfare than the current self-contained formulation allows. The embedded or constitutive kind of individuality does not build upon firm boundaries that mark territories separating self and other, nor does it abandon the connectedness that constitutes the person in the first place.

A SOCIAL PSYCHOLOGY OF EMBEDDED INDIVIDUALITY

While most deconstructive projects engage in an incessant undoing of all forms of identity, I admit to having used the deconstructive approach in order to constitute a differently structured kind of identity. While this opens my works to their own deconstruction, I find I must take that risk in order to affirm a kind of individuality better suited than the current self-contained form to the actual attainment of human welfare.

Embedded individuality requires a constitutive view of the person, re-embedding free standing modern individuals in their social worlds and thereby emphasising ensembles of relationships and communities of belongingness rather than isolated nomads. This reformulation of the individual does not take us out of the business of gathering knowledge. Furthermore, the reformulation is a perfect example of seeking to use our discipline in order to constitute a different kind of social reality. But, I persist in believing, along with Sandel (1982) and MacIntyre (1984, 1988) among others (e.g. Cahoone 1987), that an embedded individuality is not designed with current conceptions of societal management in mind; rather, it responds to a different kind of historical urgency.

GLOBALISATION

I believe that the western world is currently undergoing a dramatic historical transformation of the same order that catapulted us from the traditional into the modern world. In this case however, we are moving rapidly from the modern into the postmodern era. Numerous harbingers of this charge have already appeared: (1) social and political movements that range from the feminist perspective on personhood to the increasing sensitivity to non-western alternatives to the dominant western world view; (2) demographic patterns that force an awareness of cultural and ethnic diversity and that challenge the possibilities of homogenising that diversity under one dominant view; (3) communication technologies that make it possible to encounter world-wide events and peoples and to experience multiple realities, not just one; (4) the growing shift in human thinking from linear to nonlinear, systematic modes; (5) the emerging linked world economic system, which will be in place formally in 1992 for the European Community, but is already apparent in the vast world-wide economic networks that make the economic well-being of any one person the result of activities and policies developed somewhere else in the world; (6) the world-wide linking in matters of pollution, health, disease, and in matters of war and peace; (7) intellectual and academic movements in diverse fields which have compelled us to review our current conceptions of the individual, led in great measure by the post-structural turn to deconstructionism and its challenge to the individual as author and subject.

I believe that all of the preceding, and undoubtedly other trends I have not noted, are harbingers of a significant transition in world history. The portents for an era of interdependence are upon us. That transformation will create a transformed conception of the person: away from the no longer viable free-standing, self-contained formulation and towards something more like the embedded individuality I have sought to describe.

The tasks for the social and behavioural sciences and especially for social psychology are clear. While we continue to chart our current world, we must become visionaries open to the future that looms near on the horizon. We need to supplement our dedication to the immediacy of today with attention on tomorrow. This would give us a more future oriented social psychology, but one which as importantly places us in the forefront of the coming changes and truly in concert with issues of human welfare.

Chapter Nine

ALL HAIL THE GREAT ABSTRACTION:

STAR WARS AND THE POLITICS OF COGNITIVE PSYCHOLOGY

John Bowers

Form rhizomes and not roots, never plant! Don't sow, forage! Be neither a One nor a Many, but multiplicities! Form a line, never a point! Speed transforms the point into a line. Be fast, even while standing still! Line of chance, line of hips, line of flight. Don't arouse the General in yourself! Make maps, not photographs or drawings. Be the Pink Panther, and let your loves be like the wasp and the orchid, the cat and the baboon.

(Deleuze and Guattari 1981)

What is it for an experiment, a theory, a framework, a research program, or an explanation to be cognitive? In cognitive social psychology or cognitive psychology, what does the appending of *cognitive* add to just plain old social psychology or psychology? Sometimes it seems that cognitive is a mere honorific, meaning something like 'what we think is good or what we do here'. Othertimes, it seems that we are being presented with a new field for study and, othertimes still, that we have in the cognitive a complete approach or perspective on the whole of psychology.

White (1985) examined the reference lists of seven introductory textbooks in cognitive psychology published in 1979 and 1980. Taken together the texts cited over 3,200 references. However, of these, only 19 appeared in all seven books and only 144 publications were cited in four or more of the texts. As many as 2,620 appeared in just a single book. White takes this as evidence that there is not good agreement amongst cognitive psychologists as to just what constitutes their field and what are its basic findings.

However, being able to point out widely agreed upon 'classic', 'essential', or 'paradigmatic' (Kuhn 1962) sources is only one way in which a coherent discipline can become established (can become disciplined). Elsewhere (Bowers, forthcoming), I suggest that cognitive psychology secures its legitimacy through a set of presupposed myths and fictions. When I say myths and fictions, I do not mean that cognitivism rests on illusion, rather it has a grounding or *a priori* which is *narrated*, a set of stories or *dramas* which teachers tell pupils and researchers recount amongst themselves when the long cold nights of scepticism, self-doubt and budget cuts draw in. These dramas need not involve citations of critical experiments, indeed that might militate against their story telling function. What is important is that they are seductive in that sceptics can be drawn in, become fascinated, and come out believing that going cognitive is the right way to proceed.

These dramas are real enough. They have consequences for the way the psychology called cognitive gets done, for what might be called the texture of its theory, for the kinds of affinities and alliances cognitivism and its practitioners form or suffer: that is, for both its theory and its (political) practice. As a result of one such drama, I shall try to show that cognitive theories have a vocabulary which has affinities with militarism and which has made possible the co-option of both its metaphors and some of its advocates for work on the Strategic Defense Initiative ('Star Wars'). This slide from science to politics you might find alarming but cognitivism has always had a political existence since its formative moments in Cold War America and post-Second World War Britain (see the discussion of Broadbent's aviation work in Best 1986). Indeed, I would want to extend Jameson's (1981) thesis and claim that scientific theories, frameworks and the rest – like all texts – have a *political unconscious*, a set of political concerns – often unarticulated but which come to light at critical times and which determine what passes as neutral, disinterested, value-free science.

THE TURING TEST *OR* PRECONDITIONS ON MINDS BECOMING MACHINES

It is widely claimed that what is distinctive in the cognitive approach resides in the assumption that people are processors of information. For example, in an influential social psychological textbook, Eiser (1980: 8) explicitly says as much. In an introduction to cognitive psychology, Best (1986) devotes several

128

early pages examining what this might mean (pp. 23–9). In an extensive review article in the *Handbook of Social Cognition* series, Brewer and Nakamura (1984) document the importance of information processing psychology and particularly note Neisser's (1967) book, *Cognitive Psychology*, and its championing of computer programming and data processing analogies.

These are just a few examples of a widely disseminated claim: people can be regarded as information processing devices in some way akin to computers. Now, the question I want to ask is how the computational metaphor has become established, how it has secured legitimacy, what persuasive stories have been told about the similarity between minds and machines? After all, the computer I am using now to write this is mains powered, has a hard plastic case, a screen, a keyboard and a 'mouse-button' attached. As an information processing device, it looks in many ways quite different from me and has quite different physical properties. What stories have we been told which renders these considerations irrelevant to the appropriation of computational devices as metaphors in cognitive psychology? The Turing Test or Imitation Game is one of these stories.

In 'Computing Machinery and Intelligence', a paper first published in *Mind*, Turing begins: 'I propose to consider the question "Can machines think?"' (1950: 53). However, rather than consider the question directly, which he believes would force him to provide definitions for 'machine' and 'think', he substitutes the following scenario:

> The new form of the problem can be described in terms of a game which we can call the 'imitation game'. It is played with three people, a man (A), and woman (B), and an interrogator (C) who may be of either sex. The interrogator stays in a room apart from the other two. The object of the game for the interrogator is to determine which of the other two is the man and which is the woman. He knows them by the labels X and Y, and at the end of the game he says either 'X is A and Y is B' or 'X is B and Y is A'. The interrogator is allowed to put questions to A and B thus:
>
> C: Will X please tell me the length of his or her hair?

Now suppose X actually is A, then A must answer. It is A's object in the game to try to cause C to make the wrong identification. His answer might therefore be:

'My hair is shingled, and the longest strands are about nine inches long.'

In order that tones of voice may not help the interrogator the answers should be written, or better still, typewritten .... The object of the game for the third player (B) is to help the interrogator. The best strategy for her is probably to give truthful answers. She can add such things as 'I am the woman, don't listen to him!' to her remarks, but it will avail nothing as the man can make similar remarks.

We now ask the question, 'What will happen when a machine takes the place of A in this game?' Will the interrogator decide wrongly as often when the game is played like this as he does when the game is played between a man and a woman? These questions replace our original, 'Can machines think?'

(Turing 1950: 53–4)

Further on, Turing declares his faith:

I believe that in about fifty years' time it will be possible to program computers, with a storage capacity of 10^9, to make them play the imitation game so well that an average interrogator will not have more than 70 per cent chance of making the right identification after five minutes of questioning. The original question, 'Can machines think?' I believe to be too meaningless to deserve discussion. Nevertheless I believe that at the end of the century the use of words and general educated opinion will have altered so much that one will be able to speak of machines thinking without expecting to be contradicted.

(Turing 1950: 57)

The Turing Test as a dividing practice

The dramatic scenario Turing describes has a number of features which are worth bringing out. We can associate with the game what can be called two regimes: one of vision and one of articulation. The Test contains particular constraints of visibility. The man/machine and the woman (A and B) are removed from the interrogator (C). The interrogator stays in a separate room. In this way, it is ensured that the interrogator cannot use the act of inspection to settle the issue of who is the man/machine and who the woman. The separation of the participants into different rooms constitutes the Test's regime of vision. It sets up a boundary between the interrogator and the others. It divides and differentiates the participants.

The Test also contains particular constraints on what can be articulated. The interrogator articulates a certain sort of speech (questions) to which the man/machine and the woman are constrained to respond (with intelligible answers; Turing does not allow in his depiction of the game that they might respond with concerted disruption of the game itself). The man/machine and the woman are further constrained in terms of the medium of their answers: it is 'better' that they use a typewriter so that the physical qualities of their voices will not give the game away (*sic*). In this way, associated with the Test's constraints of visibility and complementing them, there is a regime of articulation which ensures that some forms of communication are privileged over others which are excluded.

The emphasis I have just given to regimes of visibility and articulation owes much to Foucault's work and particularly to Deleuze's (1988) interpretation of it. Foucault – in a number of studies (e.g. Foucault 1975, 1977, 1980) – has shown that forms of knowledge have associated with them forms of power-relations (see Sampson, Chapter 8, in this volume). Indeed, to insist on this, Foucault often couples power and knowledge together and speaks of power/knowledge (*pouvoir/savoir*). This insistence has a number of effects but an important one is that talking of power/knowledge should make us sceptical of claims that knowledge can exist in some pure, disinterested realm, abstracted away from particular social applications and the political questions this raises. I take Foucault as showing that claims to know are always political.

Similar comments can be passed on the Turing Test. Even though here we are talking about the seductiveness of a dramatic scenario rather than a set of actual institutional arrangements, a *narrative* and not an *institutional a priori*, we must note how the two flow together. Boundaries are defined, constraints placed upon orders of visibility and articulation, boundaries and constraints which make possible certain forms of knowledge. The boundary between interrogator on the one hand and machine and person on the other makes possible treating the latter two as similar. Without the veil of ignorance that the boundary constitutes, we would only have to *look*. Communication is restricted both in ways which ensure that the quality of a voice cannot enter into consideration, but also so that the interrogator's decisions are made non-negotiable. The game is so constructed that the interrogator decides on the identity of the participants autonomously.

Although the Turing Test is a kind of thought experiment, its imagined implementation makes possible forms of knowledge with particular properties. Accepting the fascination of the Test is productive of knowledge that is non- or anti-materialist (inspection of the stuff of which the participants are made is ruled out), knowledge that reduces language to a question and answer probing, knowledge that arises without negotiation and/or disputation between the knower and the object of knowledge. All this is built into the very fabric of the Test. These are some of the theoretical prejudices of the knowledge we call cognitivism. If you forget the constructedness of the Test or if you regard it as 'fair' in its selection of the features of the world that matter, you have already been initiated into cognitivism.

The Turing Test: abstraction and universal simulation

The Turing Test is contrived so as to force a differentiation between those features of the world that matter to the question of the similarity of thinking beings to machines and those that don't. Sets of typewritten outputs matter, the nature of the embodiment of the beings and machines under test does not. Now, the point I want to make is that carving up the world in this way makes possible treating two things which are otherwise different as the same. As long as two things (e.g. a mind and a machine) are similar with respect to the *things-that-matter*, we can treat them as being the same with respect to some newly fashioned abstract category which they are both members of: e.g. the category of intelligent artefacts (see Simon 1981). Or to put the point another way, creating abstract categories heightens our ability to say that two things are the same; abstraction is the process whereby the different gets reduced to the same. Once two things are made the same in abstraction they become exchangeable as equivalents, one can substitute for the other.

Indeed, Turing's work can be seen as marking a new phase in the historical development of abstraction. Consider De Landa's (undated) account:

> With the development of the Nazi encoding machine, the Enigma, the mechanisation of cryptology achieved an all-time high. Breaking this code required the work of some of England's most brilliant mathematicians: it also involved the incarnation of the first Turing Machine.
>
> Named after its inventor, this machine came into being as an abstract mathematical entity designed to solve extremely abstract problems in metamathematics. In particular, the increasing mechanisation of number theory, brought about by the creation of powerful formal calculi, created the need to answer certain questions about formal systems in general. These questions came to be known as Hilbert's program.
>
> Working on these problems, Turing abstracted the functions of real machines and figured out a way to define them in purely formal terms. To break the Enigma code, this machine had to be brought from its abstract existence into reality. The story of the birth of the computer is the story of how, under wartime pressure, what used to be relations between concepts became embodied in physical relations between switches and other electromechanical devices.
>
> And this is especially remarkable since Turing's was not an ordinary machine. As opposed to the Enigma machine which did only one thing – it scrambled information in complex ways – the machine designed to defeat it had to be that much more versatile. *In fact, the central idea behind the Turing machine was that it should be capable of simulating every other machine*

> (De Landa n.d.: 179–80, my italics)

De Landa's point is two-fold. First and in general, we must understand formal, abstract systems as lying within a *circuit* of abstraction and concretisation. Some metamathematical problems are given a solution through the postulation of a highly abstract machine which can stand for the functions of real, concrete machines. However, this abstraction is complemented by a concretising manoeuvre in which actual machines come into existence to break the Enigma code. Second, Turing accomplished this not by merely reconstructing the Enigma machine and – as it were – running it in reverse to decode encrypted messages. Rather, he abstracted a universal simulation device which could stand for, not just Enigma, but all other machines. In Turing then, we find the abstractive tendency, the desire to reduce the different to the same, developed to its highest form. But his very abstraction makes possible a multiplicity of (re)concretisations, equivalences and substitutions: computers as surveillance devices, as production-line automatons, as minds. De Landa's argument is consistent with our earlier reference to Foucault: along with abstract knowledge and theory, there come concrete social practices. Just as it is mistaken to think knowledge apart from power, so must we not ignore the interplay of abstraction and concretisation. To theorise abstractly is not to remove oneself from the affairs of the daily world. On the contrary, a universal simulation device can enter into indefinitely more circuits of abstraction/concretisation than can a device which substitutes only one other. As we shall see, forty years on, the Turingesque abstraction of cognitive theory has made possible new links with war, with Star Wars.

STAR WARS

The Strategic Defense Initiative (SDI or 'Star Wars') was announced by President Reagan in a speech to the American nation on 23 March 1983. In this speech Reagan outlined a research program culminating in the development of an impermeable shield to protect the United States against any incoming ballistic missile. Although much of the debate around Star Wars has focused on its technical feasibility, it is important to note the program's ideological effects. Star Wars promotes an image of work done under its auspices as defence and not aggression, and introduces the image of a fully automated war in which few soldiers need be involved. For example, in a debate in the quarterly newsletter of the UK based *Society for the Study of Artificial Intelligence and Simulation of Behaviour*, Wilks (1985: 24) suggested that 'military-oriented AI work' is less concerned with 'weapons of mass destruction' than 'with automated battlefields, robot vehicles, image identification, pilot modelling, etc. Many of these would have the function of keeping one's own people out of harm's way. If one is going to have wars at all, a strong moral [= chauvinistic?] case can be made for doing that.' Especially in the post-Vietnam American context, this last point has a considerable significance for the program's supporters. As Mosco (1987: 12) puts it:

> Ronald Reagan's Star Wars proposal may seem to us merely an expensive, if dangerous, piece of science fiction. Yet it strikes deep resonances with many aspects of our lives: the reshaping of our work; the manipulation of our yearning for security; even our nightmares, as well as the science fiction that we read. In the sense that it affects our behaviour and fears, it is already working.

The sense of the 'workability' of Star Wars that Mosco intends is at least as important as the one which underlies many of the technical debates (e.g. Parnas 1985; and see discussions in Bulkeley and Spinardi 1986, chap. 8; Thompson and Thompson 1985). Even if SDI fails in some technical sense, the existence of the program can yield success in a manifold of other ways. In particular, it contributes to the *militarisation of science*, a process with which cognitive science has particular affinities.

Artificial intelligence, cognitive science, and the Strategic Defense Initiative

It is important to realise the sheer extent of potential overlap between the research programs associated with Star Wars (especially the so-called Strategic Computing Initiative) and the concerns of cognitive psychology, artificial intelligence, etc. For example, the intense source of infra-red radiation from missiles during 'boost phase' when they ascend after launch is easily detectable, but currently existing surveillance sensors do not permit the ready discrimination of one source from another nor the tracking necessary for planned interception. Clearly, this raises issues of object perception and constancy of the sort discussed in any textbook on visual cognition (e.g. Bruce and Green 1985) and of prime importance to computational studies of vision since Marr (1975). In 1985, 32 per cent of the SDI budget was accounted for by SATKA – Surveillance, Acquisition, Tracking and Kill Assessment – (Bulkeley and Spinardi 1986: 103); and many of the major companies with private Star Wars contracts have a stake in artificial intelligence projects of this sort (e.g. Boeing, Martin Marietta, Texas Instruments and Bell Helicopter, see Mosco 1987: 18–19). Additionally, according to many proponents, visual cognition is one of the more successful applications of parallel distributed processing (PDP) modelling techniques. Though not directly through the SDI organisation, most of the US research on PDP has been supported by defence funds.

Particularly instructive (but easy to miss) are the affinities that concepts in cognitive science have with the proposed system architectures for battle management suggested to the SDI Organization by the Eastport Study Group. This group's report (Eastport Study Group 1985) contains recommendations for the structure of the computer software and hardware which would control defence against a Soviet strike. Consider the following:

> The most plausible organizations for a strategic defense battle management system are hierarchic. That is, their communication and information-processing structure can be portrayed graphically in 'tree' diagrams such as an organization chart or depiction of a chain of command. This hierarchy or tree structure of a battle management system is rooted in the command authority and branches to the sensor weapon subsystems. The properties of such hierarchic systems are very well understood both analytically and by analogy to this same organization having been adopted by living creatures and their social organizations.
>
> Such systems have the property that information sensed at the 'leaves' of the tree is processed (compressed) into more abstract representations as it is communicated toward the root, and is articulated from abstract representations to detail commands as it is communicated toward the leaves. This communication and computation structure preserves locality and allows for autonomous actions from local

subunits, which have the same tree-like structure as the
entire system.

(Eastport Study Group 1985: 7)

This passage has a number of important features which I shall
discuss in the sections below.

Hierarchy

The emphasis on hierarchy is very familiar from many models and
theoretical constructs in cognitive psychology. A selection of
examples: Craik's early and influential models of action control
(for a discussion, see Johnson-Laird 1985); artificial intelligence
work on planning (Doran, 1984, goes as far as to say that all
'effective' planning models are hierarchical); recent cognitive
psychological work on mental maps has involved suggestions that
internal representations of space are hierarchical (e.g. McNamara
1986); Taylor and Crocker's (1981) account of social schemata,
like Rumelhart and Ortony's (1977) cognitive theory, emphasises
the hierarchical embeddedness of schemata and subschemata;
hierarchical structures are emphasised for natural categories by
Rosch (e.g. 1978) and for self-categorisations by Turner and Oakes
(1986); Harré, Clarke, and DeCarlo's (1985) book is full of
suggestions for hierarchical control systems.

It would not be hard to generate fragments of plausible
cognitive-psychology-talk by substituting *central executive processor*
(in the sense of Atkinson and Shiffrin 1968) for *command authority*;
and *perceptual modules* (in the sense of Fodor 1985 and those who
have followed him) for *sensor weapon subsystems*, etc. Conversely, a
military reader of cognitive theory can derive plausible SDI-speak
by substituting in the reverse direction. As I argued above, these
substitutions and affinities are made possible by the abstraction
and universal simulation elements of the Turing Drama.

Technological structure and social relations

In the case of the Eastport Study Group's work, it is important to
note that the hierarchical structure for the software architecture is
repeatedly legitimated by reference to hierarchical (particularly
military) social systems. A number of writers in the sociology of

knowledge have tried to draw parallels between social structure and the structure of knowledge-claims and technology. This work often omits to suggest any mechanism to generate the parallelism and typically fails to show that the alleged parallelism or 'homology' is anything other than an analyst's version foisted on the material under study. However, in the passage above, it is clear that this parallel is significant for the authors of the text, not merely for us analysing it.

Indeed, it is crucial that the battle management architecture should have some points of similarity and contact with military command relations because the Study Group envisage the system as interacting with the 'command authority':

> A condensed picture of [each] local situation would be reported for purposes of threat assessment to higher authorities in the hierarchy. The higher-level battle management combines the threat assessment information from many such battle groups ... to present a condensed threat assessment to the command authority ... there must not be a loss of human control over the independent groups [of defensive weapons] ... For example, the command authority could authorize only some of the independent groups to be armed in order to match the defensive level to the type of attack.
>
> (*Eastport Study Group 1985: 24, 26*)

At the lowest levels, a multiplicity of events occur by the millisecond but at the highest level, condensed information is presented to the command authority, updated 'every second or so' (ibid.: 24). Thus, the Study Group see a hierarchical battle management system interacting with the command authority – a group of human 'end users' (ibid.: 6). This is not a fully automated war. Rather, it is a war with mechanisation at lower levels of command, where humans are substituted, their command and communicative relations being maintained in the software alongside a maintenance of human involvement at the highest levels. If, as Wilks hopes, the AI, computing and cognitive science contributions to the military 'have the function of keeping one's own people out of harm's way', it is at the cost of the responsibilities of warmongering falling to ever smaller and less accountable groups of experts and generals.

Abstraction, cognitivism, and militarism

If, as I suggested above, the abstractionism and role of simulation in the Turing Test make possible effortless translations from cognitivism to militarism, this is a rather cruel irony for some of the more politicised champions of cognitive theory. For example, Shallice (1984: 33) claims that '"general intelligence" as a concept has ideological force, because if one strips it of its technical complexities, it corresponds closely to a lay concept. Concepts like "primary memory", "logogen" and "ATN" do not. Moreover, information-processing concepts offer far less scope than, say, sociobiological ones for loose extrapolations to socially sensitive areas.' On the whole, Shallice seems to endorse the view that cognitivism is a politically progressive advance over behaviourism and that the 'social control functions of a future psychology' lie principally in cognitivism being employed not as an 'ideological justification' but as a 'technical component' (i.e. cognitive theory is used instrumentally as a means to an undesirable end).

Similarly, in the first issue of *Cognition*, Chomsky (1972), after a lengthy criticism of Skinner's (1971) *Beyond Freedom and Dignity* and Herrnstein's (1971) work on the social consequences of the inheritance of IQ, urges scientists to be aware of the ways in which their investigations are likely to be used. While thinking it unwise to prevent scientists from engaging in 'fundamental issues' of controversy, Chomsky acknowledges that researchers may often face a difficult 'conflict of values'. 'Of course, scientific curiosity should be encouraged (though fallacious argument and the investigation of silly questions should not), but it is not an absolute value' (Chomsky 1972: 42).

However, positions such as these, which emphasise the moral/political dilemmas surrounding the consequences of a theory or body of work, leave out of account what makes the theory possible in the first place, what political or institutional arrangements may be pre-supposed in the work. It is for this reason that we have emphasised the *narrative a priori* of the Turing Test, what is pre-supposed in the Test and might be tacitly agreed if the Test is found to be persuasive. We argued that the Test makes possible non-negotiable, 'third-party' (see Shotter 1987) forms of anti-materialist knowledge which mark a new phase in abstraction, permitting machines and people to be exchanged as equivalents.

These features derive from the regimes of vision and articulation which make up the Test and which cannot be separated from it. To be sure, abstractionism allows concepts removed from 'lay consciousness' (Shallice 1984) to come into existence but abstraction expands the number of concretisations which can be made, not diminishes it. Whereas 'general intelligence' could only be connected up to various crude educational programs, 'hierarchical control models' can be concretised anywhere (though perhaps over northern hemisphere theatres of war first!).

Latour (1987) suggests that we should look at 'science in action' not merely 'ready-made science'. To understand science, we have to pursue scientists in their disputes, their attempts to win over allies and keep them in line, their struggles against all manner of adversities. We should not concern ourselves only with the near-inscrutable 'black boxes' that ready-made, established science presents us with. If we follow science in action, Latour argues that we come to see science as an activity involving the construction, strengthening and extension of networks of associations. Cognitive theory has proven itself to be a particularly effective resource for the creation of long networks. In this chapter, we have seen cognitivism connect Second World War metamathematics, aviation research, social psychology, Star Wars, and a cast of thousands. Cognitivism's abstractions makes this possible.

As Latour (1987: 172) notes, it is not a strange coincidence that any body of work able to muster long networks eventually comes across the military. 'For centuries, they have enlisted people and interested them in their action, so much so that most of us are ready to obey them blindly and give up our lives if required. As far as enrolling, disciplining, drilling and keeping in line are concerned, they have proved their mettle and on a much larger scale than scientists have ever tried . . . . The similarity between the proof race and the arms race is not a metaphor, it is literally the mutual problem of *winning*.' Cognitivism, like all technoscience, is part of the late twentieth century's war machine and should be studied as such.

Chapter Ten

WHAT'S POWER GOT TO DO WITH IT?

EMPOWERMENT AND SOCIAL RESEARCH

Kum-Kum Bhavnani

There are many arguments and discussions present in contemporary European Social Psychology which suggest that the analysis of power relationships should be a central concern for social psychology:

> It is necessary to insert into social psychology a concern with problems of power, or, more precisely with relationships of power. If this is not done, ... (there is a) risk of skirting around a number of phenomena the study of which is indispensible for our understanding of certain forms of social behaviour.

> *(Deschamps 1982: 97)*

Following Deschamps, this paper argues that power within social psychological research needs to be given a greater emphasis than presently occurs. Further, it is suggested that the assumption that empowerment is necessarily synonymous with 'giving a voice' is not a valid one. Using the example of a research project about the ways in which politics is discussed by young working class people in Britain as a case-study, this paper suggests that silences, as well as 'giving a voice' can be empowering. Frequently neglected questions such as who is being empowered, and in whose interests does the empowerment serve should, it is argued, form the basis for future debates about the empowering nature of social research.

Some of the issues over the question of power have been debated within anthropology. Discussions of ethnography, and whether there can be a feminist ethnography (Stacey 1988) have implied that feminism attempts to find ways of transforming the

141

unequal power relationships within social research. Caplan (1988), in her discussion on what may constitute a feminist anthropology, argues that in the recent period there is greater understanding than previously, that 'knowledge is socially constructed', and 'that it has a power dimension' (Caplan 1988: 7). However, despite such attempts to acknowledge that the ethnographic methods can only be partial in permitting an insight into the ways in which human beings organise and discuss our lives, and despite Clifford's (1983) suggestion that the images so constituted are 'in specific historical relations of dominance and dialogue' (Clifford 1983: 119), there appears to have been little systematic exploration of the ways by which unequal power relationships are reproduced within the processes of conducting academic social research from such perspectives. Clear exceptions to this are the arguments presented about 'imperial feminism' (Amos and Parmar 1984), the boundaries of sisterhood (Carby 1983), and the ways in which feminist scholarship and colonial discourses are often intimately inscribed with each other (Mohanty 1988). Thus, although there is some work, often written by black women and women of colour which examines the 'multiple and fluid nature of power relations' (Ong 1988: 83), comparatively little has been written within social psychology about such issues. 'At times, it is as if power were a social obscenity' (Billig *et al.* 1988: 147).

DECONSTRUCTING POWER

There are a number of ways in which an analysis of power may be understood within social psychological research, and I should like to discuss three of them in this paper.

First, there is the set of power relationships between researchers and researched, or the 'subjects' of psychological research. Second, there are another set of power relationships which flow from the socially ascribed characteristics of both researcher and researched, and which carry hierarchical loadings of their own. 'Race' and gender of the researchers and those who are 'researched' are examples of these socially ascribed characteristics. The third aspect of power in social research is centred on the issue of empowerment and social research and is often the implicit rationale for the contemporary discussions on power and social research. It is the third aspect which is to be the main focus of the paper, but I shall briefly discuss the other two aspects first.

POWER RELATIONSHIPS BETWEEN RESEARCHER AND RESEARCHED

A starting point in discussing this issue is to note that it is the researcher, who, within certain confines of funding (which are clearly not unimportant), by defining the research, has power in relation to 'those researched'. This means, for example, that decisions not only about the conduct of the study, but also the write-up, the analysis, and what is determined to be peripheral or irrelevant lie, in the main, with the researcher. This power of the researcher is, however, not always noted or analysed – precisely because the power is transparent. Because of this transparency, the *processes* by which research material is omitted from either the analysis or the write-up come to be understood as natural or obvious. A certain type of material is often omitted, therefore, because of the desire and the necessity to present a clean study, which is as uncontaminated as possible.

Power may be understood a little more clearly if we force the power away from such a clean, transparent framework, and, instead, present it so that it is *seen* and, in being seen, can be examined and analysed. Some researchers who are developing a feminist analysis to examine their research methods (for example, Griffin 1986) are beginning to do precisely this. For example, by deciding to answer questions about oneself, if asked by interviewees, rather than avoid such questions (see Oakley 1981 for a sharp and witty insight into the textbook approaches to interviewing), a researcher can begin, in the very analysis of such questions, to gain an insight into the ways in which the subjects perceive the researcher. It is this type of insight which can become a central focus for the analysis of the power relationships. Thus, I am suggesting that not only is it impossible to have a clean piece of research, but, rather, that it is the very messiness, the apparently awkward questions from the researched which are desirable; it is these questions which should not be written out of any research report precisely because they can provide a starting point for the analysis of power between researchers and researched. Equally important, such 'messiness' reflects the complexities and realities of the interviewees views of themselves and the complexities of their view of the researcher – and so, may end up being a more accurate picture of their lives.

SOCIALLY ASCRIBED CHARACTERISTICS AND POWER

It is true to say that sometimes, social psychological research has ignored the power inequalities which are consequent upon the hierarchical loadings assigned to socially ascribed characteristics. Many times, however, we have tried to control for unevenness in these characteristics by ensuring that women interview women, black researchers interview black people, and so on. It is the concept of 'experimenter effect' (Rosenthal 1966) which is used to understand this 'matching' of researcher and researched. However, if it is accepted that such matching is desirable in order to minimise the impact of power inequalities in social research, the argument may be taken one step further, and suggest that, rather than sidestepping the question of power, more may be learnt about its functioning in research if the usual balance of power which flows from socially ascribed characteristics is both inverted and, therefore, subverted. A particular research project which has achieved this inversion and subversion – that is, where the more frequently encountered relationships of subordination and domination have been inverted within the research – has been discussed elsewhere (Bhavnani 1986a).

My present research, through an inversion of the more frequent balance of power, has such subversion as part of its structure. A black woman researcher interviewing black and white 16-year-old working-class people means that I, and the interviewees in the study, were inscribed within multi-faceted power relations which have both structural dominance and structural subordination in play on both sides. It is this less frequently encountered power asynchrony, or this 'messiness', which can allow for the analysis of the power relationships within social research. In addition, as *conscious* attention and interaction with the dynamics of power in research is focused upon, so a more complex view of how research subjects view themselves and their world may be available. In short, social research can avoid being synonymous with social stereotyping and, instead, become important in the construction of different sets of discursive realities about particular groups – these realities being both resonant with, and reflective of, the material realities.

EMPOWERMENT AND SOCIAL RESEARCH

The central focus of this paper, however, is to discuss issues of power from a different angle – namely that of empowerment. In order to define empowerment, it is necessary to define power.

Other writers in this book have explored the implications of the ways in which Foucault has developed arguments about power: at its crudest, Foucault's writings may be understood as questionning the widely received notion that power merely resides in powerful individuals. In his challenging approach, however, Foucault does not appear to have presented an account of the way in which the powerful make history, and nor has he systematically examined the ways in which resistances challenge that ability to make history. Flacks (1983) is helpful here, for he suggests that power may be defined as the capacity to challenge historical forces, and so, to make history; thus, power becomes the capacity to influence the condition and terms of the everyday life of a community or society. While his argument is centred around the ways in which this capacity, when realised, is disruptive of daily life, the point of using this definition within this chapter is to create a notion of power which allows that, potentially, dominated groups may have access to power.

Empowerment can then be taken as being the realisation of this capacity. Within the human sciences, oral history – both the method and the discipline – has often been cited as *the* exemplar of how social research can be empowering. The work of Paserini (1987), for example, as well as the insights provided by Wright (1985), certainly imply that historical work is very important in providing a means of understanding how the present, and possible future change, is influenced by the ways in which the past is remembered and understood. However, in many discussions of empowerment (and the above studies are an exception) there is an implicit assumption that qualitative research is an important, if not the only, means of empowerment for those who are defined as the researched – in other words, such research is seen as giving a voice to the interviewees, and is, therefore, empowering (as, for example, argued by Mishler 1986). Empowerment and 'having a voice' are not, however, the same, although the two are often conflated. For example, one can cite research which has been conducted in Britain with black residents where such research has reproduced an image of the black residents as victims or problems: this has, indeed reinforced stereotypes (see for example, Community Relations Commission 1976). Such research may be given considerable credibility because not only is there the implicit assumption that it is empowering because it is supposed to have 'given a voice' for the black residents, but also, the use of direct speech extracts confers an added, and often seen as desirable, dimension of authenticity. By using the general, as distinct from specific criteria, of 'giving a voice' or 'authenticity', such research can, however, in masking the power inequalities present within that research, be part of a disempowerment. It is a disempowerment because it reproduces social stereotypes of those who are the subjects of the research – stereotypes which have previously been important in disallowing access to power.

The problems with the general criterion of giving a voice are of two sorts. First, although it is acknowledged that some voices have been silenced, the lack of adequate attention to the reasons for this silencing means that the voices of the silenced come to be understood as being of equal value to those which have preceded them. The difficulty with this equal weighting is that the heretofore silenced voices cannot then be seen as forms of resistance or challenge to domination – their inclusion is merely seen as helpful in providing a more accurate picture. What I would argue, however, is that it is not only inaccurate to provide such a limited picture, but, also that the processes which led to the initial silencing and then the permission to speak remain unconsidered, and hence, uninterrogated. The second problem is related to this lack of interrogation. For not only is it then necessary to interrogate the ways in which the silenced voices are inscribed within unequal power relationships, but further, it is necessary to make explicit the political framework which underpins such an interrogation. If the presentation of an explicit political framework is avoided and the unstated voices are the voices of reaction, then these come to be celebrated in the same way as the voices of the dispossessed. For example, it could be argued that the post-structuralist approach which suggests that radical activity simply involves the opening up of a space for different readings is implicated in such an, at best, naïvety.

These points may be clarified, and the general argument of this paper exemplified by examining some aspects of a research study which I have conducted in the recent past (Bhavnani 1988). In so doing, I want to stress that I have no intention or desire to present it as a project which has been totally successful in negotiating such issues. I am, however, using it as a case study to demonstrate my general points about the distinction between empowerment and 'having a voice'.

The project is one which explored, using social psychological theories, the ways in which young working-class people in Britain presented and discussed their views on issues which reside within the domain of the political. Using open-ended interviewing techniques, 72 working-class sixteen year olds in Manchester, England, were interviewed between February and May 1985, about their view of society, and the political processes within it. The issues for the interviews were developed from group discussions held with approximately 90 of these young people, of whom 72 were interviewed as described. Following these 35–45 minute interviews, 60 of the group were followed up six months later, and similar interviews were conducted, most being close to 45 minutes in length. The issues covered in the interviews were employment, unemployment, the prospects for employment opportunities for young people in Britain, racism, parliamentary parties, marriage, violence against women and children, nuclear power, and their futures in ten years' time. In addition, two industrial disputes, those of the miners and schoolteachers, were discussed, these being issues which were very present in the public domain at the time of the interviews. Approximately one- third of the group were white and the other two-thirds were black – of whom half were of Afro-Caribbean origin, and half of Indian sub-continent origin. Approximately half of those interviewed were young women. Thus, the study is a social psychological analysis of the arguments presented about politics by working-class young people. The research was situated in the context of their leaving school and moving into the labour market – either as employed or as unemployed. The interviews were tape-recorded and transcribed, and some aspects not reported in this paper have been reported elsewhere (Bhavnani 1986b).

The academic discourses which analyse and describe politics amongst young people are often polarised into discourses of political activity or political apathy. It is this latter discourse, that of political apathy, which I want to look at here. Seventy per cent of the sample said they would vote in the next British General Election, meaning that 30 per cent of the sample said they would not. This mirrors levels of voting in general elections in Britain. However, it has been implied in some work (such as that of Taylor 1983, for example) that not voting is synonymous with political apathy.

KKB: What do you think of the government?

BHS44:   I don't like her (Margaret Thatcher)

KKB: What don't you like about her?

BHS44:   Don't like her – full stop.

KKB: Say a bit more...

BHS44:   There's a lot of reasons. One, she's all for herself. Two, – the cabinet. I don't like 'em. I mean they all look like a bunch of criminals even she does. I suppose she is in a way.

KKB: How do you mean?

BHS44:   I mean like she's cutting off the jobs and she's trying to say I'm trying to get more jobs in the country. There's no way she can do that. If she's cutting the jobs up, no way she's getting more jobs in. As long as she's in power there's no-one working as far as I'm concerned. I mean I can't vote. I mean I don't really understand what it's about, but I'm coming to the age that I should start thinking about it. I think if I do, I wouldn't vote Conservative.

KKB: Who would you vote for?

BHS44:   I won't vote Labour – when Heath – no the man after him – who was it – the Prime Minister – Callaghan, that's it, yeah – he promised jobs. They got nothing. I mean he was doing exactly the same as Thatcher's doing now. I mean if the two of them got together and joined as one party it'd still be the same. I mean

Kinnock's not doing much really, is he? I mean all he's doing is just sitting on his buttock . . . . I mean he promised the miners something but they didn't get it, did they? Stupid. I wouldn't vote, I reckon.

KKB: Who's the sort of person who might get your vote? What would they have to be like?

BHS44:   An MP? – Well, just say they got someone in the Labour Party – say they promised jobs and you got 'em – then I'd vote. If they promised jobs and they got the jobs I'd definitely vote for them.

From this, we can see that although the speaker has said he will not vote, it would not be accurate to say he is politically apathetic. To draw out his reference to previous prime ministers of Britain, and his analysis of the potential contributions of politicians, necessitated the use of open-ended interviewing techniques, which have demonstrated that he is an individual who is interested in party politics. To have categorised him as politically apathetic would have been to perpetuate a discursive reality which is at odds with the everyday lives and arguments of this group of young people, as seen in the above.

It would also be true to say that he has been 'given a voice' as a consequence of this project. Has he been empowered as a consequence? The positive answer to this question is based upon the use of a notion of empowerment which requires that the empowerment of subjects through social research means that in being 'given a voice' subjects may also begin to present narratives; and that through their narratives, people may be moved beyond their words to the possibility of action. That is, that they may begin to realise their capacity to create history. His comments about party politics, ending with a notion that he *may* vote in a particular situation can be analysed in this way. To be empowered, Mishler (1986) suggests, is to be speaking in one's own voice; this speaking provides a basis for applying the insights so acquired, to form a basis for action in accord with one's own interests.

In the individual second interviews, there was a substantial part in which the interviewees discussed unemployment with me.

KKB: Why do you say that there aren't many jobs around?

BHS8:   I reckon it's due to Margaret Thatcher. On telly she says she wants employment but she doesn't really.

149

KKB: What makes you say that she doesn't really – what makes you think that?

BHS8:   When you watch telly and the way she goes on [. . . .] – there was this programme we was watching on Sunday and they were talking about how the West Indians should go back to you know, their thingy, 'cause they don't want to work, and I watching that. She's like saying that and if they pass a law all the West Indians will have to go back to their own country 'cause we don't want to work, we just want to laze about – that's what the telly said. Me mum was watching – she went mad.

KKB: Why do you say it's hard to get jobs?

BHS24:   I think because a lot of people haven't got the qualifications they need really and I know that there's a lot of black people that have got good qualifications but I reckon it's because of their colour that they can't get the job they want. I thing the room is there but I think people just don't want them because of their colour. I reckon if a white person came along with less qualifications but still had a good chance of getting it, I think they'd give it to him.

These two speakers, both black, demonstrate how most of the black interviewees, in their one-to-one interviews with me, discussed racialism as an integral part of their ideas about unemployment. Again, it could be argued that in being given a voice, and using the notion of empowerment suggested earlier, the black interviewees were empowered.

Not one of the white interviewees, in their discussions of unemployment, touched on the issue of racial discrimination or racism with me. We need to ask 'why not?' The group discussions had covered the issue of racialism (initiated by the school students themselves) as had the first interviews, so the interviewees were aware that the explicit and implicit framework of the research could be to discuss racialism and racism if they so wished. Most of the white interviewees had earlier said that individual acts of racial discrimination were undesirable. From their spontaneous questions, it was clear that they had defined me as black, and, so may have assumed that, I too, had experienced such discrimination. This absence on the part of the white interviewees to initiate the discussion on racialism could be 'explained' by arguing that they had never experienced racism. However, this last explanation would ignore the point that they were all able to discuss their futures, house ownership, management of small businesses: all parts of their lives of which they had no experience. So, an experiential explanation is not sufficient to account for this absence. But, putting to one side the reasons for this absence (touched upon in Bhavnani 1986a), how may this silence be analysed?

It could be speculated that the absence of racialist views in the discussions of unemployment was empowering – both for black people and for the white interviewees. Empowering for black people because ideas which have been used to oppress have not been expressed; and empowering for white people because it demonstrates that racism is not a necessary, or, indeed, a sufficient explanation when discussing causes of unemployment. The absence of racist explanations, was empowering, in other words, because of the silence – because it was not given a voice; racism was not expressed. This argument can also be seen in Minh-ha when she states:

Silence as a will not to say or a will to unsay and as a language of its own has barely been explored.

(Minh-ha 1988: 74)

In considering empowerment in this way, it can be seen that empowerment and giving a voice are not necessarily synonymous.

CONCLUSIONS

Let me conclude by saying that I am suggesting that:

1. an analysis of power should be a part of all research, even if such an analysis is not the primary focus of the research.

2. That it is not *qualitative* research, per se, which is sufficient to provide a voice for dominated groups. Rather, it is the conceptual and theoretical basis for the research which may be the starting point when considering empowerment and social research.

151

3. I am arguing that the concept of empowerment has been overdetermined by the idea of 'giving a voice'. It is true that, often, 'giving a voice' may be a necessary step towards empowerment – using the definition of empowerment with which I began. But such an emphasis can also hide, or mask, the reasons *why* the voices are not being heard, or listened to. In other words, the idea of 'giving a voice' must provide a simultaneous analysis of those who are potential hearers, and why they do not hear.

4. Finally, it is crucial, also, to consider carefully 'who is being empowered?' In whose interests does that empowerment serve? For example, Billig's (1978) work on a social psychological analysis of fascists was aimed at *dis*empowering the group he was researching. And, so, the empowerment was aimed at those who challenge fascism, not those who espouse it.

Thus, it is clear that discussions of empowerment must be grounded in the wider nexus of political, economic, and social power relationships. For it is only as power is deconstructed, and the ways in which the inscriptions of the different elements are analysed, that it can be possible for social psychology to not claim to, as Brecht argues when discussing drama, simply represent reality, but also to suggest the possibility of the alteration of the reality. And, to paraphrase Adorno, it is necessary to begin by magnifying the splinter of glass in the eye of psychology.

NOTE

I should like to thank Ruth Frankenberg, Lata Mani, Sarah Pyett, and Jon Rust for their help and comments in writing this article. The previously published version of this chapter was published in *Text* (1988) 8 (1/2): 41–50. That paper was first presented as part of a symposium on Discourse and Power at the 3rd International Conference on Language and Social Psychology, held at Bristol, England, in July 1987.

Part Three

SUBJECTIVITY AND INDIVIDUALITY

The texts, discourses, and practices that hold social psychology together have a particular power. The deconstruction of texts and power focuses, in Part 3 on the question of subjectivity. Texts engage and trap people in a range of subject positions, and it then becomes almost as difficult for a social psychologist to escape as it is for those they study. Continuing a theme raised in Part 2, one consequence of this is that attempts to simply give a voice to subjects (or respondents or interviewees) end up reinstating the privilege a benefactor has as one who can generously bestow rights to speak. John Shotter draws attention to this problem, and takes up the idea that an alternative progressive social individuality should be pitted against the competitive, possessive subjectivity western culture has produced. Traditional social psychology always contains within it specifications for the ideal subject. These specifications are sometimes called 'models of man'. Intergroup theory is one such theoretical framework, and, put under a little pressure by Mike Michael, the supposed concern with the 'social' collapses to reveal a mechanistic picture of the (masculine) individual.

Deconstruction as a method for the subversion of texts from within has been useful to radicals in social psychology, and post-structuralism has been looked to to indicate how the work could be done. At the same time, however, a much looser sense of 'deconstruction' has been informing some critiques. This work would lie under the third meaning of deconstruction we outlined in the Introduction. David Pilgrim prefers to keep his distance from Derrida and Foucault: his work both attempts methodologically to respect the subjective reality of the participants in the study, and the topic of his research is psychotherapy – an endeavour which attempts to respect and release personal meanings. This raises some issues which then set the context for a consideration of deconstruction and psychoanalysis. What Derrida is to texts, and Foucault is to power, Lacan is to subjectivity. Janet Sayers, then, brings, together an account of Lacan's work, and situates this in an overview of psychoanalytic views of gender. Psychoanalysis has operated in a contradictory way as a set of texts and practices with regard to women. At times it is deeply reactionary, at other points (and with a selective use of Lacan's writings) it has empowered feminists, a fact which has many repercussions for the deconstruction of other disciplines which claim to be concerned with social relations.

The feminist uses of deconstruction bring us back to politics. It is not possible to engage in any critical project in the human sciences (reconstructive or deconstructive) without addressing the political implications of the theories we use. Erica Burman assesses the claims made for post-structuralist accounts of gender, and brings feminist concerns to bear on the debates. Deconstruction does open up contradictions in the discipline. The question, which is addressed in Chapter 15, is whether we should be satisfied with the perpetual conceptual housecleaning that the approach provokes or whether we should be making things more uncomfortable for social psychology by basing our deconstruction in a political critique.

Chapter Eleven

SOCIAL INDIVIDUALITY VERSUS POSSESSIVE INDIVIDUALISM:
THE SOUNDS OF SILENCE

John Shotter

'I behaved stubbornly, pursuing a semblance of order, I should have known well that there is no order in the universe.'
'But in imagining an erroneous order you still found something . . . .'

(Umberto Eco 1983: 492)

Parker (in Chapter 6, this volume) discusses some of the reasons why many of the radical alternatives to mainstream positivistic social psychology put forward in the late 1960s and early 1970s, reinforced the very isolation of individuals from social life they were intended to overcome. We now realise the problems were more deeply rooted: currently, there is something in the very nature of social life itself which works systematically to exclude many from public participation in the determination of their own future. So, although I would like to explore below another, more socially embedded (as Edward Sampson puts it in Chapter 8, this volume) image of individuality than that implicit in liberal humanism. I will not do it by providing an explicit outline of it, and arguing for its worth. Such images on their own are insufficient. The voices of those who are presently silent in social psychology, are not silenced because of its theories, but by its *professional practices* (and by the images of people and their social life implicit in them which serve to legitimate them). It is these practices which must be criticised and the image of individuality implicitly informing them changed, if social psychology is to be radically reconstructed. For otherwise, any merely theoretical alternatives are immediately annulled and controverted. Central in this criticism is an analysis of people's individual rights to speak and to have what they say taken seriously, i.e. either acted upon, or if not, responded to with some good reasons why not.

SOCIAL PSYCHOLOGY: ITS LOCATION IN TEXTS

Social psychology's most important practice might seem to be its explicit 'methodology': it is built upon the supposedly firm foundations of rational inquiry, the assumption that (proper scientific) knowledge is only acquired as a result of systematic thought and orderly investigation. But within social psychology, this 'methodology' only has sense, and only makes sense, in a context of other activities and practices. Central among these (although I shall also have a lot to say about face-to-face talk and debate later) is its production of *written texts*. All professional psychology and social psychology moves from text to text, usually beginning with the reading of already written texts, and ending with the writing of further texts.

Within the many forms of linguistic communication, the written text has a special place. This is because it can be used as a means by readers to construct a meaning solely by reference to the linguistic resources they possess within themselves. It is a carefully interwoven sequence of written sentences, structured within itself to an enormous degree by essentially intralinguistic or syntactical relations. Thus it can be said to be a (relatively) de-contextualised form of communication. The relevance of all this for us, as professional scientists, is: that whatever else a *scientific* theory is, it is always and inevitably something written and published within the context of a publicly available text. Furthermore, to the extent that all theoretical writing claims that things are not what they ordinarily seem to be, but are 'in reality' something else, the terms of a theory are not intelligible in the same way as terms in ordinary language. They need a special form of introduction: if we want to be taken seriously in our scientific claims, we need to be 'instructed' in how to see various social phenomena *as* having a certain psychological character, e.g. to see them *as* common understandings or beliefs, *as* social representations, *as* prejudices, *as* attitudes, *as* attributions, *as* learned helplessness, etc.

But in addition to these considerations, we must also add that science is conducted within a context of argumentation (Billig

1987; Popper 1963). Thus all the claims we make are made against the background of other previous textually expressed claims.

For some, the implication of this is that all of psychology without exception should be seen as moving from text to text, as solely an intertextual activity; whilst others (among whom I include myself) take a different view, that there is more to a person than can ever be expressed within the confines of a text – a view for which I shall argue below. Irrespective of one's stance upon this issue. However, it is now necessary to accept the importance of something hitherto ignored: the centrality of texts and the processes of their production in the conduct of psychology as a professional enterprise.

But this immediately arouses an anxiety, however, for as we all know, texts are nothing if not the medium *par excellence* of fiction, of story-telling. We only have to read any science fiction novel to know that what is presented and experienced as an account of an actual (but in fact imaginary) reality works, so to speak, to 'manufacture' the sense of reality it conveys. What if, because we (wrongly) believe such texts to 'contain' the true subject matter of psychology, we (wrongly) accord them more prominence *psychologically* than the social activities and practices making their production possible? Could it be that in psychology we are the victims of an enormous, corporate self- deception, and that much of what we take to be its subject matter is imaginary in the same way as the 'worlds' of science fiction?

SCIENCE AND STORYTELLING

This is where a 'deconstructive' analysis becomes relevant. For *deconstruction* in literary criticism functions, not to provide an extra gloss upon a textual production in an attempt to elaborate its (possibly unclear) meaning, but is concerned with revealing the messy, disorderly, and often socially unequal *processes* of negotiation which have gone into its formulation and construction as a finally ordered and coherent *product* (Belsey 1980; Culler 1982; Norris 1982, 1983) – processes not represented in the text itself, and about which the text of necessity is itself silent. It is precisely these social processes of negotiation (not only in the sense of bargaining but also in the sense in which one negotiates a difficult sea passage, by making use of one's limited powers and resources

157

prudently) which remain hidden behind-the-scenes in the finally polished texts professional social psychologists make publicly available. As Celia Kitzinger (Chapter 4, in this volume) says, the problem is not bad science but to some extent is to do with the nature of science itself – for, as we shall see, in 'making discoveries', rather than merely 'finding', there is more 'making' at work than we previously thought. Why is this?

Another aspect of deconstruction is relevant here. Besides emphasising the importance of the social process involved in a text's production, deconstruction also (re)emphasises the primarily *rhetorical* (and poetic) character of language – something well known in the past, but gradually forgotten as the scientific revolution took its hold (Ong 1958; Vico 1948, 1982). There are two aspects to this emphasis, one familiar and the other not: (1) the familiar aspect of rhetoric is to do with the *persuasive* function of language, the fact that it can be used materially to affect the behaviour of other people, and to 'move' them to action, or to change their perceptions in some way; (2) the other more unfamiliar aspect of rhetoric, however, is related to those aspects of language to do with 'giving' or 'lending' a *first form* to what otherwise are in fact only vaguely or partially ordered feelings and activities, or, to do with the study of how common understandings are established *before* one turns to their criticism. It is this: the realisation that, even in the face of the vague, indescribable, open, fluid, and ever changing nature of human life (its messy nature), language can work 'to make it appear as if' it is well ordered and structured, its form-giving or form-lending aspect, which is for us rhetoric's most important characteristic.

Elsewhere (Shotter 1986a), I have traced discussions of this aspect of rhetoric back to Vico. Current deconstructionists, however, often see themselves as linked to Nietzsche. De Man (1979: 105–6), for instance, in claiming that the figurative aspect of language is not just one linguistic mode among many but characterises all language as such, quotes Nietzsche as follows:

It is not difficult to demonstrate that what is called 'rhetorical' as the devices of a conscious art, is present as a device of unconscious art in language and its development . . . . No such thing as unrhetorical 'natural' language exists that could be used as a point of reference: language is itself

the result of purely rhetorical tricks and devices . . . . Tropes
are not something that can be added or subtracted from a
language at will; they are its truest nature. There is no such
thing as a proper meaning that can be communicated only in
certain particular cases.

Among the many implications of this, as De Man points out, is a
whole set of seeming *reversals* of a surprising kind. Dependencies
which we thought to be in one direction are revealed as (perhaps)
being the opposite way round. For example: (1) just at the
moment, we feel that in our 'experience', outer 'objective' events
cause inner 'subjective' effects (i.e. our perceptions of them). And
we make use of this in our theories about the nature of knowledge
and modes of inquiry: we feel some claims to truth are *certain*, not
because of the arguments given for them, but because in some way
they are caused in us or imposed upon us by the outer, objective
nature of the world. These truths can be used as 'foundations'
upon which to base our further inquiries. Deconstructive analysis,
however, shows such a belief to be an illusion. In fact, the seeing of
objects involves an active psychological process of construction
involving socially derived knowledge – doesn't it? To build
knowledge upon foundations constructed upon an analogy
between perceiving and knowing, is to see *certainty* as a matter of
the world 'outside' our human world imposing something upon
us, rather than as something we achieve in conversation between
ourselves. (2) Or again: our 'experience' of individuals as having
and speaking a language, as if their language is a possession among
other possessions which they could relinquish if they wanted to, is
also seen as an illusion; we acquire our identity by learning how to
participate in a whole mêlée of linguistically mediated communicative activities; thus, it is our language which has us and
speaks us – isn't it?

Well, yes (to a degree) and no (to a degree). It means that we
must finally face up to the lack of any pre-established orders in the
world: (1) that instead of thinking of our task as that of finding
such an order, ready-made, we must consider activities which
begin with vague, but not wholly unspecified 'tendencies' which
are then open to, or which permit a degree of actual further
specification; also (2) instead of thinking it possible for special
individuals trained in special methods simply to make 'dis-

coveries', any further specifications of states of affairs, if they are to be considered *intelligible and legitimate* to those around us, must be negotiated in a step-by-step process with them. In other words, we must now think in terms of processes of investigation involving both 'finding' *and* 'making'. I have tried to include the main aspects of the situation in Figure 11.1.

Figure 11.1

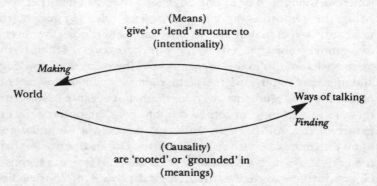

(Means)
'give' or 'lend' structure to
(intentionality)

Making

World

Ways of talking

Finding

(Causality)
are 'rooted' or 'grounded' in
(meanings)

Figure 11.1 shows that, as in classical *empiricist* approaches, we *could say* (i.e. the facts permit us to say) that our ways of talking *depend* upon the world; to the extent that our talk is rooted, or grounded in what the facts of the world will permit or allow us to say, our talk is about what we 'find' to be there. But on the other hand, in line with *hermeneutical* or interpretive views, it is equally true to say that what we take to be the nature of the world *depends* upon our ways of talking about it; thus, to the extent that it is they that 'give' or 'lend' it intelligible (and legitimate) structure and significance, it is as we 'make' it to be. And the fact is, not only that one can say both, but that one *must* assert that both are true; for as Derrida (1977) would point out, they owe their distinct existences to their *interdependency*; one claim is an *absent–presence* in 'lending' intelligibility to the other. Thus although one must say only what the facts will permit, the nature of the facts above are such that, within different systematic discourses, two equal and opposite truths can be asserted. This, of course, is precisely what Billig (1987) is now arguing in relation to the importance of rhetoric and the two-sidedness of human thinking generally.

However, we find that very difficult to accept. For all kinds of reasons in the history of philosophy (see e.g. Cassirer 1951), we are still committed to the image of knowledge as being both systematic and unitary. What other form could it have? Thus we *must* talk in terms of systems of one-way dependencies, in terms of relations of dominance. Of the two equal and opposite claims – about which is or should be the *dominant* dependency relation – we feel that it is impossible for *both* to be true. We find a two-sided truth unthinkable, and because of this think that in reality one pole of the polarity must quite 'naturally' dominate the other. This is why Derrida's (1976) work is of such importance in philosophy and the social sciences: because he shows (through a number of worked examples) how any attempt to formulate such a system of dependencies, or to argue systematically, within or through the medium of written texts, subverts itself – at work but hidden within such texts is the equal and opposite polarity of an interdependency, the repressed 'other' upon which the 'system' relies for its maintenance in existence. But in order to *legitimate* its claims to be a 'naturally' dominant order, it must repress, silence, or pretend to ignore (often without any explicit intention to do so) the 'voice' of its 'other'.

WARRANTING CLAIMS TO TRUTH: THE RIGHTS OF THE SOCIAL INDIVIDUAL

Let me discuss the reversals effected by various textual strategies further: One reversal 'undone' by a deconstructive analysis is, De Man claims, to do with the roots or grounding of language, with how one supports or warrants what one says as true. It marks a full reversal, he says (De Man 1978: 106), 'of the established priorities which traditionally root the authority of language in its adequation to an extralinguistic referent or meaning, rather than in the intralinguistic resources of figures'. The meaning of this claim can, however, be explored in two different realms: in relation to professional texts, to 'undo', so to speak, their claim that their 'truths' are well-founded; and in relation to ordinary, non-textual, conversation, to illustrate the location of its 'rootedness'.

Texts

With respect to written texts, deconstructionists themselves interpret it as meaning that no systematic texts can, in any simple way, work as truthful, non-fictional representations: they are always structured just as much (if not more) by literary devices than by supposedly independent 'empirical' realities. Thus Rorty (1980), for instance, in discussing the textual nature of modern philosophies of mind – the 'discourses of legitimation' (Lyotard 1984) upon which one way or another philosophy, and all research in psychology relies in making sense of its activities – exposes their ineradicably metaphorical nature, and how these (and not empirical facts) have determined what we think to be indubitably true about the nature of mind.

About why he chose *Philosophy and the Mirror of Nature* as the title of his book, he says that it is because:

> It is pictures rather than propositions, metaphors rather than statements which determine most of our philosophical convictions .... [And] without the notion of the mind as mirror, the notion of knowledge as accuracy of representation would not have suggested itself.

> *(Rorty 1980: 12)*

Indeed, if we were blind and had to make use either of auditory or tactile metaphors, then, for instance, we might find Wittgenstein's (1980) more practical talk about correct knowledge as being to do, not with accuracy of representation, but as a matter of 'knowing one's way about' (e.g. 1980, I, no. 549), or with being able to 'go on' (e.g. 1980, I, no. 446) without stumbling or meeting insurmountable barriers, as perfectly acceptable, not as metaphorical but 'literally' what correct knowledge is.

Conversation

These effects of 'idiom' require and have been explored further (Ortony 1979; Johnson 1987; Lakoff 1986; Lakoff and Johnson 1980). However, although many are exploring the implications of rhetoric and deconstruction in relation to the textual aspects of academic discipline (and in a moment I will mention Stam's (1986) work specifically upon social psychological texts), here I want to turn to some other implications of Rorty's work: (1) what has come to be known as his 'antifoundationalism'; and (2) his replacement of 'foundations of knowledge' by *conversation* – for this is the reversal he effects: the substitution of more everyday rhetorical or argumentative practices to replace the grounding for our claims to knowledge we have in the past found in certain philosophies. In particular, I want to explore the *non-textual* character of conversation. I want to do this for two reasons: one is that it will have a direct bearing upon the uniqueness of people's embedded individualities, and their right to speak for themselves, which I want to explore below. But the other reason is, because of deconstruction's emphasis upon 'intertextuality' – the claim that a text only ever 'makes sense' by appeals to other texts – it seems as if one must forever whirl around in a maelstrom of textual relativity. And this of course is upsetting to those of us who feel that we must take a stance towards the world, and must attempt to act rightly.

The essence of textual communication is, as already mentioned above, its intertexuality: the fact that it draws upon people's knowledge of *already formulated* meanings in the making of its own meaning – this is why texts can be understood without contexts, i.e. independently of immediate and local contexts. But as Garfinkel (1967) points out, in ordinary conversation people refuse to permit each other to understand what they are talking about in this way – as if they were assembling a meaning from a set of already pre-existing component meanings. A meaning unique to the situation and to the people in it is required. But that is not easy to negotiate. Thus, what precisely is 'being talked about' in a conversation, as we all in fact know from our own experience, is often at many points in the conversation necessarily unclear; we *must* offer each other opportunities to contribute to the making of agreed meanings.

Thus, only gradually do we come to an understanding (and even then it is often limited just to matters in hand, so to speak). As Garfinkel (1967: 40) says about such understandings, they are not objects but events, and furthermore, they are not just events which happen in an instant. Such an event is all the time developing and developed *within* the course of action which produces it, and as both process and product it is only 'known *from within* this development by both parties, each for himself [or herself] as well as on behalf of the other' – indeed, a quite special but unrecognised kind of knowledge is involved here; it is not a 'knowing-that' (theoretical knowledge) for it is practical knowledge known to us only in practice, but neither is it a 'knowing-how' (technical knowledge) for it is particular to the proprieties of its social situation. It is a third kind of knowledge of a *practical-moral* kind (Bernstein 1983; Shotter 1986a, 1986b). Ignoring it, leads us to ignore the unique nature of situations *and* of the people within them. We can thus begin to see why, when Garfinkel had his students try to talk as if words should have already determined clear meanings, it produced a morally motivated anger in the student's victims. People felt that in some way their rights had been transgressed – and as Garfinkel shows, they had!

What should we say then about the nature of words and their meanings, if we are not to see them as having already determined meanings? Perhaps, rather than *already* having a meaning, we should see the *use* of a word as a *means* (but only as *one* means among many others) in the social making of a meaning. Thus then, the 'making sense', the production of a meaning, would not be a simple 'one-pass' matter of an individual saying a sentence, but would be a complex back-and-forth process of negotiation between speaker and hearer, involving tests and assumptions, the use of the present context, the waiting for something later to make clear what was meant before, and the use of many other 'seen but unnoticed' background features of everyday scenes, all deployed according to agreed practices or 'methods'. These are in fact the properties Garfinkel claims of ordinary conversational talk. And as he says (1967: 41–2):

> People require these properties of discourse as conditions under which they are themselves entitled and entitle others to claim that they know what they are talking about, and that what they are saying is understandable and ought to be understood. In short, their seen but unnoticed presence is used to entitle persons to conduct their common conversational affairs without interference. Departures from such usages call forth immediate attempts to restore a right state of affairs.

Moral sanctions follow such transgressions. Thus, to insist words have predetermined meanings is to rob people of their rights to their own individuality. But even more than this is involved: it is to deprive one's culture of those conversational occasions in which people's individuality is constituted and reproduced. It is also to substitute the authority of professional texts in warranting claims to truth (on the basis as we now see of the unwarranted claim that they give us access to an independent, extralinguistic reality), for the *good reasons* we ordinarily give one another in our more informal conversations and debates.

POSSESSIVE INDIVIDUALISM AS A LEGITIMATING DISCOURSE

Thus clearly, there is more to learning how to be a morally acceptable (and autonomous) member of a culture in common with others, than simply discovering how to make use of a set of already determined meanings, values, or beliefs. If we are to avoid the sanctions of others, we must learn something much more complex: rather than a set of 'intersubjectively shared' meanings, we must avail ourselves of, and come to embody, a quite different set of cultural resources. But we cannot do this on our own. We require 'instruction' in how to develop the appropriate 'psychological instruments' (Shotter, in press; Vygotsky 1966), the *means* through which we must (morally) act: not only in giving form to our thoughts, actions, and utterances; but also to our perceptions; and most importantly, in regulating the effects we might have by our actions upon the other people around us. Hence the character of such culturally available resources as both (morally) enabling *and* constraining: for only if we constrain what we make of our opportunities by use of such 'ways and means', are we enabled as individuals to act both freely, *thus*, to act uniquely in a way we feel is appropriate to our own, unique circumstances.

Here is not the place to discuss the nature of the social processes involved in people's development as social rather than as 'possessive' individuals, and the nature of the 'political economy of developmental opportunities' to which it gives rise. I have discussed these issues extensively elsewhere (Shotter 1984, 1986a, in press). But once again, what I want to discuss here is the nature of the textual strategies by which a certain dominant image of individuality is maintained (and which prevents the development of an understanding of social individuality). That image is the image of possessive individualism which haunts the structure of all liberal humanistic thought. Its nature is well expressed by Macpherson (1962: 3), who twenty-five years ago was worrying about the difficulties in political theory of combining a sense of the moral worth of the individual with a sense of the moral worth of the value of community, even more relevant now than then. The difficulties of 'modern liberal democratic theory lie deeper than had been thought,' he said, the central difficulty lies in its 'possessive quality'. Where:

> Its possessive quality is found in its conception of the individual as essentially the proprietor of his own person or capacities, owing nothing to society for them. The individual was seen neither as a moral whole, nor as a part of a larger social whole, but as an owner of himself. The relation of ownership, having become for more and more men the critically important relation determining their actual freedom and actual prospect of realising their full poten- tialities, was read back into the nature of the individual.

And as I have indicated elsewhere (Shotter 1975), this concern with possession is present also in Descartes's view of science, in which he thinks of his 'method' as enabling us to 'make ourselves masters and possessors of nature' (Descartes 1968: 78). We thus have here, implicit in our philosophical talk both about the nature of individuals and of science, a taken-for-granted separation of thinking individuals (along with all their other psychological 'properties') from their social surroundings. Thus, the only legitimate linguistic currency available to us *within the profession*, irrespective of our explicit attempts to counteract it, re-enmeshes us in an isolating form of individualism. The very textual practices we *must* use, if we are to be accounted by other professionals as engaging in a properly professional critique, re-legitimates what we attack and renders our attack ineffective.

As Stam (1986) has already very clearly illustrated the effect of these textual practices in social psychology – in relation also to our concern here with how people experience their autonomy and individuality – let me now turn to a brief exposition of his work. He discusses three areas: (1) the locus of control construct (e.g. Rotter 1966); (2) learned helplessness theory (e.g. Abramson, Seligman, and Teasdale 1978); and (3) self-efficacy theory (e.g. Bandura

1977). The general tenor of his analysis can be illustrated by what he has to say about learned helplessness theory. As is well known, the theory was first used to describe the impaired escape–avoidance behaviour of dogs, following their exposure to uncontrollable shocks. Rather than simply in terms of learned 'expectations' the theory has now been reformulated in terms of attribution theory to apply to human beings: the current *attributions* people make for past noncontingencies between their responses and outcomes, are said to influence their expectations of future noncontingency. This formulation is, as Stam points out, avowedly asocial. Thus when the theory is applied, as it is now increasingly to depression, its asocial nature leads only to a limited set of suggestions for therapy. As Stam (1986: 141) says:

> therapy consists of various philanthropic welfare arrange-ments (e.g. housing), relinquishing unattainable goals, and changing 'unrealistic attributions' (Abramson *et al.* 1978). Note, however, that none of these proposals involves giving the depressed person more control over their contingencies. The question of the social origins of learned helplessness remains unaddressed as does the very constitution of the social world. Rather it is deemed both irrelevant and determined. It is the individual who must change and adapt in his/her isolation.

But what are the textual practices which sustain this state of affairs? Stam (1986, following Wexler 1983) describes them as: *desocialisation, deproblematisation, deinstitutionalisation,* and *dehistori-cisation*. All essentially result in re-contextualising social psycho-logical issues by separating them from the actual socio-historical contexts within which they occur and re-situating them within a new intralinguistic, textually, *and professionally* created 'social reality'; but to motivate the reading of Stam's important article I will not here elaborate upon them further. Instead, I will describe the 'three tricks for the production of "ruling illusions"' men-tioned by Marx and Engels (1977: 67), which seem to me to parallel exactly the recommended 'methodology' in social psychological research. No. 1 is to separate, in its writing down, the data one collects from the particular individuals who enact it and the particular situations in which it is enacted. (This is done by setting up the conditions said to be required for the controlled observation of regularities.) No. 2 is to 'find' an order in the data and to present it as a 'scientific discovery'. (This is done textually, in a number of different ways, usually by relating the data to the supposed 'empirical' implications of a particular theory – but see Smedslund (1978), who shows such implications to be also purely linguistic.) No. 3 is where the order is now 'explained' as being due to a certain causal agent, something within us which 'rules' our conduct. It is in this way that the real social and political conditions of our lives are rendered invisible, and furthermore, we ourselves (as ordinary people) are silenced in our attempts to speak about them. For, without instruction in the proper professional procedures, one is not taken seriously. But – and I hesitate to make the accusation for it is a serious one – is it 'ruling illusions' such as these which are the commodities (professionally chartered) social psychologists are 'manufacturing' for sale upon the open market? If not, what other account can they give of themselves?

CONCLUSIONS: SOCIAL INDIVIDUALITY

I have been exploring above a non-cognitive, social constructionist (Gergen 1982, 1985; Harré 1983; Shotter 1984) – and non-systematic – approach to human individuality. And implicitly, I have been making (what some may see as paradoxical) the claim that it can afford us an understanding of people's rights as *unique* individuals denied us by our current approaches to social psychology – given their scientistic, and inter- and intra-individualistic, cognitive biases. It currently denies us such an understanding, not because of its exclusion of such theories, but by its insistence upon certain 'professional' textual practices. Thus, no matter how benevolent as a professional psychologist one may be towards those one studies, no matter how concerned with 'their' liberation, with 'their' betterment, with preventing 'their' victimisation, etc., the fact is that 'their' lives are not made sense of in 'their' terms. While what they say is treated as 'data', they themselves are not treated seriously as being able to speak the truth about their own lives; their claims cannot pass the appropriate institutional tests (see Dreyfus and Rabinow 1982: 47–8). The terms in which their behaviour is described do, however, make sense to those who 'rule' them: for the very form of a social scientific 'finding', as a cause–effect, as a conditions–consequence relation, indicates a relation of domination, one which is often rendered ineffective, luckily, by its (mysteriously hidden) lack of scope.

So, in terms of social justice alone, there is cause for complaint: there is no place in which the unique 'voices' of nonprofessional individuals can be heard and taken seriously in their talk about their lives. But there is a further issue which some might think even more important: the social constructionist approach above can be extended to explain, not only why we as a matter of fact possess unique social identities, but also why (morally) it is *necessary* for us to do so. For only if we are *all* able (i.e. are allowed the opportunities) to express our social 'position' in our actions in relation to the set of 'positions' constituting 'the way of life' to which we belong, can we responsibly contribute to its reproduction in our actions (Giddens 1984; Shotter 1984).

Thus those who see a danger in Thatcherism's explicit contempt for communal enterprises (and for non-professional individuals), and who are worried by its reshaping of education as a commodity for sale in a market of possessive individuals, have cause for more than just humanitarian concern: it neglects the intricately negotiated, rhetorically developed and culturally transmitted, means and devices by which people sustain their way of life (and the forms of mentality it makes available to them), and by which in turn, amongst themselves they sustain their individuality. Society is more than an accidental collection of individual men and women, and of families. It is a set of practices and procedures, of orderly institutions giving rise to structures of thought and feeling, all deriving their sense from their rooting in the 'bustle' of everyday public life (Wittgenstein 1980, II, nos. 624, 625, 626, 629). Our society's achievements, our ways of doing things, our customs and laws, our industries and our sciences, and crucially our words, depend for their significance just as much upon the common and collective sense of the people as upon the refined claims of professional researchers. People's (unpaid) contributions to the bustle of everyday life are the sounds of silence we do not at the moment dare share in, for fear of losing our professional status.

Chapter Twelve

INTERGROUP THEORY AND DECONSTRUCTION

Mike Michael

Since the revitalisation of intergroup research in the early seventies, a substantial body of work has been generated that links up with two particularly 'productive' areas of social psychology: attribution theory (and the psychology of ordinary explanations) and social representations. This convergence, if not outright integration, embraces a variety of traditional social psychological concerns including social perception, identity and self, the relation of the individual to group and society, motivational parameters (such as the needs for familiarity, control and self-esteem), and cognitive processes (such as categorisation, memory, and attention). Intergroup theory constitutes a major component in contemporary European social psychology. To deconstruct it is therefore to embark on a strategic critique of modern social psychology at one of its ostensibly more social frontiers.

In this chapter, there will first be a brief summary of intergroup theory. While special attention is paid to the recent elaborations of Turner, an outline of some of the major research trends within the field will also be presented. From this I will distill what will be generically called intergroup theory (IGT). Before launching into the deconstruction, I will consider some of the more general parallels that can be drawn between deconstruction and IGT.

Through deconstruction it will be shown that IGT has systematically neglected content, preferring to illuminate the processes or mechanisms underlying intergroup behaviour. By demonstrating how some of IGT's pivotal concepts exclude other concepts while simultaneously being constituted through this process of exclusion, the importance of content is revealed. In other words, the abstract processes invoked by IGT are shown to be content-laden. The significance of this is that the historicity of these concepts, and the processes they purport to describe, are laid bare. Three elements of IGT will be addressed. Drawing on Billig's (1985) and Williams' (1984) important critiques, the privileging of categorisation and prejudice, and IGT's masculine bias, are the first and second elements. The third addresses IGT's model of the individual as non-reflexive.

INTERGROUP THEORY

In exploring the minimal conditions for intergroup discrimination, Tajfel (Tajfel *et al.* 1971; Billig and Tajfel 1973) showed that by simply categorising subjects in one or other group (even when this was conducted on a completely arbitrary basis), subjects would exhibit gross in-group favouritism. This was manifested as maximum differentiation in which the out-group was maximally deprived of rewards, even where this resulted in a relative loss in the in-group's profit. However, Turner (1975, 1978a, 1981) found that categorisation *per se* could not account for these findings. By introducing the possibility of rewarding the self, where the choice of rewarding either self, out-group or in-group preceded the choice of rewarding between in-group and out-group, the out-group discrimination effect diminished significantly. Turner interpreted his results as showing that social identity, as well as categorisation, affected intergroup behaviour: that is, subjects had first to identify with the categories imposed by the experimenter before the pattern of in-group favouritism and out-group discrimination manifested itself.

On the basis of this work, Tajfel (1978) formulated social identity theory. Turner (1982, 1984, 1985, 1987) has since elaborated a cognitive definition of the social group. Accordingly, individuals define themselves in terms of distinct social categories, learning the stereotypic norms of that category and the behaviours that are criterial attributes for category membership. Actors assign norms to themselves in the same way that they assign stereotypic traits to others; in other words, there is involved in group identification a process of self-stereotyping. As category membership becomes more salient, behaviour becomes more normative and conformist. Under these circumstances social identity is positively enhanced.

To this end the following processes should come into play: (1) individuals will tend to evaluate distinctive (in-)category characteristics positively; (2) conflict with out-groups will be manifested for the purposes of distinguishing the in-group from out-groups; (3) within the in-group, individuals will move (and claim to be) closer to the group norm and thereby assert that they are superior to other group members.

So, the desire for positive self-esteem is partially fulfilled in membership of the group. Self-categorisation leads individuals to identify with groups, to differentiate their group from and to compete against others. In consequence, self-esteem is enhanced. Social situational factors affect the salience of self-categories (self-images) and group membership. It is in the process of social interaction that such factors arise and evoke the relevant categories. Thus social identity simultaneously draws upon the social (i.e. individuals are 'embodiments of historical, cultural and politico-ideological forces', Turner and Oakes 1986: 249); mediates the social (incorporates social norms making interaction meaningful); and contributes to the social by 'inducing uniformities of action' (p. 249).

In explicating Turner's work in particular, there is inevitably an injustice done to the diversity of IGT as a whole. In both empirical and theoretical domains there are major differences of accent. For example, categorisation is accorded primary importance in the work of some researchers (e.g. Deschamps 1984; Doise 1978). Others have attempted to specify the conditions which mediate or affect intergroup differentiation: similarity with the out-group (Turner 1978b; Brown 1984); individuation of the out-group (Wilder 1978); perception of the in-group's position in relevant status hierarchies (Ng 1980); cross-category membership (e.g. Doise 1978); superior conformity of the self (Codol 1975); stereotyping (Huici 1984). In addition to these theoretical concerns are those studies which have applied the intergroup approach to concrete social phenomena such as: racism (Milner 1981); class and education (Hewstone *et al.* 1982); the women's movement (Williams and Giles 1978); a factory workforce (Brown 1978); a riot (Reicher 1984); political parties (Mummendey and Schreiber 1984). Moreover, there is an increasing urgency in the critical awareness that intergroup theory needs to be fundamentally integrated with social phenomena that have remained largely outside its purview. These would include ideology and social structure (Billig 1976), discourse and power (Henriques *et al.* 1984), myth (Tajfel 1984), socio-historical conditions (Taylor and McKirnan 1984).

This partial survey of the IGT research endeavour, while giving a flavour of its richness, should not detract from the fact that, with the exception of a handful of critiques, contemporary IGT research draws upon a core model of the individual (group-research member). Turner's work has painstakingly illuminated the nature of this individual, and it is in his elegant theoretical formulations and empirical investigations that this figure emerges most clearly delineated.

DECONSTRUCTION AND IGT: POINTS OF COLLISION

Deconstruction is the technique of teasing out the strategically neglected part of a text. By fixing on a given set of theories, concepts, ideas, etc., a text solidifies, fixes and asserts its objectivity. This is managed by a process of exclusion in which the excluded concepts shape those entailed in the text. This is the essence of Derrida's *différance* (Derrida 1976, 1978, 1982b; Culler 1982). Deconstruction's task is to recover the excluded term by which the present(ed) term is formulated.

This procedure allows access to the hidden presuppositions of a text. The major advance claimed for deconstruction is that it apprehends the immanent categories of a text; it attacks a text on its own grounds, drawing out the hidden terms logically entailed by the present(ed) terms (Ryan 1982). However, these grounds are necessarily historically contingent. What the deconstructionist perceives as the core differences and traces are a product of his or her socio-historical position. The intelligibility and warrantability of a deconstructive analysis, that is, in general terms, its force or potency, derives from the like positioning of the reader. This is not to render any reading relative, but to situate its force historically (Derrida 1982b; Rorty 1980; Bernstein 1986).

In the deconstruction of a text, the central or pivotal terms are identified and counterposed to their 'differences', that is, those suppressed terms which simultaneously oppose them and give them meaning. Derrida's project is to reassert the suppressed terms, to show how they are always covertly incorporated into a text, shaping the present(ed) terms through their absence. The intermediate goal of deconstruction is to overturn the hierarchy of present and absent terms; the eventual aim is to neutralise the opposition by, for example, developing a transcendent term. However, as Derrida also points out, this is a delicate operation. To proceed too quickly to the transcendent term might negate any effective intervention in the text. No attempt will be made to generate or derive neutralising terms, though I will suggest how some of these oppositions might better cohabit. However, before this, some similarities and contrasts between IGT and deconstruction will be presented.

The above elementary characterisation of deconstruction hints at an intergroup analysis of deconstructive practice: that is, the traces, differences, counter-terms excluded by a text emerge only with the aid of the deconstructionist's group-membership. For example, Williams' (1984) persuasive analysis of the masculine bias in social identity theory is partly a result of her own gender-related experiences. At a more general level, this book is an exercise in group identification, the group being that of 'deconstruction-sympathisers'; indeed, Gergen (1985) has identified a social constructionist movement in social psychology. On this score, Rose (1984) has accused various post-modernist thinkers, Derrida included, of over-differentiating themselves from their predecessors. Differentiation is one of the defining characteristics of intergroup behaviour. It is important to reflect on whether deconstruction as the basis of a social identity might not lead deconstructionists to differentiate to the point of severing links with related intellectual and political traditions (see Bernstein 1986).

A potentially more fruitful tack concerns the resemblance between the process of intergroup differentiation and the play of differences in a text or a language. At the academic level, the intergroup theorist perceives society as a multitude of groups of differential status and power, embroiled in a generalised struggle (Tajfel 1978, 1981; Tajfel and Turner 1979) which involves comparison, competition and conflict. Here, deconstruction can analyse the way that social identity (seen as a text) is generated through differentiation, by considering the range of terms/ identities that are excluded. This would be tied to the potency of given 'terms', that is, identities, comparison dimensions, status and economic hierarchies, and so on. For example, Deschamps (1982) has suggested that the dominant white, middle-class male group partially maintains its position by monopolising what is currently a highly potent comparison dimension, what might be called 'individuality'. By describing in-group members in terms of their individual traits and out-group members (e.g. women, 'minority' races/cultures, working class) in terms of their group characteristics, out-group members are downgraded. Deconstruction would show, in this instance, how this individuality derives its power by simultaneously excluding its own group characteristics, while at the same time incorporating them as the unspoken ground on which individuality is based and which this individuality serves to sustain. In brief, the processes of intergroup differentiation would be considered as the play of difference, each group being a text which, more or less explicitly, defines itself by asserting its difference from other groups-cum-texts.

The analogy between IGT and deconstruction is, of course, simplistic and it would be unwise to conflate these disciplines given their different source interests. However, similarities persist. Thus, physical violence is a ready option in the cause of intergroup competition. The play of differences in a text is somewhat more sedate. And yet, it too is grounded in violence, as terms are 'forcibly' excluded from the text. This latter point suggests that the visceral experience of group membership also pervades, though in a dissipated form, a text. This is one of the reasons some critics of deconstruction feel that it is itself a violent intrusion into an actually unitary text (see Culler 1982).

Lack of space precludes the development of the above points here. The rest of the chapter will consist of a partial deconstruction of IGT.

DECONSTRUCTING INTERGROUP THEORY

To briefly summarise, IGT is a theory of process and can be represented step-wise. Individuals perceive the world in terms of social categories. They identify with some of these, classifying themselves in terms of social identities. These social identities are collective, that is, shared by a group. Individuals grow up associated with, and members of, groups. Social identity is made cognitively available by particular social circumstances. It is fundamentally tied to self esteem. In pursuing self-esteem, individuals attempt to enhance their social identity and the standing of their group. This is managed by differentiation from and comparison and competition with out-groups. Social comparison processes depend on the relation of the in-group to the out- group, for example, similarity and relative status. Various means of comparison are deployed, such as derogation of the out-group by shifting to more favourable comparison dimensions, or positively re-evaluating dimensions or characteristics that are downgraded by out-groups.

This theory is process oriented because the content of the categories or identities has little bearing on how intergroup comparison, competition, and so on, are conducted. The influence of content is largely quantitative, affecting the degree as opposed to the very presence and form of comparison.

The exclusion of content serves to elevate process, to make it appear that the processes described are universal. By asserting the formative role of content, we are showing that the process described by a text is not primary, that is, is not the sole origin of the behaviour being explained. That is, processes are tied to different contents, and the variety of content-process patterns needs to be presented for a proper understanding of a given phenomenon, in this case intergroup behaviour. The reinstatement of content can highlight the social dimension of presented concepts that is often only implicit in Derrida's more philosophical projects (Ryan 1982). The content that is relevant in the present context refers to actual social identities (e.g. as a nurse, policeman, etc.). In general, the argument is that these identities will affect the type of behaviour in which the group engages. So, not only does self-categorisation and the need for positive social identity shape group identity by accentuating and/or diminishing certain of its characteristics, but the content of the identity will influence the way comparison and, indeed, co-operation is conducted, and the way self-esteem is generated. Inevitably, these identities are historical and socially conditioned. To understand them in relation to intergroup processes it is therefore necessary to have some explicit social theory to hand. In other words, to situate the dialectic between intergroup content and process, there is a need for some theory of the relation that exists between particular groups, and for the socio-historical circumstances that have given rise to relevant identities (e.g. gender, class, race, etc.). This is in marked contrast to IGT research where peculiar contents often merely *illustrate* intergroup processes.

Three aspects of intergroup theory will be deconstructed. Two will draw on the exemplary analyses of Billig (1985) on the interaction of tolerance, prejudice, categorisation, and particularisation; and Williams (1984) on the relation of gender to intergroup processes. The third deconstruction will focus on the role of reflexivity.

Categorisation and prejudice

Billig (1985) has produced a detailed critique of the priority accorded categorisation in the social psychological production of prejudice. He is especially concerned with the way that categorisation, as a cognitive process, serves to render simplification and distortion, and thus stereotyping, inevitable. The overview of IGT presented earlier on indicated that categorisation and stereotyping are an inherent part of intergroup behaviour. The social world is categorised and some of these categories constitute social identities. Through the dynamics of comparison, differentiation and competition, social categories are internally simplified and polarised from other (similar) categories. This process of stereotyping occurs both for the self and others (Tajfel 1981; Turner 1982). As Billig observes of Tajfel, 'prejudice (is viewed) as an outgrowth of normal thought, is seen as inevitable' (p. 82). Against categorisation, Billig sets, in dialectical opposition, the process of particularisation in which a stimulus is distinguished from a general category and from other stimuli. Billig aligns the process of particularisation with tolerance. It is this axis of particularisation–tolerance which Billig counterposes to the dominant axis within IGT of categorisation–prejudice.

But Billig goes beyond this opposition to emphasise the role of language and its capacity to both simplify and enrich, and to warn against any simplistic one-to-one correspondence between categorisation and prejudice, and particularisation and tolerance. He goes on to show how each cognitive process can be allied to both social behaviours. For example, prejudice can be buoyed up by particularisation: as Pettigrew (1979) has argued, an out-group member who exhibits positively evaluated behaviour can be particularised, his or her personal peculiarities being used to differentiate the individual from his or her own group, thereby consolidating the negative representation of the out-group. This is, of course, a version of the 'exception that proves the rule' ploy.

To account for this unruly combination of cognitive and social processes, Billig opts for a form of analysis that examines the rhetoric involved in categorisation. It requires that the fluidities of thought and the ambiguities of language are directly addressed. Such a project is of necessity social and requires, in the intergroup context, an analysis of the way in which the content of a particular category constrains fluidities and ambiguities to the point where it generates intergroup behaviour.

Here, then, the implied third term is rhetoric, which transcends the opposing axes. In IGT, this would mark a shift in resources from the stultified arena of minimal group experiments and the like, to the close and critical analysis of group members' talk and actions (a project exemplified by Billig's study of fascists, 1978). An IGT up to this task would have to accommodate these fluidities as they occur on various levels, including that of theory. Thus, for example, alternative, similarly fluid, conceptions of the self and self-esteem would need to be incorporated (e.g. Sampson 1983b; Gergen 1984).

Masculinity

Williams (1984) has analysed the way that intergroup behaviour manifests what she views as a predominantly masculine style. Focusing on Tajfel's (1978) social identity theory, she notes that it does not take fully into account affiliation and attachment processes which might undermine the potency of intergroup discrimination. She points to evidence that men tend to engage in social identification processes more so than do women, and that women are more involved in communal processes such as helping other groups. The latter involves a form of agency somewhat different from that typical in the masculine role; this will affect the sort of group identity and processes that women might develop. For Williams, then, the social identity posited by social identity theory is 'an analogue type of personal identity encouraged in males' – that is, 'an agentic identity' (p. 313). In other words, she shows how the putatively universal processes of IGT are in fact tied to a specifiable content: masculinity. Overall, this theoretical sex-bias suggests 'that the relationship between identity and intergroup behavior is more complex than that proposed by the original formulation of (social identity theory)' (p. 314). Extending Williams' observation a little further, this complexity cannot be confined merely to the role of gender identity, but can be extended to class, caste, race, and age related identities.

Williams has produced a deconstruction in which she has examined modes of intergroup behaviour and their conceptual-isation that IGT has failed to address. As with psychoanalysis (e.g. Easthope 1986), it might be the case that IGT presents a workable portrayal of masculinity in its intergroup context. However, through exclusion, this portrayal has been rendered paradigmatic for both sexes.

To place the predominance of the masculine in IGT in its social context, it can be pointed out that intergroup theorists are themselves engaged in the group membership of the academic or scientific community. Social psychology has for some time now pursued natural scientific status (Gergen 1982; Farr 1981). Both social psychology and natural science have been taken to task for their overbearingly masculine character (e.g. Sampson 1978; Fee 1983; Henderson 1983). This is not to reduce IGT to its institutional bases, merely to show that there is a possible, no doubt obtuse, causal relation between the experiences of social psychologists and their theorisation of intergroup behaviour (see also Reicher and Potter 1985).

Reflexivity

In IGT as a whole there is a general absence of a theorisation of reflexivity, though it is tapped by the occasional ad hoc use of post-experiment questionnaires and interviews. However, this is a poor substitute for the sort of concerted investigation of reflexivity practised by, for example, ethogenics (Harré and Secord 1972; Harré 1979).

Reflexivity can be briefly described as the, more or less, critical review of one's premises (Lawson 1984) and can take the extreme form of a loss of belief in fundamentals whether these be epistemological, moral or aesthetic. In this extreme case, all premises are permanently open to revision. Such a process is facilitated by the capacity to take up new perspectives from which to review previous commitments. It has been argued that this loss (or impermanence) of foundations characterises the present epoch (e.g. Lyotard 1984; Deleuze and Guattari 1983; Jameson 1984). Of course, such an analysis is contentious but it will nevertheless be deployed for the purpose of illustrating both the historicity of the intergroup process and a mode of behaviour which it has thus far suppressed.

IGT tends to presuppose non-reflexivity insofar as it does not theoretically accommodate the conscious questioning of the premises and constituents of one's identity. Assuming that reflexivity is latent in all behaviour (e.g. Harré 1979), that is, there is always the option of an adoption of alternative vantage points, then IGT may be seen as a theorisation of the 'freezing' of reflexivity. The processes of differentiation, comparison, competition, and so on, are essentially seen as expressions of non-reflexivity; they are mechanistic. This is because they are practised by group-members that are thoroughly entrenched (or are attempting to better immerse themselves) in their group identity. It is from within this social identity that all relevant other identities are apprehended; it is from behind the in-group barricades that the characteristics and behaviours of the out-group are evaluated. To reflect can entail the taking up of an out-group's perspective. Intergroup theory does to some extent address this possibility, but this is related to status effects, with lower status groups finding themselves utilising the comparison dimensions provided by higher status groups. However, as Tajfel and Turner (1979) make clear, the impetus is towards reasserting internal criteria of comparison.

The reflexive apprehension of an out-group's perspective might strike the reader as a highly idealistic proposal, especially when contrasted with IGT's earthy realism. However, this would be a gross misreading of the present argument. Reflexivity is materialistically grounded in the specific conditions of the present epoch (e.g. advances in communication systems; accelerated dynamics of capitalism). IGT leaves no space for a 'drifting' (or quantum leaping) from social identity to social identity that an aggravated reflexivity might engender.

In the light of these points, IGT embodies a dual relation to reflexivity. On the one hand, it excludes it from its concerns. Yet, simultaneously, it engages reflexivity by theorising a social behavioural strategy for containing the reflexive process. It describes one mode of resistance to the uncertainty that reflexivity engenders. It has been ventured that there is currently a breakdown of identity and self (e.g. Deleuze and Guattari 1983). This is more prominent for some classes of individual than for others: it is the former that will most likely engage in intergroup processes for the 'self-fixing' they afford. Williams' identification of the masculine bias in IGT suggests that one such class is men. Indeed, there is some evidence that men's identity is indeed more prone to this sort of disintegration under prevailing conditions. (e.g. Metcalf and Humphries 1985).

In historically relating reflexivity to IGT, it is not intended that the relationships be confined to the present period. It is taken for granted that the relationship will shift, change, and repeat itself over time. The main aim is to stress the historical mediation of intergroup processes in contrast to the social psychological temptation to explain them in terms of cognitive and motivational universals. Introducing reflexivity into the equation shows how historically contingent these processes are.

CONCLUDING REMARKS

In this chapter, IGT has been subjected to a partial deconstruction and the dominance of three terms — masculinity, categorisation, and non-reflexivity — has been examined. The counter-terms have been shown to undermine IGT's claims to universality. However, these are not the sole oppositions coursing through the body of IGT: other deconstructions might fix on IGT's conceptions of the self, self-esteem and self-interest, or the posited relation of individual to society.

As regard the present analysis, it was previously mentioned that there would be no attempt to define the third term to neutralize the deconstructed oppositions. Instead, it was suggested that opposing terms might be reconciled in some way. This might proceed by showing how they interact in dialectical tension. Thus categorisation and particularisation, masculinity and femininity (or agentic and communal styles), and reflexivity and non-reflexivity, are conceived as part of a contradictory unity or totality. Social psychology would entail the close scrutiny of the dynamics of these oppositions as they appear in both concrete social behaviours and the commentaries on them (whether they be in the form of lay talk or academic text). As hinted in Billig's work (see Chapter 3, in this volume), to approach social psychology in this way is to recognise the 'rhetorical' intent of both behaviour and text, that is to access the 'use' to which they are put. 'Use' cannot be confined to the individual intention of actors or authors, but must also be located in terms of objective historico-social conditions into which it feeds and on which it draws. Of course, this approach is hardly exempt from the processes it attempts to characterise: any analysis is subject to the same forces. Nevertheless, the awareness of one's own historical contingency serves as a vital counterbalance to the blithe universalism of much social psychology: the 'use-fulness' or effectiveness of this (or any) perspective rests not on some abstract objectivity, but on the prevailing pattern of social forces. The fact that this book has appeared now suggests that we might be in the midst of fundamental social change.

Chapter Thirteen

RESEARCHING PSYCHOTHERAPY IN BRITAIN:
THE LIMITS OF A PSYCHOLOGICAL APPROACH

David Pilgrim

In this chapter, I will try to explore some of the difficulties entailed in British psychologists researching psychotherapy. At first sight, such limitations should be few in number given the defensible assumptions that psychotherapy is a psychological process and that the latter is scrutinised optimally, therefore, by researchers trained in academic psychology. However, these are dubious assumptions for three reasons. First, although psychotherapy is an inter-personal process, its own roots of phenomenology and hermen-eutics have enjoyed only limited legitimacy within British psychology. For this reason, the research psychologist may approach the topic of psychotherapy with a sense of uncertainty if their core training has eschewed such areas of knowledge.

Second, the certainties surrounding quantitative method-ologies underpinned by positivism and empiricism may take the psychotherapy researcher so far, in terms of studying therapeutic outcome, and the relationship between process and outcome, but at some stage a living sense of therapy-in-action can only be illuminated by alternative research strategies. Once more the research psychologist may be wary to take up such a challenge if their core training has provided them with neither the knowledge nor the confidence in such alternatives. My third doubt about psychologists being well placed to study psychotherapy relates to the issue of psychology *ipso facto* being *psychological*, when psychotherapy is a form of practice which is shaped in form and content by its *social* context. The latter can only be illuminated by stepping outside of psychology into sociology, social history and economics.

These problems are outlined in this form to present the essence of my argument (that psychologists may not be as well placed as they often assume they are to study psychotherapy). However, such a presentation is rather general and certainly without supporting arguments. To concretise the presentation, I will outline a piece of research I carried out alone (a relevant point) into the practice of National Health Service (NHS) psychotherapy. A full version of this research is written up as my Ph.D. thesis (Pilgrim 1986). However what I outline below is a precis of the research along with some confessions not fully expressed in the formal write-up. (I assume that all formal accounts within the academic discourse contain these sub-texts, whether or not they are subsequently revealed.)

AN OUTLINE OF THE STUDY

In the early stages of the research my intention was to try to investigate something of the rhetoric of the therapists, i.e. whether or not therapists do what they claim to do in theory, or in *post hoc* accounts of their work with clients. At the time (1982), I was working in a regional NHS psychotherapy unit outside of London, as a clinical psychologist. What preoccupied me, and the subjects I began to have exploratory negotiations with, to the point of distraction from my original intentions, were wider and deeper aspects of the role of state-employed therapists in Britain, outside of London, operating in a mental health service undergoing structural changes and inheriting intra- and inter-professional tensions. Thus the pressing contemporary occupational concerns of my prospective subjects (most of which I shared) shaped the research focus.

At this point I decided to interview therapists about their work in much the same way that an industrial sociologist might collect partial occupational biographies in order to clarify the day to day functioning of a trade or profession (see Benyon 1970; Bertaux and Bertaux-Wiame 1981). The problem for me was that I was not a sociologist, and though sympathetic to a biographical perspective on life (as a therapist), I felt uncertain as a research psychologist to proceed using a biographical approach, given that the latter seemed not to be 'proper' science within the discourse of my core training. Thus I felt unskilled in a qualitative approach to research and uncertain about the legitimacy of such an approach.

Whilst my supervisor quickly allayed anxieties in the latter realm, by pointing me to erudite sources and noting the need to negotiate a sympathetic external examiner, these tricks of the academic trade could only smooth the path and ensure the correct impression when writing up the research. What still remained was any sense of *genuine* competence in pursuing my research interest.

Nonetheless, I started to interview therapists (nurses, psychologists, and psychiatrists) about their work, whilst at the same time trying to read about the main sources within social psychology and sociology (many of which were untouched in my core training) which had something to say about the relevance of personal accounts in human science. For clarity, although these tasks were carried through concurrently, it may be useful to describe them separately.

I interviewed ten subjects and collected over fifty hours worth of taped material which was transcribed. This process produced three times the number of words in transcribed verbatim accounts that were permissible in terms of thesis length, under university regulations. Consequently substantial editing had to take place to reduce the material down to manageable and permissible proportions, in addition to removing redundancy from the material and disguising names and places. Also, I had to attempt to make sense of the material presented by my interviewees and opted to analyse the themes emerging in my first subjects' sessions. These themes were not indwelling to his account but reflected a negotiation between us, and the *post hoc* interpretive decisions I made about selecting themes and illustrative vignettes of tape (Plummer 1983). At this stage some doubts and guilt remained about the legitimacy of claiming that this constituted proper research.

The (five) themes settled on and pursued with other subjects related to: how the subjects became therapists; the relationship between the therapists and their parent or core profession; the relationships between the three professions; problems in establishing a psychotherapy service in the NHS outside of London; and the impact of particular clinical settings on the practice of therapists. What was touched on by the subjects, but I did not ask them to elaborate, was the minutiae of their work with patients. This represented such a large area, that it seemed to constitute a research topic in itself and was, therefore, unmanageable within the limits of a Ph.D. which, by now, was pursuing the occupational, professional, and organisational aspects of a sub-system of the mental health service in Britain, at a particular historical juncture.

I will now outline the concurrent task of reading the existing sources on biographical material, personal accounts, and ordinary language or common-sense emphases in social psychology and sociology. This task eventually was transformed into a review of the personal account research for the thesis but in practice the final approach ('dialectical reasoning' below) was of use to me in the main. The others either emphasise ordinary accounts of motivation (Peters 1959), or emphasise the need to situate or contextualise accounts (Mills 1940), or justify the central legitimacy of personal accounts for human science (Harré and Secord 1972; Garfinkel 1967; Cicourel 1974). These guidelines and bases for justifying the research's legitimacy were important in an overall sense, but impinged little on my awareness when conducting the interviews and analysing or interpreting and editing the data.

As a clinician social-psychological, sociological, and anthropological sources were mainly new and were always challenging if not trying. (This is not a case of personal special pleading but is an acknowledgement that the academic sub-division of labour (Braverman 1974) tends to lead to uncertainty and challenge, when a researcher strays over their own professional boundary into other bodies of knowledge.) Nonetheless, the work of Sartre and Geertz did seem to offer the real basis of making sense of my research focus, in such a way, that a coherent, and hopefully useful, account of NHS psychotherapy could be given. What Sartre and Geertz advocate is a research process that entails tacking to and fro between personal accounts and their social context. This process facilitates the reciprocal understanding of the context from the account and the account from the context.

If such a precarious task is adjudged to have been carried through successfully, then an understanding of both the subjective life of actors in the world and objective aspects of their world are enriched. This process of enrichment or illumination redefines research goals away from generating knowledge claims based upon hypothesis testing, within the traditional empiricist–positivist paradigm. Moreover, the emphasis on context pre-empts, arguably, the charge against personal accounts research of being

186

individualistic or homocentric (see Lemert 1979). Accounts are only seemingly individualistic because, provided that they are situated or contextualised, they, or their narrators, can be used as paradigms or prototypes, which can be used through interpretation, to uncover common discursive and organisational aspects of a shared social reality.

Returning then to the details of this particular piece of research, how did the orientation of Geertz and Sartre help me? Essentially, I took the five main themes about the working lives of the therapists (noted above), and alternated attention between my primary source (the accounts) and secondary sources, which provided me with some knowledge of the supra-personal features of the world inhabited by the narrators. These secondary sources included: social histories of British psychiatry, psychology, and nursing; writings on the sociology of the professions; official publications of the three professions under investigation; material on social and economic changes in post-war welfarism; publications on mental health reform, and the balance between biological and psychological approaches to treatment.

The conclusions I drew from this process of oscillating between psychotherapy and its modern NHS context can be summarised as follows:

1. The core mental health professions contain psychotherapy in ways which both advocate its practice and development, and inhibit them. The dominance of biological models in British psychiatry and methodological empiricism in clinical psychology have marginalised but not excluded psychotherapy. The professions have integrated psychotherapy in an eclectic way. This has superceded the purging of it as a humanistic protest by medicine, and its derision as pre-scientific by psychology, during the 1960s.

2. Psychotherapy is the focus of both intra- and inter-professional conflicts both in terms of its legitimacy as a psychiatric treatment, and in terms of its managerial regulation. In particular the role of medical dominance in the NHS is a vital political factor when understanding the control of psychotherapy. However, the dominance of the medical profession inside the mental health services is being subverted presently by the increased professionalisation of psychology and by the loss of the territorial base of the Victorian asylum. The latter is being phased out in most

localities. Where funded, the new mental health facilities in the community are becoming the focus of ideological and professional tensions.

3. Large variations exist between localities in the provision of NHS psychotherapy and the bulk of such provision is in the metropolis. Since the mid-1970s however, there has been a gradual expansion in the stock of psychotherapeutic knowledge in the NHS.

4. An ideological tension exists in Britain between private and NHS practice. Whilst the former is more likely to provide more appropriate setting conditions conducive to the proper practice of psychotherapy, many practitioners opt to work in the public sector. In the light of a psychoanalytical ghetto emerging in London, following the pre-war entry of the Freuds and Klein, even NHS psychotherapy is tilted in availability towards London, with many consultant psychotherapists working in the NHS part time in addition to their private practice.

5. Given the traditional structural dependency of nursing on medicine, where nurses have developed psychotherapeutic skills, they have tended to follow medical leads. This is true both in terms of their employing medically-managed structures and in terms of who trained them. As with other health practices, the impression is one of nursing following the professional contours of medicine.

6. In contrast to nursing, the newer profession of clinical psychology has followed medical contours less. As it possesses an alternative body of knowledge, psychology has represented a greater challenge to medical hegemony. Following a brief period of initial dependency, clinical psychology developed professionally in an autonomous direction, which culminated in repeated disputes with the psychiatric profession.

7. Changes in mental health policy since the nineteenth century have altered the degree of legitimacy enjoyed by 'softer' forms of social control, such as psychotherapy. In Victorian times, more treatment (the precursor of psychotherapy) fitted badly with the custodial regime of the State asylum. Instead, a bio-determinist model in psychiatry, with its treatments acting upon the bodies of emotional deviants, fitted better with the policy of warehousing the mad. At this stage, the marginalisation of psychological approaches within psychiatry was functional for this state-funded and directed warehousing policy and for the development of

medical dominance. (An epistemology which asserted bio-determinism gave power exclusively to medical practitioners.)

Subsequently, in the twentieth century, this mutually rewarding relationship between the medical profession and the State system of custodial management of emotional deviance remained during the inter-war periods in particular, and the biological emphasis within British psychiatry was consolidated. However, during both world wars, psychodynamic approaches within psychiatry came to the fore more in response to the need to treat battle neurosis and the need to sharpen up military selection practices.

After the Second World War, the asylum/bio-determinism relationship temporarily re-stabilised but the costs to welfare capitalism of continuing to warehouse deviance began to be too great for the state to bear. Gradually policies developed advocating hospital run-down. Despite 'community care' policies dominating governmental thinking over the past thirty years, it is only very recently, in the context of a deep and lengthy economic recession, that health authorities are saving money by closing down psychiatric hospitals. In this contemporary context, psycho-therapists are embroiled, as a result of organisational inertia, in intra- and inter-professional disputes (noted above) and yet are facing a future in which their knowledge may be deployed more than in the psychiatric hospital, when, and if, community mental health projects are funded.

8. The deductions made, by tacking between therapists accounts and secondary sources of knowledge, could be enriched by further research, which takes accounts from other interested parties, such as patients and even staff antagonistic to the practice of psychotherapy.

On the basis of the outlined conclusions drawn above, at the end of the research (1986), I tried to make tentative predictions about the future of NHS psychotherapy (in the knowledge that making predictions outside of the laboratory is risky).

DISCUSSION

Having outlined, in an inevitably sketchy manner, for reasons of space, the content and process of the piece of research, I would now like to explore some wider reflections arising during and following its completion. Returning to the points made at the outset, I experienced insecurity on all three counts as a consequence of being a British psychologist attempting to make sense of psychotherapy in its social context. My basic academic training in undergraduate and clinical psychology had provided me neither with the skills nor confidence to pursue research which could examine reflexively my own professional culture. Moreover, the state of the art of psychotherapy research itself had only relatively recently recognised the need to sharpen up qualitative exploration of the processes within therapy. This newer research did not extend to exploring the actual context of therapy, although a few recognised that psychotherapy did not take place in a vacuum (e.g. Berman and Segal 1982).

Although I was comfortable with a phenomenological and interpretive approach to decoding the accounts of psychotherapy clients, this did not generalise to using such an approach to understand fellow therapists as an occupational peer group working in an organisational context involved in substantial reform. This seems to indicate that despite the reflexive potential of phenomenology and hermeneutical systems rooted in depth psychology, such reflexivity is severely limited. As Ferraroti (1981) has noted, a biographical approach to understanding society involves methodologies which go beyond the individual to groups of peers (neighbours, work colleagues, families, etc.), and must invoke knowledge of supra-personal features of their situating time and place.

The psychotherapies are themselves predicated on the lengthy study of biographical material but tend to negotiate its understanding primarily with individuals in the consulting room, rather than with groups of individuals in a shared daily living context. Moreover, hermeneutical systems derived from depth psychology, as well as being preoccupied by the understanding of the psyche via a diadic therapeutic relationship, have *a priori* assumptions about the context of the client, which predominantly are in the past (childhood), and are limited by the boundaries of a theory-constructed context (the nuclear family). In the non-psychodynamic traditions of therapy, such as Rogers' client-centred approach, there is a preoccupation with the facilitive conditions for individual growth. Thus phenomenological and hermeneutic systems underpinning varieties of psychotherapeutic practice have collectively contributed to the construction of individual mental distress. The centring of attention on individual psychopathology and the more general reification of the individual thus produces practitioners who are psychologically sophisticated and sociologically weak or incompetent in their analyses of distress-in-context. Psychological reductionism thus becomes an occupational hazard for the psychotherapist.

To make my position clear on this, I should emphasise that phenomenological and hermeneutical strategies help therapists understand their clients but they do not enable therapists to understand their own practice in a socio-political context. Whilst Freud's reification of the family, Jung's reification of the self within the individual, and Rogers' interest in individual potential may have provided therapists with working guidelines for their therapy, they are limited in accounting for the very existence at a particular time and place of psychotherapeutic practice. Whilst not wanting to detract from the genuine wisdom and ameliorative advantages, implicit to psychotherapeutic theory and practice, for the human condition, it has to be acknowledged that they have little or nothing to say about the social determination of their own existence. When attempts are made to trace the roots of practising therapy, psychologistic reasoning is put forward (for instance, in the notion of the 'wounded healer' or the 'helping profession syndrome' (Pilgrim 1987)). Such psychological reductionism can only be pre-empted by attempting instead to develop a sociology of psychotherapeutic knowledge. The most coherent attempt to date of this sort, with regard to psychotherapy and personality theory, is *Self and Social Context* (Holland 1978). (A related corrective to psychotherapeutic enthusiasm and reductionism is *Social Amnesia* (Jacoby 1975).)

The reconciliation of the study of the subjective perspective of actors and the study of the social context of those actors is highly problematic. The variety of positions within the social sciences, which emphasise objectivity on one side and subjectivity on the other (what Marx described as 'false antinomies'), shows the difficulty in generating an academic consensus on the value and weighting to be attached to psychological versus sociological processes and subjective perspectives versus objective conditions, by the two professions. (Although these tensions operate in their most acute form in the human sciences they are also hotly debated

191

in the philosophy of science. For an overview of the positions in the debate between relativism and objectivism, see Bernstein 1983.)

Given the difficulties surrounding reconciling subjective and objective factors, and psychological and sociological processes within personal account research, it is not surprising that there is a significant inertia within British psychology about departing from the certainties entailed in objectivist–positivist methodologies. British psychology has certainly produced *justifications* for personal account research and discursive analysis (e.g. Shotter 1984) but inertia still seems to surround actually *doing* this type of research. Undergraduate training in psychology for instance does not equip students to be confident in collecting and interpreting accounts, deploying interpretive methods or textual analysis. There exists in other words not only a tradition of methodological empiricism because of our British intellectual culture (Hearnshaw 1964; Anderson 1969) but also, in consequence, a poor stock of knowledge about alternative research methods. Significantly, it took a philosopher (Harré) rather than a psychologist to advocate new methods in Britain within the profession, such is the impact of the past on the present.

Thus a parallel seems to exist, in Britain, between the professional status of a biographical approach to psychiatric treatment (psychotherapy) and a biographical approach to social psychological research. In both cases such an approach is not actually illegitimate but it remains sufficiently marginal to produce a picture of theoretical justifications, but only slow and tentative *practical* consequences. Theoreticians, such as Shotter and Harré, may have accumulated a justifiable international reputation, but their impact on the practice of research within Britain is still marginal. Analogously, innovations in psychotherapy such as the object-relations theory of Winnicott and Fairbairn, the therapeutic community experiments in British military hospitals and British anti-psychiatry are more noteworthy for their *international* reputation than their impact on native mental health practices. Psychoanalytical theory and practice have been consistently derogated and derided as being pre-scientific (Eysenck 1952 and since). The therapeutic community movement has been marginal in British psychiatry throughout the post-war period and has now sharply declined (Trauer 1984). As for the anti-psychiatrists, they were expelled from state psychiatry and their ideas rejected by the core of the profession (Cooper 1967). A less charitable interpretation of such events was that the psychiatric radicals chose to seek greener pastures (Ingleby 1987). What then are the lessons to be drawn for psychotherapy research, in the light of the above diverse discussion? They can be sketched as follows:

1. Non-positivist research into psychotherapy is likely to progress in a faltering manner, given that the professional ethos of the British mental health professions (the so-called 'psy-complex') has been dominated in Britain by methodological empiricism in psychology and biological reductionism in medicine. A biographical approach to therapy and research will nonetheless exist, to some degree of lesser or greater marginality, as the scientistic excesses of British empiricism continue to provoke a legitimation crisis and a critical response. Such a response has emerged over the past twenty five years, in British psychology and psychiatry, in such an intellectually sophisticated form, that its elimination from the academic discourse is now highly unlikely.

2. If psychotherapy research, using qualitative methods, is to go beyond the limited frame of the therapeutic relationship, then an understanding of the synchronic and diachronic features of that relationship's social context must be pursued, drawing upon bodies of knowledge outside of psychology. As psychotherapy researchers have at last confronted the limits of the positivistic examination of therapeutic process and outcome using quanti-tative methods (e.g. Elliott 1983), the next step is to enlarge the frame under investigation.

Given the disability accruing from the sub-division of in-tellectual labour, such a task may be beyond the abilities of psychologists operating alone. A more efficient alternative might be to join with other human scientists (especially in sociology and anthropology) in inter-disciplinary projects as a first step towards developing a trans-disciplinary appreciation of psychotherapy in various contemporary contexts. This has two implications for psychotherapy research. First, such an expansion of the frame of investigation would seek a greater contextualised understanding of stasis and change in the lives of distressed people, which includes, but is not limited to, the processes existing inside the therapeutic sessions. Second, an enlargement of the research frame would increase the likelihood of psychotherapy as a social practice being illuminated, as connections would be made with the therapy's situating and sustaining context.

3. If psychologists are to participate efficiently in such projects, then their own basic training will need reforming. In particular, a shift from the manipulation of variables in a closed-system experimental or observational framework, to the uncertainties of open-systems research will require new skills and assumptions. As has been noted above, there is no lack of recognition of such a need, at the theoretical level, within versions of social psychology. What may be needed now is a form of education for psychologists which facilitates *practical skills* in conducting field research. In the light of the importance of participant-observation experience, it may be that the age of the student and their extra-academic life experience may influence the facility with which they can go on, as a researcher, to cope with a particular area of investigation.

4. Related to these educational implications about skills is a further point about value-engagement and *a priori* assumptions held by researchers. In Britain, as academic and applied psychology have become increasingly professionalised in the second half of this century, legitimacy and scientificity have become almost synonymous. The British empiricist definition of scientificity, by and large, is predicated on the rules and rituals of the natural sciences. Given that until relatively recently, even sociologists of scientific knowledge have been content to follow their founding fathers (Marx and Durkheim) in pursuing value analysis in the *Geisteswissenschaften* only (Mulkay 1979), it is a little surprising that psychologists generally have been professionally socialised into assuming that their empiricism clothes them in disinterestedness and neutrality.

If the biographical method is to be properly pursued by psychologists studying psychotherapy, their *a priori* assumptions and value preferences will require examination and declaration (see Taylor 1979; and Gadamer 1975). This uncovering process itself may need to become a new and vital aspect of psychotherapy research.

A point of departure for this chapter is the role of psychotherapy research itself (of old or new paradigm variety) contributing to the individualisation of distress. In the light of my earlier arguments that psychotherapies reify the individual this must surely mean that researching these practices in their own terms further legitimises this process. The *degree* to which this is true represents an interesting research topic in itself. It may be that all cats are grey in the dark if a post- structuralist account of the psy complex is to be accepted, with Victorian moral treatment and modern psychotherapies representing voluntary relationships which merely constitute alternative versions of psychiatric oppression and surveillance (Castel 1983). Notwithstanding my doubts expressed above about therapists being socially blinkered and psychologically reductionist, I still believe that psychotherapy represents a progressive alternative to pills, hypodermics, and electricity.

Chapter Fourteen

PSYCHOANALYTIC FEMINISM:
DECONSTRUCTING POWER IN THEORY AND THERAPY

Janet Sayers

Feminism has adopted a variety of perspectives and strategies from psychology, as well as from other disciplines, in seeking to understand and remedy the ills done women by existing sexual inequalities and divisions in society. In this chapter I shall be concerned particularly with feminism's use of psychoanalytic psychology. I shall start with its structuralist, and subsequent post-structuralist use of Freudian theory, and end with recent uses of post-Freudian British School psychoanalysis within feminist theory and therapy.

My specific focus will be the place of psychoanalysis as a means of deconstructing the fantasy, understood as transferred from parental figures on to the therapist, that all power resides 'in' the individual – in the self or other, child or parent, patient or therapist. This will involve tracing a shift that has occurred in psychoanalysis from Freudian attention to the transference into therapy of infantile fantasies of omnipotence and patriarchal authority to post-Freudian attention to mothering understood variously in terms of power and nurturance. It also serves as an example to social psychology of the deconstruction of power in social relationships, in this case in the social relationships structuring psychoanalytic practice.

FREUDIANISM AND PATRIARCHY

Freud explicitly rejected the reduction to power of psychoanalytic concern with parent–child, therapist–patient relations. (It was on this point that he broke with his erstwhile follower, Alfred Adler.) Arguably, however, issues of power were central to the genesis and

196

development of Freud's technique. In *Studies in Hysteria*, Freud, (1895) describes giving up hypnotism as a means of recovering the otherwise unconscious memories fuelling hysterical symptoms because his patients resisted his authority in seeking to hypnotise them. Instead, he pressurised them to recall in full consciousness the memories associated with the first occurrence of their symptoms. This, in turn, led to the development of psycho-analysis's 'fundamental rule', free association. Using this method, Freud (1896) soon found patients recalled scenes of sexual seduction in infancy in association to their symptoms. Later, largely on the basis of his own self-analysis, he came to understand these memories as constituted by Oedipal fantasies of sexual possession of the mother in rivalry with the father. Freud (1923) hypothesised that all children – girls as well as boys – initially construe genital sex difference as signifying the father's power to punish with castration the child's realisation of its desire for the mother.

Freud (1912) had already traced the resistance of patients to obeying his rule of free association to an effect of their transferring on to him the power they first invested in the father – men resisting this rule out of rivalry with him as father-figure, women resisting it in so far as they fell in love with him as they had first fallen in love with the powerful figure of the father in infancy. Later, Freud (1937) observed that cure can founder in men due to their unconsciously equating submission to the analyst's treatment as tantamount to submitting to castration by the father. On the other hand, he said, cure in women can fail in so far as they entertain the fantasy that only by acquiring a penis – as it were from the therapist as father – can they get better.

Given the obstacles to cure posed by his patriarchal authority – an authority arguably equally used in the directiveness of today's behaviour and cognitive behaviour therapy – Freud (1912) sought to turn this disadvantage to good effect by interpreting and seeking to make conscious the 'transference' into therapy of patients' fantasies about the power and authority of their actual father.

This father-centred and phallocentric approach hardly seems promising stuff out of which to forge feminist theory and practice! The Left, however, has long looked to psychoanalysis and its account of psychology and subjectivity as means of supplementing

Marxism and its seeming one-sided focus on economics to the neglect of subjectivity. Psychoanalysis has seemed particularly promising in this respect because, like Marxism but unlike non-psychoanalytic psychology, it recognises the dialectical interplay of appearance and reality. In Marxism this is theorised in terms of the contradictions of economic base and ideological superstructure, in psychoanalysis in terms of the contradictions of unconscious and conscious thought (Sayers 1986) – contradictions often repressed in orthodox (and radical) social psychology.

In the late 1960s, especially under the influence of French structuralist Marxist Louis Althusser's essay 'Freud and Lacan', it seemed that Freudian psychoanalysis offered feminism a means of explaining the persistence and reproduction, at the level of psychology and ideology, of patriarchy. For it seemed, according to the researches of anthropologist Claude Lévi-Strauss, that, whatever the variations between societies in their surface appearance, the underlying structure determining relations both within and between societies is always one of patriarchal kinship exchange of women by men.

Structuralist psychoanalyst, Jacques Lacan, had sought to integrate this observation with Freudian theory. And it was this approach that Juliet Mitchell (1974) took up in *Psychoanalysis and Feminism*. Like Lacan she described the child as initially entertaining the fantasy of being everything the mother desires, this being represented by the phallus in patriarchal society. True, we are generally unaware of this fantasy. The reason for this unconsciousness, and here Mitchell reiterated Freud, is that we repress it from consciousness in infancy as a result of then interpreting sexual difference as signifying the father's power to punish with castration this fantasy's realisation.

Freud's theory of the Oedipus and castration complex, Mitchell asserted, thus explains the psychological acquisition and reproduction of patriarchal relations from one generation to the next. As a result of these complexes the boy comes to identify with his father's authority. He foregoes possession of the mother in recognition of this power with the promise of eventually acceding to it. By contrast, the girl, construing her lack of a penis as signifying that she can never realise patriarchal power in her own right, turns from the mother to the father and subsequently to other men to achieve indirectly the power the penis seemingly conveys.

Since the early 1970s post-structuralists have taken issue with structuralist psychoanalysis and Althusserian Marxism to the extent that they seemingly mistake patriarchy and capitalism as more monolithic than they are in fact. In part inspired by the then plethora of political movements – of women, Blacks, gays, and so on – seemingly only tangentially related to the centrality accorded by Marxism to class struggle, French historian Michel Foucault and his followers insisted that power is not located in a single site, or class. Instead, they argued, power is everywhere. It is produced and resisted equally in all walks of life, domestic and occupational alike. Specifically, they maintained, power is produced and resisted through the disciplines and discursive practices whereby each area of social life seeks to demarcate itself from the next.

Psychoanalysis, Foucault (1979a) claimed, is no different from other discursive practices in this respect. In particular he likened it to the Catholic confessional. Like the priest, he observed, the analyst institutes a veritable inquisition into the analysand's most intimate experience. In the name not of religious but of psychoanalytic doctrine – namely the supposed curative effect of making conscious the unconscious – analysts incite analysands to free associate and talk about their experience in sexual terms. Psychoanalysis thereby marks out a discursive domain – the body and its pleasures as essentially sexual – a domain in which power is exercised through analysts encouraging and analysands resisting talking about their experience or accepting the analyst's interpretation of it as sexual.

Individual subjectivity – even the seemingly innermost sexual heart of the self – is thus understood by Foucault not as preceding social and linguistic relations but as produced by them. Adoption of this approach within feminism went along with increasing attention to Lacan's account of language. Mitchell had emphasised the structuralist aspects of his work, his recasting of Freud's theory of the Oedipus and castration complex in terms of the reproduction, at the level of ideology, of the patriarchal structures described as universal by Lévi-Strauss. Increasingly poststructuralist-minded feminists concentrated on Lacan's deconstruction, in terms of language, both of our narcissistic self-regard as whole and undivided and of our persistent tendency to conflate power with its symbolic and bodily representation, to reify it as though it resided 'in' particular individuals, in men say.

199

Lacan (1977), read now as a post-structuralist, developed Freud's account of infantile narcissism into what he termed the theory of 'the mirror stage'. According to this theory, the toddler, still experiencing itself as in bits and pieces – as plaything of every passing bodily whim and passion – becomes enraptured by its reflection in the mirror. For its reflection presents itself to itself not as fragmented but as integrated and whole. Lacan claims that it is the infant's identification with this reflection, that is with an image that is actually external and alien to itself, that initiates the illusion of the self as whole. It also originates, he says, the capacity to represent oneself outside oneself in language by the personal pronoun, 'I'. He thereby deconstructs the omnipotent fantasy of the self as whole and undivided, showing it instead to be founded in the illusory elision of division – of inner and outer – at its very inception.

As well as adopting Lacan's mirror stage theory, post-structuralist feminism also adopted his account of the castration complex to deconstruct the otherwise fixed seeming meaning of words and symbols. This involved reiterating Lacan's insistence on disabusing the persistent illusion, described by Freud (1915) in his essay 'The unconscious', that words are one and the same as the things they represent. In Lacan's terms, this is to collapse the signifier into the signified, to mistake man, say – or the penis – for the power or phallus he represents when, in fact, the penis is not the phallus. Instead, he insisted, the meaning of the phallus, like all terms in language, is given by the antithesis of the presence/absence of that which it signifies, in this case the penis. Reiterating Freud, Lacan asserts that this antithesis, and the power of the father that it represents, is first recognised in the castration complex of late infancy. And, again like Freud, he argues that it is this complex, and the recognition of patriarchal power it involves, that first forces a gap between the infant and its initial omnipotent fantasy of being one with the mother. It thereby also initiates the use of words to signify this gap.

Lacan views psychoanalysis as quintessentially 'a talking cure', as operating through the analysands' capacity to use words to signify the separation between themselves and their desire. Only by articulating the gap between what one wants and what one has, it seems, can one take effective action to begin to bridge it. And this involves dealing with the painful fact that gratification in reality is always more limited than in fantasy.

POST-FREUDIANISM AND MOTHERING

Lacan might have insisted that psychoanalysis is essentially a talking cure. Meanwhile psychoanalytic therapy had generally moved on from this, Freud and Breuer's (1895) early characterisation of their approach to therapy. Indeed Lacan's 'return to Freud' was in large measure a reaction against this post-Freudian development – a development that included increasing attention to the therapeutic value of not necessarily verbalising but bearing with, and containing the analysand's anxieties. These anxieties, in turn, were now understood less in terms of sex, desire, and a patriarchally-oriented castration complex than in terms of mother-related conflicts of love and hate. And the containing, as opposed to verbalising, function of the analyst was likened to that of the mother in holding and caring for her baby, both physically and emotionally.

This move from focus on the place of the analyst as powerful father to that of the analyst as mother, understood not only in terms of nurturance but also in terms of power, was determined by a number of factors. Within psychoanalysis it was fostered by the extension of its techniques to the treatment of children – an extension pioneered by Anna Freud and Melanie Klein on the basis of the teaching and mothering experience socially accorded their sex. Using the insights afforded by this experience Klein and her followers in the so-called 'British School' of psychoanalysis increasingly drew attention to the place of the mother – often somewhat neglected by the father-centredness of Freudian theory – in conditioning our psychology and subjectivity.

This new-found emphasis on mothering was also reinforced by factors external to psychoanalysis. Concern about rising urban crime led to the establishment, in the 1920s, of Child Guidance Clinics aimed at advising mothers how best to bring up their children without risk of their becoming delinquent. Mothers, it seemed, were the best targets for this advice given their greater physical involvement in child-rearing. In a sense, however, this development involved the state appropriating the erstwhile disciplinary power of men in their role as *pater familias*. This power was now mediated via the advice given to mothers by experts such as psychologists and social workers – a development since documented by Foucault's followers (see Donzelot 1979; Rose 1985). Analysts also contributed to this movement. Many became involved in working with, and writing about delinquency (see Aichorn 1925; Bowlby 1944; Anna Freud 1949; Klein 1927; Schmideberg 1933; Winnicott 1943). And their work was often central to the training of Child Guidance staff. It was also often cited in legitimation of the closure of the day nurseries instituted to enable women to contribute to the War effort of 1939–45 (see Riley 1983).

Other developments during the war years also strengthened the focus of psychoanalysis on the mother. Psychoanalysis now increasingly joined forces with non-analytic psychiatry, as it had in the First World War, in treating the psychological casualties of war. In the process psychoanalysts found themselves increasingly involved in treating psychotic as well as neurotic conditions. Freud had argued that the lack of transference in psychosis makes it impervious to psychoanalytic treatment. Since then, and with the development of child analysis in the inter-War years, analysts increasingly came to view psychosis in children (see e.g. Klein 1930) and adults as effect not of problems in relation to the father (as Freud, 1911, had implied in the Schreber case), but as a product of disturbance in the infant's earliest, pre-Oedipal relation to the mother. Many argued that such disturbance called for the supplementing of verbal interpretation by empathic mirroring and nurturant mothering. And this approach in turn has now come to inform analytic treatment of neurotic as well as psychotic conditions.

Faced with this mother-centred shift of psychoanalysis some feminists, as indicated above, have insisted on the value of returning to the more father-centred stance of early Freudian analysis as a means of understanding, in order to combat, the psychological persistence and reproduction of patriarchal power and authority. Many more have reacted against Freud's patriarchalism and phallocentrism – especially against his penis-envy theory of women's psychology. Some reject psychoanalysis altogether on this account. Others have adopted the ready-made alternative to Freudian father-centredness furnished by the mother-centred theory and practice of post-Freudian, British School analysts such as Klein and Winnicott.

It is this approach that informs feminist therapy, at least as practised at London's Women's Therapy Centre. The Centre's 1976 co-founders, Susie Orbach and Louise Eichenbaum, use US sociologist Nancy Chodorow's (1978) Winnicott-influenced description of daughters' identification with, and sons' separation from the mother. They go on to argue that women's relative powerlessness and consequent dependence on securing men's emotional and economic support results in their quickly learning to serve the needs of men and others before their own. As a result, they say, women often become unable to recognise their needs either in themselves or as seemingly reflected in their daughters. They thereby often fail empathically to mirror, recognise, or meet their daughters' needs in the 'good enough' sense described by Winnicott. As a result the daughter's 'true self', as Winnicott (1960) might have put it, her 'needy little girl self', as Eichenbaum and Orbach (1985) put it, readily goes into hiding.

The solution, they argue, is to counter the social processes that cause women to become split off from their 'true self' needs. This, say Eichenbaum and Orbach (1987), includes refusing to adopt a Freudian stance, which they characterise as disqualifying as unrealisable pre-Oedipal desire women's longing to have their unmet infantile needs of the mother satisfied. Instead, they argue, therapists should interpret and make conscious the resistance stemming from such repudiation of women's needs as this resistance is transferred on to the therapist *qua* mother. Otherwise women are liable prematurely to quit therapy in the belief that their needs are not sufficiently important, or out of fear lest they offend and tire the therapist as in infancy they seemingly tired and upset their mothers.

Other therapists at the Centre equally insist on the importance of interpreting the transference into therapy of feelings first apparently experienced in relation to the mother. But in a sense they seek to deconstruct rather than shore up the fantasy of the all-nurturant mother/therapist who, but for patriarchy's disqualification of women's needs, has the wherewithal fully to meet her daughter's/patient's every need.

In addition, Sheila Ernst (1977) draws attention to the negative aspect of women's sense of mergence with their mothers as described by Chodorow. She cites the histories of several of her patients to illustrate the harm done women by remaining wedded to the first relation with the mother, to the mother's childhood image of them. Far from fostering infantile sense of fusion with the mother, Ernst implies, therapy should help women overcome its crippling and constraining effects by becoming separate and independent. This involves the therapist gradually disillusioning the patient of the fantasy of identifying with, of being one with the therapist, just as Winnicott says the mother, after an initial period of absolute adaptation to the infant's needs, gradually fails perfectly to adapt to its needs thereby disillusioning it of the omnipotent fantasy of having the whole world at its command.

Therapy, according to Ernst again following Winnicott, also involves interpreting and making conscious – deconstructing – the grandiose illusion whereby recognition of the mother's separateness, and awareness of the dependence on her to which this recognition gives rise, is denied and refused in relation to the therapist. The task of therapy, in Ernst's terms, thus becomes one of freeing women from the alluring fantasy of omnipotence and grandiosity involved in feeling fused with the mother so as to escape and become independent of this feeling's all too real constraints. But this is no easy task, she says, given the tenacity with which mothers often hold on to their daughters as a result of the lack of power socially allotted them beyond home and family.

Resistance to the reality of separation and difference, writes fellow-therapist Marie Maguire (1987), is also fuelled by the considerable power invested in fantasy in the mother beyond the limited power actually accorded her as primary caregiver. She argues that recognition of difference from the mother initially evokes the feeling, described by Klein, that the mother is all-powerful container of everything good, the child feeling entirely empty by comparison. While boys are able to deal constructively with this feeling, says Maguire, through realising themselves as different but equal through achievements in work outside the maternal domain of hearth and home, girls are forced to compare themselves on this self-same ground with their mothers in so far as they too are encouraged to become mothers. They are therefore more likely, says Maguire to react negatively to perception of difference and separation from the mother by enviously seeking to spoil the mother's seeming goodness. In this they seek to do away with the seeming difference between them and their mothers that evokes such painful feelings of emptiness and depletion. This in turn gives rise to the fantasy, claims Maguire following Klein, of the mother as retaliating and envious destroyer of the daughter. Only by interpreting, working through – and thus deconstructing – these omnipotent fantasies, as transferred into therapy, of the self and mother as containing all that is destructive and bad, or all that is nurturant and good, she implies, can women begin to realise the reality of limitation, separateness, and difference that these fantasies otherwise impede.

CONCLUSION – FORGETTING THE FATHER?

But where are the actualities of power in all this? Feminist therapists, as I have sought to show, clearly address issues of sexual inequality in their theories. Yet why does their practice seemingly pay so much attention to deconstructing the power – both actual and fantasied – of infant and mother to the neglect of that of the father? Why does it too singularly fail to recognise ways in which patriarchal authority and sexual difference and inequality also determine mothering, including the child's dawning awareness of separation from the mother?

It is not even as though British School analysts, from whom the feminist therapists I have been discussing derive much of their mother-centred approach, altogether neglect the place of the father. Marion Milner, for instance, attributes the source of her patient Susan's omnipotent fantasy of being everything to her mother not only to her mother's repeatedly shoring up this fantasy – addressing her 'Oh Moon of my Delight', and inciting her to love her, 'Yes, the whole world' (Milner 1969: 325, 420n) – but also to her mother's failure to acknowledge that the lodger was Susan's father. Hence, according to Milner, Susan's fascination with and repeated acquiescence as a child in an elderly neighbour's exhibitionism. For the sight of his penis served to reassure her that all power – including that of the phallus – did not reside in her.

Some reasons have already been indicated why developments both within and outside psychoanalysis led to its greater attention to mothering. The exaggeration in feminist theory and practice of this focus to the neglect of the place of the father is however surprising given feminism's commitment to bringing to public consciousness the iniquities of patriarchy. Furthermore, and paradoxically, feminism's new-found emphasis on mothering comes perilously close to repeating the compelling tendency of much non-feminist psychology toward mother-blaming.

On the other hand, psychoanalytic feminism's current attention to mothering is an understandable reaction against patriarchalism, including that of Freudian psychoanalysis. It is in keeping with feminism's concern to right the wrongs of patriarchy by developing a woman-centred, 'woman-identified-woman' theory and practice in the interests of forging the solidarity and caring warmth between women, including mothers and daughters, necessary to women banding together to improve their social lot.

The focus of feminist therapy on mothering is also not surprising given the lack of any obvious father-figure in woman-woman therapy in which the woman therapist – because of the social equation of her sex with mothering – is much more likely and immediately to elicit issues relating to the mother, and to become the target of issues concerning power just as the actual mother does because of her greater physical presence in the child's early life. As analysts Herman and Lewis observe:

> It is our impression, based on clinical experience, that daughters often displace their anger at their critical, aloof, neglectful, or absent fathers onto their mothers. Fathers' lack of interest in their daughters is accepted as an inevitable, even natural state of affairs, while any slight on the part of the mother is bitterly resented.

(Herman and Lewis 1986: 155–6)

However understandable, the focus of feminist therapy on the mother carries the risk, as described in the family by Herman and Lewis and as in non-feminist psychoanalysis, of attending so much to power relations – both fantasied and real – operating within the parent–child, therapist–patient dyad that all sight is lost of the real inequalities of power by sex, race, and class that also conditions this dyad from without.

In a sense, Foucault glosses over this problem to the extent that he refuses any distinctions of power – including presumably those of inner and outer, fantasy and reality. Instead he insists that power is produced everywhere the same, inside and outside therapy alike. By contrast, and even though it sometimes focuses so much on internal fantasy to the neglect of external reality, psychoanalysis rightly recognises that there is a distinction. And it is here, as I have sought to demonstrate, that its value to the deconstructionist project of Foucault and his feminist followers lies; namely in deconstructing and disabusing us of the fantasies of power, as transferred into therapy, that otherwise so obstruct our effectively challenging the realities of its actual unequal distribution (Frosh 1987). Here lies, by the same token, the value of feminist psychoanalysis to the deconstruction of the power relations social psychology arguably needs to attend to outside therapy.

Chapter Fifteen

DIFFERING WITH DECONSTRUCTION:
A FEMINIST CRITIQUE

Erica Burman

As this book testifies, deconstruction, and associated post-structuralist ideas have been used in psychology in a number of ways. As a feminist I have felt wary and even hostile to these approaches, and not only because of the complexity and commitment to theory that its deployment presupposed. In this chapter I outline the political challenges presented by deconstruction, not only those through which they are used to critique psychology, but also the difficulties that the use of these methods present to the maintenance of a progressive politics. It is worth, however, briefly summarising deconstruction's progressive possibilities before moving on to look at the problems.

PROMISES

1. Attention is drawn to the materiality of language: discourse is seen as constitutive of and linked to practice, hence it is possible to theorise psychology's relationship to social practices as both reflective and productive. Rose (1985), for example, highlights how the domain of 'individual psychology', focused around the key concepts of 'ability' and 'temperament', developed to provide the technology to segregate and classify people through personality and intelligence testing; to differentiate the 'fit' from the 'feebleminded', and to diagnose indications of 'degeneracy' and 'delinquency'. Thus its subsequent history traces the struggle to legitimise that 'expertise', to maintain its monopoly on its administration.

2. The approach succeeds in relativising psychology, and highlighting the historical variability of discursive relations. This affords a clearer method and perspective of theorising our own

positions in relation to psychological practices, and enables us to identify progressive or reactionary features of discourses according to our purposes. For example, the 'human rights' discourse of 'normalisation' which is so prevalent in mental handicap can be seen to be gender insensitive (Adcock and Newbigging 1990); the discourse of protection and violation of innocence surrounding child abuse denies childhood sexuality and correspondingly positions a 'knowing' child as culpable (Kitzinger 1988); the child-centred discourse of 'natural needs' can skate over issues of school racism as 'adolescent peer group problems' (Warren 1988).

3. Deconstruction focuses on dominance, contradiction and difference: in highlighting the multiplicity of positions afforded by competing discourses and their contradictory effects, it enables us to envisage ways of disrupting the dominant discourse and to construct positions of resistance. So, for example, Steedman (1982) points out how young girls can use their extending symbolic repertoire to reflect upon and transcend their social positions; Walden and Walkerdine (1982) highlight the gendered culture of early education as providing an environment in which girls are supported and encouraged to be successful (in marked contrast with later schooling); and Hudson (1984) suggests that young women adopt the discourse of 'adolescence' as a strategy to escape the more confining definitions of behaviour and opportunities permitted by 'femininity'.

4. Deconstruction also introduces a politics of subjectivity: This accounts for the dynamics of subordination, including female 'narcissism' and even 'masochism' as constructed through cultural forces, and it has prompted powerful analyses of pornography and media representations of women, as well as more theoretical analysis of women's excursion from systems of representation as their constitutive feature. This work is empowering in so far as it avoids positioning women as passive victims. Now women are beginning to challenge the traditional relations and idealised images set up in technologies of representation (Spence 1986). Moreover, these accounts highlight the absences, resistances and denials of psychology as a gendered practice.

5. When Foucault's (1979a) work is brought in, it provides a description of power. What we can gain, then, from post-structuralist critiques in psychology is a framework to trace, theorise and talk about the power relations it both participates in

and gives rise to. So, for example, Walkerdine (1981) accounts for a group of three-year-old boys' verbal sexual harassment of their nursery school teacher in terms of their strategic adoption of masculine discourse, which positions them as dominant in relation to a female teacher, to counter their otherwise subordinate position as pupils. The teacher, however, is disempowered from resisting through her subscription to a 'childand-centred' pedagogy which positions her as powerless to interfere in the 'natural' course of children's development. Three major issues follow from this analysis: first, the child-centred model, arising out of post-Darwinian evolutionary theory, presents an asocial model of development as an organic unfolding of inherent abilities (Venn and Walkerdine 1978) which denies or neglects gender relations and specificities (Urwin 1986). Second, drawing attention to the gendered culture of early (and in different ways later) education has implications for our understanding of the relative progress and achievements of girls and boys. Third, the discourse of child-centredness, with its notions of 'readiness', 'treating each child as an individual', 'learning through play', and 'interest-driven learning' accords so little agency to teachers or schools as responsible for children's educational progress that the only explanation available to account for failure is one which lapses into a cultural or class deficit model (Sharp and Green 1975). Hence 'progressive education' as enshrined in the 'positive discriminatory' policies of the Plowden Report is shown to slip into victim blaming, taking the child as responsible for their disadvantage and treating this as an unalterable quality of the individual which is unamenable to intervention.

These, then are some of the powerful analyses made available by deconstruction and post-structuralism. Yet despite the powerful practical and conceptual apparatus these offer to a feminist critique of psychology, there are also areas in which post-structuralists and fellow travellers and the now attendant culture of deconstruction − postmodernity − are fundamentally at variance with this project.

CONFLICTS AND COMMONALITIES

The overall problem concerns the approach's inability to ally itself with any explicit political position; and following from this, a deliberate distancing and 'deconstruction' of any progressive political program. Indeed, a key feature of 'deconstruction' is its explicit critique and proscription of any commitment to a conception of history as moving forwards. Teleology is seen as one of the key characteristics of the modernist movement it seeks to deconstruct, and all utopias are branded as idealist, unattainable and metaphysical. This is all very well when we want to use deconstruction to highlight the underlying political program of psychology as reproducing and perpetuating a liberal humanist ideology of the rational uniform subject. Here deconstruction allows us to highlight the default politics at work, the cultural imperialism, the individualisation and denial of oppression, and ultimately the reinstatement of the mind–body, self–other, emotion–reason oppositions that have structured western philosophy and politics since the 'coincidental meeting' of Descartes and capitalism. Unfortunately it also rules out building a feminist or socialist politics into the deconstructive enterprise. For deconstruction to join forces with feminism and socialism would be to prioritise particular textual readings in a way that is utterly antithetical to its intent.

This issue has largely been elaborated in terms of current debates about the nature of postmodernity and the future of socialism. Drawing upon Lyotard's (1984) distinction between 'grand' and 'little narratives', we can see that there are continuities as well as conflicts between feminism and deconstruction. This opposition between narratives mirrors a tension within feminism, that of the problem of integrating the 'little stories' of individual women with the wider narratives of history and patriarchy – a tension heightened by the fact that a feminist politics is premised on the necessity and possibility of articulating the two (hence 'the personal is political'). Marxist analyses have also addressed this issue by trying to link the history of the working classes and understanding of capitalism with the activities of the workers. But while in Marxism the tension between the personal and the grand narrative is bridged or articulated primarily through notions of a 'vanguard' (with all the problems this entails), feminism goes further by threatening (deconstructing) the opposition through developing new ways of organising. In this way feminism can be seen to problematise the hierarchical nature of most left organisations and Marxist politics, showing how they are in danger of reproducing precisely those inequalities they are against.

However, there is one area where feminism's partiality for the personal may lead it into the same political cul-de-sac as deconstruction. In particular we can notice continuities between the cultural corollary of deconstruction, postmodernism, and current tendencies in feminism. Just as the post-modern subject is said to be caught in a static series of presents rather than history, capable only of pastiche rather than parody, pleasure rather than politics, is individualised rather than collective, so too we can interpret and evaluate 'identity politics' as leading towards an individualisation and depoliticisation of experience with a corresponding shift from questions of oppression to identity (Bourne 1987; Burman, in press).

DILEMMAS

Not only are there conceptual problems in trying to mesh together feminism and deconstruction, but there are also more immediate tactical dilemmas that feminist involvement in deconstruction poses. Much of the impetus for the deconstructive enterprise in psychology, as elsewhere, has come from feminists. However, there is a danger that deconstruction may be appropriating feminist critiques, through claiming to incorporate and thus rendering irrationally invisible a specifically feminist contribution and project. In social psychology this is illustrated through the ways feminist research and methodological critiques have been assimilated into 'new paradigm' research, which draws heavily on, but rarely acknowledges, a much longer tradition of feminist work. As Reason and Rowan put it, in a section of their introduction entitled 'The feminism issue', '. . . there seems to be a real danger that in new paradigm research men will take a "female" view of looking at the world, and turn it into another "male way of seeing it"' (Reason and Rowan 1981: xxiii). Indeed, it is interesting that this danger was highlighted by the (male) editors of a 'handbook' of 'new research methods' which was guilty of precisely this inadvertent disenfranchisement of feminist research, and even more significant that in the follow-up book (Reason 1988) neither 'feminism' nor 'feminist research' appear in the index and the only references are in fact cited within a general rubric of 'post-positivism' (Reason 1988: 3).

This argument has parallels in the broader arena in which deconstruction critiques arise before gradually percolating into psychology. It may have taken the insights of post-structuralist psychoanalysis to *theorise* women's subversion of the patriarchal order, but this powerful critique is predicated on the prior existence of women's resistance. Psychoanalysis may have facilitated *recognition* of women's oppositional relation to as well as (and by virtue of) our exclusion from dominant systems of representation. Drawing on Irigaray's (1977) analysis of the speculum as the symbol of how masculine practices are shaped by the feminine void they seek to master, we might even go further to posit the category of the feminine as their suppressed/repressed constituting force. However, there is no reason why feminists should necessarily defer to a theoretical framework such as deconstruction simply because it lends some credence or legitimacy to our demands. Nor is it clear that these analyses of 'femininity' necessarily have anything to do with feminist politics unless they are linked to theories of both resistance and change. Indeed, deconstruction could well become a new technology to colonise women's critical and revolutionary potential.

While it may be tactically useful to adopt deconstructive approaches for progressive political projects, this could be done at the expense of failing to advance the underlying feminist and radical project through lack of explicit commitment to it. Hence we marginalise those feminists who do not seek refuge under deconstruction's 'facilitating' mantle, and at the same time surrender the expression of our own motivations to be cast within its own terms. This raises then the question of dangers from within of being recuperated into a new kind of orthodoxy or subject position.

DANGERS

The main danger deconstruction holds for feminists is that of depoliticisation. There are a number of subtle ways in which this possibility arises, some of which I have already touched upon. Here I want to concentrate on one main issue: the political consequences of deconstruction's celebration of 'difference'.

Difference (with '*différance*') is perhaps the key term in the deconstructive lexicon (Derrida 1982b); its methodology is to adopt the devalued term of the opposition it identifies to highlight the metaphysical dynamic of its construction. However, just as 'affirmative' movements have their limitations as political strategy, so too the principal danger with deconstruction is that difference may become a substitute rather than a starting point for resistance. Hence it is in relation to this issue that debates about deconstruction and feminism are most closely intertwined.

The post-structuralist package of Derrida, Foucault and Lacan offers critiques and insights into the constitution of dominant patriarchal discourses and constructions of feminine positions, but leaves feminists in some confusion as to what action follows from this analysis of women's relation to the symbolic. As Toril Moi's (1985) account of Kristeva's analysis of the implications of post-Lacanian psychoanalysis for feminism points out, there are three possible avenues for feminist politics. The first of these, women's demands for equal access to the symbolic order, can broadly be equated with 'equal opportunities'. This is liberal feminism, where equality is defined in terms of male (patriarchal) norms, and as such is clearly insufficient to dismantle patriarchy. The second position is that of radical feminism, where women reject the male symbolic order in the name of difference. This glorification of the (formerly devalued term of) femininity can be seen as congruent with the practice of deconstruction, and is epitomised in the writing of Hélène Cixous. However, this position, through its undoubtedly empowering celebration of women's bodily and psychological qualities, lapses into biologism and essentialism, and treats difference as universal and timeless. Equally, as Moi's critique of Irigaray demonstrates, ignoring material and historical specificities of women's relation to power permits the essentialisation of women's experiences, reduces us to our bodies, individualises our struggles and positions us as uniformly powerless within the dominant order so that resistance from within cannot be envisaged.

This is perhaps the primary danger of deconstructive critiques, a danger that is acknowledged in wider discussions of post-modernism where the subject is depicted as alienated from a collective politics, as able to sustain only a momentary criticality, and as ultimately stranded in a timeless present that maintains and constitutes itself only by carnivalesque allusion to past genres (Jameson 1984). At the theoretical level, we have seen how deconstruction is fundamentally committed to a liberal pluralism which renders each of its deconstructive readings as equally valid, and paralyses political motivation. Again, there are some connections to be made with contemporary debates in the women's movement, most notably around theorising differences of culture and heritage through 'identity politics', and the politics and ethics of women's sexuality as in addressing sado-masochism.

Deconstruction, like some varieties of feminism, seeks to undo or reject the dichotomy between masculine and feminine by demonstrating its metaphysical (and, for feminists, political) basis (this is Moi's third position). As Moi points out, while it is *politically* essential that feminists defend women as women to counteract our oppression as women under patriarchy, 'an "undeconstructed" form of "stage two" feminism, unaware of the metaphysical nature of gender identities, runs the risk of . . . uncritically taking over the very metaphysical categories set up by patriarchy in order to keep women in their places, despite attempts to attach new feminist values to these categories' (1985: 13).

DILUTIONS

As well as its inherently problematic nature for radicals, there are also difficulties associated with introducing post-structuralist ideas into social psychology. I will confine myself to two examples here.

The psychological concept of 'androgeny' is perhaps the shining example of the career of an undeconstructed critique of 'masculinity' and 'femininity', yet which nevertheless anticipates some of deconstruction's rhetoric. Formulated as a way of escaping the restrictive confines of polarised psychological sex roles, it has been hailed as a visionary promise of what life without sex typing could be like. What it notably fails to theorise though, through its equal valuing of qualities traditionally associated with masculinity and femininity, is the initial inequality of gendered positions. It thus renders oppression as simply a feature of individual incompetence or unwillingness to change (Carrigan *et al.* 1987). Like postmodernism, 'androgeny' needs to be seen in the context of the market needs of late capitalism, and that this is recognised (even welcomed) by its advocates is seen by one of the paradigmatic examples of androgenous behaviour offered by Bem (1976): the ability to sack an employee 'with sensitivity' (Billig

1982). This is no rejection of the masculinity/femininity distinction as metaphysical, but a simple exploitation and construction of human potential to meet the demands of capital.

Second, one of the primary routes by which deconstruction has found its way into social psychology has been through 'discourse analysis'. Perhaps the paradigmatic case of the consequences of this is the construction and reception of Potter and Wetherell's *Discourse and Social Psychology* (1987), which has created a first legitimate foothold for post-structuralist critiques in mainstream social psychology. The book holds within itself a number of contradictory positions, sometimes claiming that the role of discourse analysis is to comment on and critique social psychology, and at other times asserting that it is part and parcel of the proper business of social psychology. Moreover, the sample analyses of transcripts reveal a reluctance to deconstruct their own discourse as researchers (Bowers 1988). So far so good: strategy may prevail over logic; sometimes there are good reasons for not wanting to entirely undermine authorial authority, particularly when seeking to make a credible case for innovation. However, it would have been better to acknowledge properly the post-structuralist inspiration for their approach. Although Foucault and Derrida are briefly cited, the potential of discourse analysis to surprise, disrupt and unsettle psychology is instead safely attributed to developments in ethnomethodology, ordinary language philosophy and linguistics. (Psychoanalysis, let alone Lacan, does not get a mention.) Deconstruction may be watered down to such an extent that it can easily be assimilated into prevailing paradigms, and renders even more difficult the project to bring the full force of these critiques to bear on the practice of psychology.

DIVERSIONS

There is a further sense in which post-structuralism could be seen to be diversionary rather than simply dangerous, particularly in the seduction of form. (Of course, this reintroduction of the form-content opposition is heresy to deconstruction.) It is easy to be hypnotised by the aesthetic of argument, to create a kind of conceptual analysis for pleasure rather than for politics (indeed such is the dynamic of deconstruction proper). Just as anti-nuclear activists can become fascinated by the details of the horror of weapons of mass destruction, so too we can become so absorbed in analysing the technology of symbolic domination that we come to treat the discursive as a *purely* symbolic relation, and forget the material and historical basis of oppression.

Of course, this argument could be turned against me to suggest that the account I have presented here is motivated by an unconscious desire simply to deconstruct deconstruction rather than subject it to a thoroughgoing political critique. But how are we to judge? Am I answerable to history? To a wider community of feminists? Or, as current vogue would have it, to my therapist (should I have one – should I have one?)? Perhaps speculation of this kind is symptomatic of the priority individual reflection is accorded over action through a politics informed by deconstruction. At the very least, the lack of specification of a political accountability should be good grounds for suspicion.

Deconstruction's avowed focus on the materiality of discourse can have other effects too: it is easy to over-interpret interventions at the level of discourse as necessarily having political implications and to divert political projects into discursive ones, misrecognising full-blown political resistance in every momentary contradiction.

At a wider level, the cultural correlate of deconstruction in wider society, postmodernism, is characterised by a political apathy and disengagement that itself mocks politics as 'post'. This resignation and indifference should lead us to be wary of the current moves to see in popular culture and consumption a 'political' resistance. Further, the contemporary left rhetoric of 'new times' and, still worse, 'new realism' can be seen to reflect the same political fatalism and preoccupation with ephemera that postmodernism engenders.

CONVERSES AND CONCLUSIONS

Given the arguments and issues outlined in this chapter, it is not surprising that the feminist response to post-structuralist ideas in the social sciences is far from uniform. Some feminists are in the forefront of developing deconstructive techniques and some give it an enthusiastic reception as a political tool (Weedon 1987), while others find it possible to develop a progressive political practice within psychology without invoking a post-structuralist framework (Sayers 1986), or are actively hostile to it as an elitist and intellectualist substitute for politics (Stanley and Wise 1983).

As far as social psychology is concerned, like Humpty Dumpty, deconstruction takes it apart and refuses to let it be reconstituted. Rather, it comments on the political undesirability and theoretical impossibility of such an enterprise. For to 'reconstruct' psychology is to tie it to the limits of our current vision, to foreclose possibilities for change, and to return us to a static and essential social psychology that counters any genuinely historical and materialist analysis.

At the level of theory, deconstruction seems to be a sharp but dangerous tool. The political impasses and consequences of a commitment to the deconstructive enterprise seem to take away as much as they offer. In fact the problems and pitfalls of post-structuralism as a whole for a radical critique of social psychology derive from precisely those features which I outlined at the beginning as potentially most promising: highlighting the materiality of language carries with it the danger of tackling the representation at the expense of engaging with the political reality; using the multiplicity of readings to indicate ideological operation of dominant discourses opens the project up to liberal pluralism; acclaiming the subject's multiple positioning in discourse as facilitating contradiction and resistance also presents the prospect of fragmentation and incipient dissipation of political energies; and focusing on a politics of subjectivity can lead to a celebration of difference rather than a galvanising into action.

In terms of practice, the recent history of the uptake of these ideas in British psychology provides some instructive lessons. While they were initially circulated through the shortlived but influential radical journal *Ideology and Consciousness* (later *I & C*) in the late 1970s, they were first collected together to mount a sustained and specific critique of psychology in *Changing the Subject* (Henriques *et al.* 1984). The reception and effects of this book present in microcosm the dilemmas posed by post-structuralism in psychology. A striking feature is its highly uncharacteristic publishing history: like any other book, its sales started with an initial peak which gradually declined, but unlike many others it has reproduced this pattern several times over the last five years, almost as though it is rediscovered by successive cohorts of radical psychologists. However the dangers of producing a 'new orthodoxy' which simply replaces the old were epitomised by what, with hindsight, sound like complacent and mistaken claims made for it as marking a new era in psychology (Ingleby 1984). Nevertheless the book, and the ideas contained within it, did become the focus of debate by some psychologists, although others found the meetings alienating, academic and insufficiently linked to action. Ultimately the networks created have largely become a forum for postgraduates doing similar research, hence reinstating with an over-elaborate if potentially progressive theory the traditional division of labour and interests between academics and practitioners. The endeavours that have tried to follow the real political reverberations in psychology accompanying deconstruction have so far been dogged by its theoretical reputation, which has, paradoxically – in terms of the substance of the ideas – foreclosed further radical political developments.

POST-WORD

As I finish this chapter, I am no longer certain whether my account has dispensed with deconstruction by showing some of its political impasses; or has in fact reinstated it through employing deconstructive methods to highlight its own limitations. Have I deconstructed my own resistance to deconstruction through using its methodology to critique it? Or still yet fallen prey to the charge of subordinating a feminist politics to deconstruction? Or both of these?

I suggested earlier that the danger of deconstruction is that it invites us to let difference stand in for political action. Writing now at the brink of the 1990s and in the middle of third-term Thatcher Britain, understanding 'race', class, and sex subject positions in relation to power is more than academic. And yet I am drawn back to the question that the political critique both afforded and problematised by deconstruction poses for feminists: How can we resist the seductiveness of difference? Should we resist post-structuralism or can we appropriate its analysis of sexual difference to inform our own struggles? If post-structuralism has anything useful to tell us it can illuminate the processes of objectification and idealism that construct and maintain prevailing (patriarchal) power relations. To take up deconstruction's interpretation of difference and *différance* poses two major challenges to a feminist politics: to re-envisage subject positions that are capable of change

219

beyond merely reproducing the inverse of what they are not; and to take seriously our own claims that discourses are practices which lie beyond as well as within language.

Deconstruction offers a notion of difference that resists closure and is always provisional. Yet part of the very popularity of its ideas must be understood in terms of its emergence at a particular juncture in late capitalism. Indeed it is the very discourse of discourse that makes it possible to speak of its effects. Rather than allowing deconstruction to function as a defence, a displacement used to defer political engagement, a feminist position on deconstruction, as with every other dominant social/symbolic practice, can only be one of a strategic marginality and subversion.

NOTE

I would like to thank Jonathan Potter for his helpful comments on an earlier version of this chapter.

REFERENCES

Abercrombie, N. (1980) *Class, Structure and Knowledge: Problems in the Sociology of Knowledge*, Oxford: Basil Blackwell.

Abrams, P. (1968) *The Origins of British Sociology 1834–1914*, Chicago: University of Chicago Press.

Abramson, L. Y., Seligman, M. E. P., and Teasdale, J. (1978) 'Learned helplessness in humans: critique and reformulation', *Psychological Review* 87: 49–74.

Adcock, C. and Newbigging, K. (1990) 'Women in the shadows: clinical psychology, women and feminism', in E. Burman (ed.) *Feminists and Psychological Practice*, London: Sage.

Adorno, T. W. (1967) 'Sociology and psychology', *New Left Review* 46: 63–80.

Adorno, T. W. (1973) *Negative Dialectics*, New York: Seabury Press.

Aichorn, A. (1935 [1925]) *Wayward Youth*, New York: Viking.

Althusser, L. (1971) 'Freud and Lacan', in *Lenin and Philosophy and Other Essays*, London: New Left Books.

Amos, V. and Parmar, P. (1984) 'Challenging imperial feminism', *Feminist Review* 17: 3–19.

Anderson, P. (1969) 'Components of the national culture', *New Left Review* 50.

Archibald, W. P. (1978) *Social Psychology as Political Economy*, Toronto: McGraw-Hill Ryerson.

Aristotle (1909) *Rhetorica*, trans. R. Claverhouse, Cambridge: Cambridge University Press.

Armistead, N. (ed.) (1974) *Reconstructing Social Psychology*, Harmondsworth: Penguin.

Arney, W. R. (1982) *Power and the Profession of Obstetrics*, Chicago: University of Chicago Press.

Aronson, E. (1988) *The Social Animal (5th Edition)*, New York: Freeman.

Atkinson, R. C. and Shiffrin, R. M. (1968) 'Human memory: a proposed system and its control processes' in W. K. Spence and J. T. Spence (eds) *The Psychology of Learning and Motivation: Advances in Research and Theory* (vol. 1), New York: Academic Press.

Austin, J. L. (1962) *How to do Things with Words*, Oxford: Clarendon Press.

Bandura, A. (1977) 'Self-efficacy: toward a unifying theory of behavioural change', *Psychological Review* 84: 191–215.

Banks, J. A. (1979) 'Sociological theories, methods and research techniques – a personal viewpoint', *Sociological Review* 27 (3): 561–77.

Baron, R. A., Byrne, D., and Griffit, W. (1974) *Social Psychology*, Boston: Allyn and Bacon.

Bazarman, C. (1987) 'Codifying the social scientific style: the APA *Publication Manual* as a behaviorist rhetoric', in J. S. Nelson, A. Megill and D. N. McCloskey (eds) *The Rhetoric of the Human Sciences*, Wisconsin: University of Wisconsin.

Belsey, C. (1980) *Critical Practice*, London: Methuen.

Bem, S. (1976) 'Probing the promise of androgeny', in A. G. Kaplan and J. P. Bean (eds) *Beyond Sex Roles: Readings Towards a Psychology of Androgeny*, Boston: Little, Brown and Co.

Bem, S. (1983) 'Gender schema theory and its implications for child development: raising gender-aschematic children in a gender-schematic society', *Signs* 8: 598–616.

Bem, S. (1984) 'Reply to Morgan and Ayim', *Signs* 10: 197–9.

Bentler, P. M. and Abramson, P. R. (1981) 'The science of sex research: some methodological considerations', *Archives of Sexual Behavior* 10: 225–51.

Benyon, H. (1970) *Working for Ford*, Harmondsworth: Penguin.

Berkowitz, L. (1980) *A Survey of Social Psychology (2nd Edition)* New York: Holt, Rinehart and Winston.

Berman, E. and Segal, R. (1982) 'The captive client', *Psychotherapy, Research and Practice*, 19: 31–6.

Bernstein, R. J. (1983) *Beyond Objectivism and Relativism*, Oxford: Basil Blackwell.

Bernstein, R. J. (1986) *Philosophical Profiles*, Cambridge: Polity Press.

Bertaux, D. and Bertaux-Wiame, I. (1981) 'Life stories in the baker's trade', in D. Bertaux (ed.) *Biography and Society*, Beverley Hills: Sage.

Best, J. B. (1986) *Cognitive Psychology*, St. Paul: West.

Bhavnani, K-K. (1986a) 'Power and the research process', paper given at British Psychological Society, Social Psychology Section Annual Conference, University of Sussex.

Bhavnani, K-K. (1986b) 'Political youth? Young people and social representations of politics', paper given at Simpsio Internacional: Juventud, Trabajo y Desempleo, Toledo.

Bhavnani, K-K. (1988) 'A Social Psychological Analysis of Young Working Class People's Views of Politics', unpublished Ph.D. Thesis, University of Cambridge.

Billig, M. (1976) *Social Psychology and Intergroup Relations*, London: Academic Press.

Billig, M. (1978) *Fascists: A Social-psychological Analysis of the National Front*, London: Academic Press.

Billig, M. (1982) *Ideology and Social Psychology: Extension, Moderation and*

Contradiction, Oxford: Basil Blackwell.

Billig, M. (1985) 'Prejudice, categorization and particularization: from a perceptual to a rhetorical approach', *European Journal of Social Psychology* 15: 79–103.

Billig, M. (1987) *Arguing and Thinking: A Rhetorical Approach to Social Psychology*, Cambridge: Cambridge University Press.

Billig, M. (1988a) 'Rhetorical and historical aspects of attitudes: the case of the British monarchy', *Philosophical Psychology* 1: 83–103.

Billig, M. (1988b) 'Social representation, anchoring and objectification: a rhetorical analysis', *Social Behaviour* 3: 1–16.

Billig, M. (1988c) 'Common-places of the British Royal Family: a rhetorical analysis of plain and argumentative sense', *Text* 8.

Billig, M. (in press) 'Studying the thinking society' in G. Breakwell and D. Canter (eds) *Empirical Approaches to Social Representations*, Oxford: Oxford University Press.

Billig, M. and Tajfel, H. (1973) 'Social categorization and intergroup behaviour', *European Journal of Social Psychology* 3: 27–52.

Billig, M., Condor, S., Edwards, D., Gane, M., Middleton, D., and Radley, A. R. (1988) *Ideological Dilemmas*, London: Sage.

Birke, L. (1980) 'From zero to infinity: scientific views of lesbians', in Brighton Women and Science Group (ed.) *Alice Through the Microscope: The Power of Science over Women's Lives*, London: Virago.

Blum, J. M. (1978) *Pseudoscience and Mental Ability: The Origins and Fallacies of the IQ Controversy*, New York: Monthly Review Press.

Borges, J. L. (1985) *Fictions*, London: John Calder.

Bourne, J. (1987) 'Homelands of the mind: Jewish feminism and identity politics', *Race and Class* 29 (1): 1–24.

Bowers, J. M. (1988) 'Review Essay on *Discourse and Social Psychology*', *British Journal of Social Psychology* 27: 185–92.

Bowers, J. M. (forthcoming) *The Narrative Legitimation of Cognitive Science*.

Bowlby, J. (1944) 'Forty-four juvenile thieves: their characters and home lives', *International Journal of Psycho-Analysis* 25: 19–53, 107–28.

Braudel, F. (1985) *Civilization and Capitalism*, vol. 2, London: Fontana.

Braverman, H. (1974) *Labor and Monopoly Capital*, New York: Monthly Review Press.

Brewer, W. and Nakamura, G. (1984) 'The nature and functions of schemas', in R. Wyer and T. Srull (eds) *Handbook of Social Cognition* (vol. 2), Hillsdale: Erlbaum.

Brighton Women and Science Group (1980) 'Introduction' in Brighton Women and Science Group (ed.) *Alice Through the Microscope: The Power of Science over Women's Lives*, London: Virago.

British Psychological Society (1988) *The Future of the Psychological Sciences: Horizons and Opportunities for British Psychology*, Leicester: British Psychological Society.

Broad, W. and Wade, N. (1983) *The Betrayers of Truth* London: Century.

Brown, R. (1965) *Social Psychology*, London: Collier-Macmillan.

Brown, R. (1986) *Social Psychology: The Second Edition*, New York: The Free Press.

Brown, R. J. (1978) 'Divided we fall: an analysis of relations between sections of a factory workforce', in H. Tajfel (ed.) *Differentiation Between Social Groups*, London: Academic Press.

Brown, R. J. (1984) 'The role of similarity in intergroup relations', in H. Tajfel (ed.) *The Social Dimension*, Cambridge: Cambridge University Press.

Browning, C. (1984) 'Changing theories of lesbianism: challenging the stereotypes', in T. Darty and S. Potter (eds.) *Women-Identified Women*, Palo Alto, California: Mayfield Publications.

Bruce, V. and Green, P. (1985) *Visual Perception: Physiology, Psychology and Ecology*, London: Erlbaum.

Bulkeley, R. and Spinardi, G. (1986) *Space Weapons*, Cambridge: Polity Press.

Burman, E. (in press) 'Identity crisis, political cop-out or cultural affirmation?: the Jewish feminism debate', in G. Chester and others *An Anthology of British Jewish Feminist Writing*, London: Women's Press.

Cahoone, L. E. (1988) *The Dilemma of Modernity: Philosophy, Culture and Anti-culture*, Albany, NY: State University of New York Press.

Callon, M. (1986) 'Some elements of a sociology of translation', in J. Law (ed.) *Power, Action and Belief*, London: Routledge & Kegan Paul.

Canguilhem, G. (1980) 'What is psychology?', *Ideology and Consciousness* 7: 37–50.

Caplan, P. (1988) 'Genderising anthropology: possibilities and necessities for a feminist anthropology', seminar presented at University of Bradford, November.

Carby, H. (1983) 'White women listen! the boundaries of sisterhood', in Centre for Contemporary Cultural Studies (eds) *The Empire Strikes Back*, London: Hutchinson.

Carrigan, T., Connell, B. and Lee, J. (1987) 'The "sex-role" framework and the sociology of masculinity', in G. Weiner and M. Arnot (eds) *Gender Under Scrutiny: New Inquiries in Education*, London: Hutchinson.

Carson's Consolation (1978) quoted in J. Green (ed.) *A Dictionary of Contemporary Quotations*, London: Pan.

Carter, A. (1985) *Nights at the Circus*, London: Picador.

Cassirer, E. (1951) *The Philosophy of the Enlightenment*, New Jersey: Princeton University Press.

Castel, R. (1983) 'Moral treatment: mental therapy and social control in the nineteenth century', in S. Cohen and A. Scull (eds) *Social Control and the State*, Oxford: Basil Blackwell.

Chodorow, N. (1978) *The Reproduction of Mothering*, Berkeley: University of California Press.

Chomsky, N. (1972) 'Psychology and ideology', *Cognition* 1: 11–46.

Cicourel, A. V. (1974) *Cognitive Sociology*, New York: Free Press.

Clifford, J. (1983) 'On ethnographic authority', *Representations* 2: 118–46.

Codol, J. -P. (1975) 'On the so-called "superior conformity of the self" behaviour', *European Journal of Social Psychology* 5: 457–501.

Collins, H. M., and Pinch, T. J. (1979) 'The construction of the paranormal: nothing unscientific is happening', in R. Wallis (ed.) *On the Margins of Science*, Keele: University of Keele Press.

Community Relations Commission (1976) *Between Two Cultures: A Study of Relationships in the Asian Community in Britain*, London: CRC.

Condor, S. (1986a) 'The eye of the beholder and the myopia of the researcher: social psychological approaches to 'stereotypes' and stereotyping', paper given at British Psychological Society Social Psychology Section Conference: Cambridge University.

Condor, S. (1986b) 'Sex role beliefs and 'traditional psychology', in S. Wilkinson, (ed.) *Feminist Social Psychology*, Milton Keynes: Open University Press.

Cooper, D. (1967) *Psychiatry and Anti-Psychiatry*, London: Tavistock.

Craig, P. and Cadogan, M. (1981) *The Lady Investigates*, London: Gollancz.

Cullen, M. (1975) *The Statistical Movement in Early Victorian Britain*, Hassocks, Sussex, Harvester.

Culler, J. (1982) *On Deconstruction: Theory and Criticism After Structuralism*, Ithaca, NY: Cornell University Press.

Davis, M. (1971) '"That's interesting!" towards a phenomenology of sociology and a sociology of phenomenology', *Philosophy of the Social Sciences* 1: 309–44.

Deaux, K. and Wrightsman, L. S. (1984) *Social Psychology in the 80s* (4th edn) Monterey, California: Brooks/Cole.

De Cecco, J. P. and Shively, M. G. (1984) 'From sexual identity to sexual relationships: a context shift', *Journal of Homosexuality* 9: 1–26.

De Landa, M. (undated) 'Policing the spectrum', *Zone* 1/2: 176–87.

Deleuze, G. (1988) *Foucault*, Minneapolis: University of Minnesota Press.

Deleuze, G. and Guattari, F. (1981) 'Rhizome', *I & C* 8: 49–71.

Deleuze, G. and Guattari, F. (1983) *Anti-Oedipus: Capitalism and Schizophrenia*, London: Athlone Press.

De Man, P. (1979) *Allegories of Reading*, New Haven: Yale University Press.

Derrida, J. (1976) *Of Grammatology*, Baltimore and London: Johns Hopkins University Press.

Derrida, J. (1978) *Writing and Difference*, London: Routledge & Kegan Paul

Derrida, J. (1982a) 'Signature event context', in *Margins of Philosophy*, Brighton: Harvester.

Derrida, J. (1982b) *Positions*, London: Athlone Press.

Derrida, J. (1987) *The Post Card: From Socrates to Freud and Beyond*, Chicago: University of Chicago Press.

Derrida, J. (1988) 'Interview (1983)' in D. Wood and R. Bernasconi (eds) *Derrida and Différance*, Evanston, Ill: Northwestern University Press.

Descartes, R. (1968) *Discourse on Method and Other Writings* (trans. with intro. by F. E. Sutcliffe), Harmondsworth: Penguin.

Deschamps, J. -C. (1982) 'Social identity and relations of power between groups', in H. Tajfel (ed.) *Social Identity and Intergroup Relations*, Cambridge: Cambridge University Press.

Deschamps, J. -C. (1984) 'The social psychology of intergroup relations and categorical differentiation', in H. Tajfel (ed.) *The Social Dimension*, Cambridge: Cambridge University Press.

Deutscher, I. (1968) 'On social science and the sociology of knowledge', *American Sociologist* 3: 291–2.

de Villiers, P. and de Villiers, J. (1979) *Early Language*, London: Fontana/Open Books.

Doise, W. (1978) *Groups and Individuals*, Cambridge: Cambridge University Press.

Doise, W. and Moscovici, S. (1984) 'Les Décisions en groupes', in S. Moscovici (ed.) *Psychologie Sociale*, Paris: Universitaires de France.

Donzelot, J. (1979) *The Policing of Families*, with a foreword by G. Deleuze, London: Hutchinson.

Doran, J. (1984) 'Coordinating agents: The TEAMWORK project', in G. N. Gilbert and C. Heath (eds) *Social Action and Artificial Intelligence*, London: Macmillan.

Dreyfus, H. L. and Rabinow, P. (1982) *Michel Foucault: Beyond Structuralism and Hermeneutics*, Hassocks, Sussex: Harvester Press.

Easthope, A. (1986) *What a Man's Gotta Do*, London: Paladin.

Easthope, A. (1988) *British Post-Structuralism: Since 1968*, London: Routledge.

Eastport Study Group (1985) *Summer Study 1985* (A report to the Director, Strategic Defense Initiative Organisation.)

Eco, U. (1983) *The Name of the Rose*, London: Picador.

Edmondson, R. (1984) *Rhetoric in Sociology*, London: Macmillan.

Elliott, R. (1983) 'Fitting process research to the practising therapist', *Psychotherapy, Research and Practice* 20: 47–55.

Eichenbaum, L. and Orbach, S. (1985) *Understanding Women*, Harmondsworth: Penguin.

Eichenbaum, L. and Orbach, S. (1987) 'Separation and Intimacy', in S. Ernst and M. Maguire (eds) *Living With the Sphinx*, London: Women's Press.

Eiser, J. R. (1980) *Cognitive Social Psychology*, London: McGraw Hill.

Ernst, S. (1987) 'Can a daughter be a woman?' in S. Ernst and M. Maguire (eds) *Living With the Sphinx*, London: Women's Press.

Eskola, A. (1971) *Sosiaalipsykologia*, Helsinki: Tammi.

Eysenck, H. J. (1952) 'The effects of psychotherapy: an evaluation', *Journal of Consulting Psychology*, 16: 319–24.

Farley, J. and Geison, G. L. (1974) 'Science, politics and spontaneous generation in nineteenth-century France: the Pasteur–Pouchet debate', *Bulletin of the History of Medicine* 48: 161–98.

Farr, R. M. (1981) 'On the nature of human nature and the science of behaviour', in P. Heelas and A. Lock (eds) *Indigenous Psychologies: the Anthropology of the Self*, London: Academic Press.

Farr, R. M. and Moscovici, S. (eds) (1984) *Social Representations*, Cambridge: Cambridge University Press.

Fee, E. (1983) 'Women's nature and scientific objectivity', in M. Lowe and R. Hubbard (eds) *Women's Nature,* New York: Pergamon Press.

Ferraroti, F. (1981) 'On the autonomy of the biographical method', in D. Bertaux (ed.) *Biography and Society,* Beverley Hills: Sage.

Fiske, J. (1982) *Introduction to Communication Studies,* London: Methuen.

Fiske, S. T. and Taylor, S. E. (1984) *Social Cognition,* New York: Random House.

Flacks, R. (1983) 'Moral commitment, privatism and activism: notes on a research program', in N. Haan, R. Bellah, P. Rabinow and W. Sullivan (eds) *Social Science as Moral Inquiry,* New York: Columbia University Press.

Fleck, L. (1979) *The Genesis and Development of a Scientific Fact,* Chicago: University of Chicago Press.

Fodor, J. (1985) *Modularity of Mind,* Cambridge, Mass.: MIT Press.

Forquet, F. (1980) *Les Comptes de la Puissance,* Encres: Editions Recherches.

Foucault, M. (1972) *The Archaeology of Knowledge,* London: Tavistock.

Foucault, M. (1975) *The Birth of the Clinic,* New York: Random House.

Foucault, M. (1977) *Discipline and Punish: The Birth of the Prison,* London: Allen Lane.

Foucault, M. (1979a) *The History of Sexuality. Vol. I: An Introduction,* London: Allen Lane.

Foucault, M. (1979b) 'On governmentality', *I & C:* 6, 5–21.

Foucault, M. (1980) *Power/Knowledge: Selected Interviews and Other Writings 1972–1977,* Hassocks, Sussex: Harvester Press.

Foucault, M. (1981) 'Omnes et singulatim: towards a criticism of "political reason"', in S. McMurrin (ed.) *The Tanner Lectures on Human Values II,* Salt Lake City: University of Utah Press.

Foucault, M. (1982) 'The subject and power'. Afterword to H. Dreyfus and P. Rabinow, *Michel Foucault: Beyond Structuralism and Hermeneutics,* Hassocks, Sussex: Harvester Press.

Foucault, M. (1988) 'Technologies of the self', in L. H. Martin, H. Gutman and P. H. Hutton (eds) *Technologies of the Self,* London: Tavistock.

Franklin, D. (1987) 'The politics of masochism', *Psychology Today,* January.

Fraser, C. and Foster, D. (1982) 'Social groups, nonsense groups and group polarization', in H. Tajfel (ed.) *The Social Dimension,* Cambridge: Cambridge University Press.

Fraser, C., Gouge, C., and Billig, M. (1971) 'Risky shifts, cautious shifts and group polarisation', *European Journal of Social Psychology* 1: 7–30.

Freud, A. (1949) 'Certain types and stages of social maladjustment', in K. R. Eissler (ed.) *Searchlights on Delinquency,* New York: International Universities Press.

Freud, S. (1895) with J. Breuer *Studies on Hysteria,* SE II.

Freud, S. (1896) 'The aetiology of hysteria', SE III.

Freud, S. (1905) *Jokes and their Relation to the Unconscious,* SE VII.

Freud, S. (1911) 'Psycho-analytic notes on an autobiographical account

227

of a case of paranoia (dementia paranoides)', SE XII.

Freud, S. (1912) 'The dynamics of transference', SE XII.

Freud, S. (1914) 'On narcissism: an introduction', SE XIII.

Freud, S. (1915) 'The unconscious', SE XIV.

Freud, S. (1920) *Beyond the Pleasure Principle*, SE XVIII.

Freud, S. (1923) 'The infantile genital organization', SE XIX.

Freud, S. (1937) 'Analysis terminable and interminable', SE XVIII.

Freud, S. (1953–74) *The Standard Edition of the Complete Psychological Works of Sigmund Freud* (24 vols.), ed. J. Strachey, London: The Hogarth Press and The Institute of Psycho-Analysis.

Frosh, S. (1987) *The Politics of Psychoanalysis*, London: Macmillan.

Fryer, P. (1937) 'Pseudo-scientific racism', in D. Gill and L. Levidow (eds) *Anti-Racist Science Teaching*, London: Free Association Books.

Furfey, P. H. (1971) 'The sociologist and scientific objectivity', in E. A. Tiryakin (ed.) *The Phenomenon of Sociology*, New York: Appleton-Century-Crofts.

Furnham, A. (1983) 'Social psychology as common sense', *Bulletin of the British Psychological Society*, 36: 105–9.

Gadamer, H. -G. (1975) *Truth and Method*, New York: Seabury Press.

Garfinkel, H. (1967) *Studies in Ethnomethodology*, New York: Prentice-Hall.

Geertz, C. (1975) *The Interpretation of Cultures*, London: Hutchinson.

Geertz, C. (1983) *Local Knowledge: Further Essays in Interpretive Anthropology*, New York: Basic Books.

Gergen, J. (1982) *Toward Transformation in Social Knowledge*, New York: Springer Verlag.

Gergen, K. J. (1984) 'Theory of the self: impasse and evolution', *Advances in Experimental Social Psychology*, 19: 49–115.

Gergen, K. J. (1985) 'The social constructionist movement in modern psychology', *American Psychologist* 40: 266–75.

Gergen, K. J. and Gergen, M. M. (1981) *Social Psychology*, New York: Harcourt Brace Jovanivitch.

Gerth, H. H. and Mills, C. W. (1946) *From Max Weber: Essays in Sociology*, New York: Oxford University Press.

Giddens, A. (1984) *The Constitution of Society*, Cambridge: Polity Press.

Gilbert, G. N. and Mulkay, M. (1982) 'Warranting scientific belief', *Social Studies of Science* 12: 383–408.

Gilligan, C. (1982) *In a Different Voice: Psychological Theory and Women's Development*, Cambridge, MA: Harvard University Press.

Goffman, E. (1971) *The Presentation of Self in Everyday Life*, Harmondsworth: Penguin.

Goldstein, J. H. (1980) *Social Psychology*, New York: Academic Press.

Gonsiorek, J. C. (1981) 'Introduction: Present and Future Directions in Gay/Lesbian Mental Health', *Journal of Homosexuality* 7: 5–7.

Goodman, G., Lakey, G., Lashof, J., and Thorne, E. (1983) *No Turning Back: Lesbian and Gay Liberation for the '80s*, Philadelphia: New Society Publishers.

Gordon, C. (1987) 'The soul of the citizen: Max Weber and Michel

Foucault on rationality and government', in S. Lash and S. Whimster (eds), *Max Weber, Rationality and Modernity*, London: Allen and Unwin.

Green, J. and LeFanu, S. (1985) *Dispatches From the Frontiers of the Female Mind*, London: Women's Press.

Griffin, C. (1986) 'It's different for girls', in H. Beloff (ed.) *Getting Into Life*, London: Methuen.

Habermas, J. (1984) *Theory of Communicative Action*, London: Heinemann.

Habermas, J. (1987) *The Philosophical Discourse of Modernity*, Cambridge: Polity Press.

Hacking, I. (1986) 'Making up people', in T. C. Heller *et al.* (eds) *Reconstructing Individualism*, Stanford, CA: Stanford University Press.

Hall, G. S. (1919) 'Some possible effects of the war on American psychology', *Psychological Bulletin* 16: 48–9.

Hamilton, D. L. and Trolier, T. K. (1986) 'Stereotypes and stereotyping: an overview of the cognitive approach', in J. F. Dovidio and S. L. Gaertner (eds) *Prejudice, Discrimination and Racism*, Orlando: Academic Press.

Haney, C. and Zimbardo, P. (1976) 'Social roles and role-playing: observations from the Stanford Prison Study', in E. Hollander and R. Hunt (eds) *Current Perspectives in Social Psychology*, New York: Oxford University Press.

Harding, S. (1986) *The Science Question in Feminism*, Ithaca: Cornell University Press.

Hare, E. H. (1962) 'Masturbatory insanity: the history of an idea', *Journal of Mental Science*, 108: 1–25.

Harré, R. (1979) *Social Being: A Theory for Social Psychology*, Oxford: Basil Blackwell.

Harré, R. (1981) 'Rituals, rhetoric and social cognition', in J. P. Forgas (ed.) *Social Cognition*, London: Academic Press.

Harré, R. (1983) *Personal Being: A Theory for Individual Psychology*, Oxford: Basil Blackwell.

Harré, R., Clarke, D., and DeCarlo, N. (1985) *Motives and Mechanisms: An Introduction to the Psychology of Action*, London: Methuen.

Harré, R. and Secord, P. F. (1972) *The Explanation of Social Behaviour*, Oxford: Basil Blackwell.

Hawkes, T. (1977) *Structuralism and Semiotics*, London: Methuen.

Hearnshaw, L. (1964) *A Short History of British Psychology*, London: Methuen.

Heelas, P. and Lock, A. (1981) *Indigenous Psychologies: The anthropology of the Self*, London: Academic Press.

Heider, F. (1958) *The Psychology of Interpersonal Relations*, New York: Wiley.

Henderson, H. (1983) 'The warp and the weft: The coming synthesis of eco-philosophy and eco-feminism', in L. Caldecott and S. Leland (eds) *Reclaim the Earth*, London: Women's Press.

Henriques, J., Hollway, W., Urwin, C., Venn, C., and Walkerdine, W.

(1984) *Changing the Subject: Psychology, Social Regulation and Subjectivity*, London: Methuen.

Herman, J. and Lewis, H. B. (1986) 'Anger in the mother–daughter relationship', in T. Bernay and D. W. Cantor (eds) *The Psychology of Today's Woman*, Hillsdale, New Jersey: Analytic Press.

Herrnstein, R. (1971) 'IQ', *The Atlantic* September: 43–64.

Hewstone, M., Jaspers, J. and Lalljee, M. (1982) 'Social representation, social attribution and social identity: the intergroup images of public and comprehensive schoolboys', *European Journal of Social Psychology* 12: 241–69.

Hines, T. (1988) *Pseudoscience and the Paranormal: A Critical Examination of the Evidence*, London: Prometheus Books.

Holland, R. (1978) *Self and Social Context*, London: Macmillan.

Horkheimer, M. and Adorno, T. W. (1972) *Dialectic of Enlightenment*, New York: Seabury Press.

Hudson, B. (1984) 'Femininity and adolescence', in A. McRobbie and M. Nava (eds) *Gender and Generation*, Basingstoke: Macmillan.

Huici, C. (1984) 'The individual and social functions of sex- role stereotypes', in H. Tajfel (ed.) *The Social Dimension*, Cambridge: Cambridge University Press.

Ingleby, D. (1974) 'The job psychologists do', in N. Armistead (ed.) *Reconstructing Social Psychology*, Harmondsworth: Penguin.

Ingleby, D. (1984) 'Development in social context', Paper given at British Psychological Society Developmental Psychology Section Conference, University of Lancaster.

Ingleby, D. (1987) personal communication to D. Pilgrim.

Irigaray, L. (1977) 'Women's exile', *Ideology and Consciousness* 1: 62–76.

Jacoby, R. (1975) *Social Amnesia: A Critique of Conformist Psychology from Adler to Laing*, New York: Beacon Press.

Jakobson, R. (1960) 'Poetics and linguistics', in T. A. Sebeok (ed.) *Style in Language*, Cambridge, Mass,: MIT Press.

Jakobson, R. and Halle, M. (1956) *Fundamentals of Language*, The Hague: Mouton.

James, P. (1986) 'A taste for death', *Time*, October 16th.

Jameson, F. (1981) *The Political Unconscious*, London: Methuen.

Jameson, F. (1984) 'Postmodernism, or the cultural logic of late capitalism', *New Left Review* 146: 53–92.

Jaspers, J. (1983) 'The task of social psychology: some historical reflections', *British Journal of Social Psychology*, 22: 277–88.

Jodelet, D. (1984) 'Representation sociale, phénomèmes, concept et théorie', in S. Moscovici (ed.) *Psychologie Sociale*, Paris: Presses Universitaires de France.

Johnson, M. (1987) *The Body in the Mind*, Chicago: University of Chicago Press.

Johnson-Laird, P. (1985) *Mental Models*, Cambridge: Cambridge University Press.

Jones, K. and William son, K. (1979) 'The birth of the schoolroom', *I & C* 6: 59–110.

Jones, R. S. (1973) 'Proving Blacks inferior: the sociology of knowledge', in J. A. Ladner (ed.) *The Death of White Sociology*, New York: Random House.

Kameny, F. E. (1971) 'Gay liberation and psychiatry', *Psychiatric Opinion* 8: 18–27.

Kamin, L. (1974) *The Science and Politics of IQ*, Harmondsworth: Penguin.

Karlen, A. (1972) 'A discussion of "homosexuality as a mental illness"', *International Journal of Psychiatry* 10: 108–13.

Kelley, H. H. (1972) 'Causal schemata and the attribution process', in E. E. Jones, D. E. Kanouse, H. H. Kelley, R. E. Nisbett, S. Valins, and B. Weiner (eds) *Attribution: Perceiving the Causes of Behavior*, Morristown: General Learning Press.

Kelley, H. H. and Michela, J. L. (1980) 'Attribution theory and research', *Annual Review of Psychology* 31: 457–501.

Kirk, R. (1961) 'Is social science scientific?' *New York Times Magazine*, Section 6 (25 June): 15–16.

Kitzinger, C. (1987) *The Social Construction of Lesbianism*, London: Sage.

Kitzinger, J. (1988) 'Defending innocence: ideologies of childhood', *Feminist Review* 28: 77–87.

Klein, M. (1975 [1927]) 'Criminal tendencies in normal children', *Writings. vol. I*, London: Hogarth Press.

Klein, M. (1975 [1930]) 'The importance of symbol formation in the development of the ego', in J. Mitchell (ed.) *The Selected Melanie Klein*, Harmondsworth: Penguin.

Kohn, A. (1986) *False Prophets*, Oxford: Basil Blackwell.

Kronemeyer, R. (1980) *Overcoming Homosexuality*, New York: Macmillan.

Kuhn, T. (1962) *The Structure of Scientific Revolutions*, Chicago: University of Chicago Press.

Lacan, J. (1977) *Ecrits*, London: Tavistock.

Lakoff, G. (1986) *Women, Fire, and Other Dangerous Things*, Chicago: University of Chicago Press.

Lakoff, G. and Johnson, M. (1980) *Metaphors We Live By*, Chicago: University of Chicago Press.

Lalljee, M., Brown, L. B. and Ginsberg, G. P. (1984) 'Attitudes: disposition, behaviour or evaluation', *British Journal of Social Psychology* 23: 233–44.

Lapsley, R. and Westlake, M. (1987) *Film Theory: An Introduction*, Manchester: Manchester University Press.

Lastrucci, C. L. (1970) 'Looking forward: the case for hard-nosed methodology', *American Sociologist* 5: 273–5.

Latour, B. (1984) *Les Microbes, Guerre et Paix, followed by Irreductions*, Paris: Metailie (forthcoming as *The Pasteurisation of French Society*, Cambridge, MA: Harvard University Press).

Latour, B. (1986a) 'Visualisation and cognition: thinking with eyes and hands', *Knowledge and Society: Studies in the Sociology of Culture Past and Present* 6: 1–40.

Latour, B. (1986b) 'The powers of association', in J. Law (ed.) *Power, Action and Belief*, London: Routledge & Kegan Paul.

Latour, B. (1987) *Science in Action*, Milton Keynes: Open University Press.

Law, J. (ed.) (1986) *Power, Action and Belief*, London: Routledge & Kegan Paul.

Law, J. (1987) 'Technology and heterogeneous engineering: the case of Portuguese expansion', in W. Bijker, T. P. Hughes and T. Pinch (eds) *The Social Construction of Technological Systems*, Cambridge, MA: MIT Press.

Lawson, H. (1984) *Reflexivity: the Postmodern Predicament*, London: Hutchinson.

Le Bon, G. (1896) *The Crowd: A Study of the Popular Mind*, London: Ernest Benn Ltd.

Leff, M. C. (1987) 'Modern sophistic and the unity of rhetoric', in J. S. Nelson, A. Megill and D. N. McCloskey (eds) *The Rhetoric of the Human Sciences*, Wisconsin: University of Wisconsin.

Lemert, C. C. (1979) *Sociology and the Twilight of Man*, Carbondale: Southern Illinois University Press.

Levidow, L. (1987) 'Racism in scientific innovation', in D. Gill and L. Levidow (eds) *Anti-Racist Science Teaching*, London: Free Association Books.

Lévy-Leboyer, C. (1988) 'Success and failure in applying psychology', *American Psychologist*, 43 (10): 779–85.

Lykes, M. B. (1985) 'Gender and individualistic vs. collectivist bases for notions about the self, *Journal of Personality*, 53: 356–83.

Lynch, M. and Woolgar, S. (1988) 'Sociological orientations to representational practices in science', Introduction to M. Lynch and S. Woolgar (eds) *Representational Practices in the Natural Sciences*, Special Issue of *Human Studies*, February 1988.

Lyotard, J.-F. (1984) *The Postmodern Condition: A Report on Knowledge*, Manchester: Manchester University Press.

McGrath, J. E. (1980) 'What are the social issues? Timeliness and treatment of topics in the Journal of Social Issues', *Journal of Social Issues* 36: 98–124.

Machan, T. R. (1974) *The Pseudo-Science of B. F. Skinner*, New York: Arlington House Publishers.

MacIntyre, A. (1984) *After Virtue (2nd Edition)*, Notre Dame, Indiana: University of Notre Dame Press.

MacIntyre, A. (1988) *Whose Justice? Which Rationality?*, Notre Dame, Indiana: University of Notre Dame Press.

McKinlay, A. and Potter, J. (1987) 'Social representations: a conceptual critique', *Journal for the Theory of Social Behaviour* 17: 471–88.

McNamara, T. (1986) 'Mental representation of spatial relations', *Cognitive Psychology* 18: 87–121.

Macpherson, C. B. (1962) *The Political Theory of Possessive Individualism: Hobbes to Locke*, Oxford: Oxford University Press.

Maguire, M. (1987) 'Casting the evil eye – women and envy', in S. Ernst and M. Maguire (eds) *Living With the Sphinx*, London: Women's Press.

Mahler, M., Pine, F., and Bergman, A. (1975) *The Psychological Birth of the Human Infant: Symbiosis and Individuation*, New York: Basic Books.

Mahoney, M. J. (1977) 'Publication prejudices', *Cognitive Therapy and Research* 1: 161–75.

Mandel, E. (1978) *Late Capitalism*, London: Verso.

Mann, J. (1981) *Deadlier Than the Male*, London: David and Charles.

Marcus, L. (1987) '"Enough about you, let's talk about me": recent autobiographical writing', *New Formations* 1: 77–94.

Marcuse, H. (1964) *One Dimensional Man*, Boston: Beacon Press.

Marcuse, H. (1966) *Eros and Civilization*, Boston: Beacon Press.

Marr, D. (1975) *Analyzing Natural Images*, Cambridge, Mass: MIT Press.

Marx, K. and Engels, F. (1977) *The German Ideology (part one)*, London: Lawrence and Wishart.

Mazure, A. (1968) 'The Littlest Science', *American Sociologist* 3: 196–9.

Mead, G. H. (1934) *Mind, Self and Society: From the Standpoint of a Social Behaviourist*, Chicago: University of Chicago Press.

Merton, R. K. (1968) *Social Theory and Social Structure*, New York: Free Press.

Metcalf, A. and Humphries, M. (eds) (1985) *The Sexuality of Men*, London: Pluto Press.

Meyer, J. (1986) 'The self and the life course: institutionalization and its effects', in A. Sørensen, F. Weinert and L. Sherrod (eds) *Human Development and the Life-Course*, Hillsdale, NJ: Erlbaum.

Middlebrook, P. N. (1980) *Social Psychology and Modern Life (2nd Edition)*, New York: Alfred Knopf.

Milgram, S. (1963) 'Behavioural study of obedience', *Journal of Abnormal and Social Psychology* 67: 371–8.

Miller, J. G. (1984) 'Culture and the development of everyday social explanation', *Journal of Personality and Social Psychology* 46: 961–78.

Miller, P. (1987) *Domination and Power*, London: Routledge & Kegan Paul.

Miller, P. and O'Leary, T. (1987) 'Accounting and the construction of the governable person', *Accounting, Organizations and Society*, 235–65.

Miller, P. and O'Leary, T. (forthcoming) 'Hierarchies and American ideals, 1900–1940', *Academy of Management Review*, April 1989.

Miller, P. and Rose, N. (1988) 'The Tavistock programme: governing subjectivity and social life', *Sociology* 22: 171–92.

Miller, P. and Rose, N. (forthcoming) *Rationalities and technologies of government*.

Mills, C. W. (1940) 'Situated actions and the vocabulary of motives', *American Sociological Review* 5: 904–13.

Milner, D. (1981) 'Racial prejudice', in J. C. Turner and H. Giles (eds) *Intergroup Behaviour*, Oxford: Basil Blackwell.

Milner, M. (1988 [1969]) *The Hands of the Living God*, London: Virago.

Minh-ha, T. (1988) 'Not you/like you: post-colonial women and the interlocking questions of identity and difference', in 'Feminism and the critique of colonial discourse', *Inscriptions* 3/4: 71–8.

Mishler, E. (1986) *Research Interviewing, Context and Narrative*,

Cambridge, Mass: Harvard University Press.

Mitchell, J. (1974) *Psychoanalysis and Feminism*, Harmondsworth: Penguin.

Moberly, E. R. (1983) *Psychogenesis: The Early Development of Gender Identity*, London: Routledge & Kegan Paul.

Moghaddam, F. M. (1987) 'Psychology in the Three Worlds: as reflected by the "crisis" in social psychology and the move towards indigenous Third World psychology', *American Psychologist* 47: 912–20.

Mohanty, C. (1988) 'Under western eyes: feminist scholarship and colonial discourses', *Feminist Review* 30: 61–88.

Moi, T. (1985) *Sexual/Textual Politics: Feminist Literary Theory*, London: Methuen.

Mosco, V. (1987) 'Star wars is already working', *Science as Culture*, pilot issue: 12–34.

Moscovici, S. (1972) 'Society and theory in social psychology', in J. Israel and H. Tajfel (eds) *The Context of Social Psychology: A Critical Assessment*, London: Academic Press.

Moscovici, S. (1976) *Social Influence and Social Change*, London: Academic Press.

Moscovici, S. (1982) 'The coming era of representations', in J. -P. Codol and J. -P. Leyens (eds) *Cognitive Analysis of Social Behaviour*, The Hague: Martinus Nijhoff.

Moscovici, S. (1984a) 'The phenomenon of social representations, in R. M. Farr and S. Moscovici (eds) *Social Representations*, Cambridge: Cambridge University Press.

Moscovici, S. (1984b) 'The myth of the lonely paradigm', *Social Research* 51: 939–67.

Moscovici, S. (1987) *Answers and questions*', *Journal for the Theory of Social Behaviour*, 17: 513–29.

Moscovici, S. and Zavalloni, M. (1969) 'The group as a polarizer of attitudes', *Journal of Personality and Social Psychology* 12: 125–35.

Mulkay, M. (1979) *Science and the Sociology of Knowledge*, London: George Allen and Unwin.

Mummendey, A. and Schreiber, H. -S. (1984) '"Different" just means "better": Some obvious and hidden pathways to ingroup favouritism', *British Journal of Social Psychology* 23: 363–8.

Neisser, U. (1967) *Cognitive Psychology*, New York: Appleton-Century-Crofts.

Nelson, J. S., Megill, A., and McCloskey, D. N. (1987) 'Rhetoric of inquiry', in J. S. Nelson, A. Megill, and D. N. McCloskey (eds) *The Rhetoric of the Human Sciences*, Wisconsin: University of Wisconsin.

Ng, S. H. (1980) *The Social Psychology of Power*, London: Academic Press.

Nisbett, R. E. and Ross, L. (1980) *Human Inference*, New Jersey: Prentice-Hall.

Norris, C. (1982) *Deconstruction: Theory and Practice*, London: Methuen.

Norris, C. (1983) *The Deconstructive Turn*, London: Methuen.

Oakley, A. (1979) 'The baby blues', *New Society*, April.

Oakley, A. (1981) 'Interviewing women: a contradiction in terms', in H. Roberts (ed.) *Doing Feminist Research*, London: Routledge & Kegan Paul.

Oestreich, G. (1982) *Neostoicism and the Modern State*, Cambridge: Cambridge University Press.

Ong, A. (1988) 'Colonialism and modernity: feminist re-presentations of women in non-western societies', *Inscriptions* 3/4: 79–93.

Ong, W. J. (1958) Ramus: Method and the Decay of Dialogue, Cambridge, MA: Harvard University Press.

Ortony, A. (1979) *Metaphor and Thought*, Cambridge: Cambridge University Press.

Ossorio, P. (1981) 'Ex post facto: the source of intractable origin problems', Boulder Colorado: Linguistic Research Institute Reports N. 28.

Parker, I. (1987) 'Social representations': social psychology's (mis)use of sociology', *Journal for the Theory of Social Behaviour* 17 (4): 447–69.

Parker, I. (1989) *The Crisis in Modern Social Psychology, And How to End It*, London: Routledge.

Parker, I. (1990) 'Discourse discourse: social psychology and postmodernity', unpublished MS.

Parkes, C. (1972) *Bereavement*, London: Tavistock.

Parnas, D. (1985) *Software Aspects of Strategic Defense Systems*, University of Victoria, Department of Computer Science Research Report DCS-47-IR, July.

Parrinder, P. (1980) *Science Fiction: Its Criticisms and Teaching*, London: Methuen.

Paserini, L. (1987) *Fascism in Popular Memory: The Cultural Experience of the Turin Working Class*, Cambridge: Cambridge University Press.

Pasquino, P. (1978) 'Theatrum Politicum. The genealogy of capital – police and the state of prosperity', *Ideology and Consciousness* 4: 41–54.

Perelman, C. (1979) *The New Rhetoric and the Humanities*, Dordrecht: D. Reidel.

Perelman, C. and Olbrechts-Tyteca, L. (1971) *The New Rhetoric*, Notre Dame, Indiana: University of Notre Dame.

Perrin, S. and Spencer, C. (1980) 'The Asch effect – a child of its time?', *Bulletin of the British Psychological Society* 32: 405–6.

Peters, R. S. (1959) *The Concept of Motivation*, London: Routledge & Kegan Paul.

Pettigrew, T. F. (1979) 'The ultimate attribution error: Extending Allport's cognitive analysis of prejudice', *Personality and Social Psychology Bulletin* 5: 464–78.

Pilgrim, D. (1986) *NHS Psychotherapy: Personal Accounts*, unpublished Ph.D. thesis, University of Nottingham.

Pilgrim, D. (1987) 'The psychology of helping: a critical review', in E. Karas (ed.) *Current Issues in Clinical Psychology*, London: Plenum Press.

Plummer, K. (1983) *Documents of Life*, London: George Allen and Unwin.

Popper, K. (1963) *Conjectures and Refutations*, London: Routledge &

Kegan Paul.

Popper, K. (1988) 'The allure of the open future', extracted from a lecture given to the World Congress of Philosophy, Brighton, *The Guardian*, 29 August: 8.

Potter, J. (1988) 'Cutting cakes: a study of psychologists' categorisations', *Philosophical Psychology* 1: 17–32.

Potter, J. and Litton, I. (1985) 'Some problems underlying the theory of social representations', *British Journal of Sociology* 24: 81–90.

Potter, J. and McKinlay, A. (1987) 'Model discourse: interpretive repertoires in scientists' conference talk', *Social Studies of Science* 17: 443–63.

Potter, J., Stringer, P., and Wetherell, M. (1984) *Social Texts and Context: Literature and Social Psychology*, London: Routledge & Kegan Paul.

Potter, J. and Wetherell, M. (1987) *Discourse and Social Psychology: Beyond Attitudes and Behaviour*, London: Sage.

Rachman, S. (1978) 'Little Hans', *Bulletin of the British Psychological Society*, 31: 394.

Raven, B. H. and Rubin, J. Z. (1976) *Social Psychology: People in Groups*, New York: Wiley.

Rawls, J. (1971) *A Theory of Justice*, Cambridge MA: Belknap Press of Harvard University Press.

Reason, P. (ed.) (1988) *Human Inquiry in Action: Developments in New Paradigm Research*, London: Sage.

Reason, P. and Rowan, J. (eds) (1981) *Human Inquiry: A Sourcebook of New Paradigm Research*, Chichester: Wiley.

Reicher, S. D. (1984) 'The St Paul's riots: an explanation of the limits of crowd action in terms of a social identity model', *European Journal of Social Psychology* 14: 1–21.

Reicher, S. D. (1988) 'Review essay on *Arguing and Thinking*', *British Journal of Social Psychology* 27: 283–8.

Reicher, S. D. and Potter, J. (1985) 'Psychological theory as intergroup perspective: A comparative analysis of "scientific" and "lay" accounts of crowd behaviour', *Human Relations*, 38: 167–89.

Reynolds, L. T. (1966) 'A note on the perpetuation of a "scientific" fiction', Sociometry 29: 85–8.

Ridgway, J. and Benjamin, M. (1987) *Psi Fi: Psychological Theories and Science Fictions*, Leicester: British Psychological Society.

Riley, D. (1983) *War in Nursery*, London: Virago.

Rogers, T. B. (1980) in H. J. Stam, T. B. Rogers, and K. J. Gergen (eds) *The Analysis of Psychological Theory: Metapsychological Perspectives*, Washington: Hemisphere.

Rorty, R. (1980) *Philosophy and the Mirror of Nature*, Oxford: Basil Blackwell.

Rorty, R. (1987) 'Science as solidarity', in J. S. Nelson, A. Megill, and D. N. McCloskey (eds) *The Rhetoric of the Human Sciences*, Wisconsin: University of Wisconsin.

Rosch, E. (1978) 'Principles of categorization', in E. Rosch and B. Lloyd (eds) *Cognition and Categorization*, New Jersey: Erlbaum.

Rose, G. (1984) *Dialectic of Nihilism*, Oxford: Basil Blackwell.

Rose, N. (1979) 'The psychological complex: mental measurement and social administration', *Ideology and Consciousness* 5: 5–68.

Rose, N. (1985) *The Psychological Complex*, London: Routledge & Kegan Paul.

Rose, N. (1988) 'Calculable minds and manageable individuals', *History of the Human Sciences* 1: 179–200.

Rose, N. (1989) *Governing the Soul: Technologies of Human Subjectivity*, London: Routledge.

Rosenblatt, P. C. and Miller, M. (1972) 'Problems and anxieties in research design and analysis', in C. G. McClintock (ed.) *Experimental Social Psychology*, New York: Holt, Rinehart and Winston.

Rosenthal, R. (1966) *Experimenter Effects in Behavioral Research*, New York: Appleton.

Rotter, J. B. (1966) 'Generalized expectancies for internal versus external control of reinforcement', *Psychological Monographs* 80 (1, Whole No. 609).

Rumelhart, D. and Ortony, A. (1977) 'The representation of knowledge in memory', in R. Anderson, J. Spiro, and W. Montagu (eds) *Schooling and the Acquisition of Knowledge*, Hillsdale: Erlbaum.

Russ, J. (1985) *The Female Man*, London: Women's Press.

Ryan, M. (1982) *Marxism and Deconstruction*, Baltimore: Johns Hopkins Press.

Sabini, J. and Silver, M. (1982) *Moralities of Everyday Life*, New York: Oxford University Press.

Said, E. (1985) *Orientalism*, Harmondsworth: Penguin.

Sampson, E. E. (1976) *Social Psychology and Contemporary Society* (2nd edn) New York: Wiley.

Sampson, E. E. (1977) 'Psychology and the American ideal', *Journal of Personality and Social Psychology* 35: 767–82.

Sampson, E. E. (1978) 'Scientific paradigms and social values: Wanted – a scientific revolution', Journal of Personality and Social Psychology 36: 1332–43.

Sampson, E. E. (1983a) *Justice and the Critique of Pure Psychology*, New York: Plenum.

Sampson, E. E. (1983b) 'Deconstructing psychology's subject', *Journal of Mind and Behaviour* 4: 136–64.

Sampson, E. E. (1985) 'The decentralization of identity: towards a revised concept of personal and social order', *American Psychologist* 40: 1203–11.

Sampson, E. E. (1988) 'The debate on individualism: indigenous psychologies of the individual and their role in personal and societal functioning', *American Psychologist* 43: 15–22.

Sandel, M. J. (1982) *Liberalism and Limits of Justice*, Cambridge, England: Cambridge University Press.

Sartre, J. -P. (1963) *Search for a Method*, New York: Knopf.

Saussure, F. de (1974) *Course in General Linguistics*, London: Fontana.

Sayers, J. (1986) *Sexual Contradictions: Psychology, Psychoanalysis, and*

Feminism, London: Tavistock.

Schmideberg, M. (1933) 'The psychoanalytic treatment of asocial children', *New Era* 14: 87–90.

Schneider, D. J. (1976) *Social Psychology*, Reading, Mass: Addison-Wesley.

Schumpeter, J. A. (1954) *History of Economic Analysis*, New York: Oxford University Press.

Seidenberg, B. and Snadowsky, A. (1976) *Social Psychology: An Introduction*, New York: The Free Press.

Shallice, T. (1984) 'Psychology and social control', *Cognition* 17: 29–48.

Shannon, C. E. and Weaver, W. (1949) *The Mathematical Theory of Communication*, Urbana: University of Illinois Press.

Sharp, R. and Green, A. (1975) *Education and Social Control*, London: Routledge & Kegan Paul.

Shotter, J. (1975) *Images of Man in Psychological Research*, London: Methuen.

Shotter, J. (1984) *Social Accountability and Selfhood*, Oxford: Basil Blackwell.

Shotter, J. (1986a) 'A Sense of place: Vico and the production of social identities', *British Journal of Social Psychology* 25: 199–211.

Shotter, J. (1986b) 'Speaking practically: Whorf, the formative function of language, and knowing of the third kind', in R. Rosnow and M. Georgoudi (eds) *Contextualism and Understanding in the Behavioural Sciences*, New York: Praeger.

Shotter, J. (1987) 'Cognitive psychology, "Taylorism", and the manufacture of unemployment', in A. Costall and A. Still (eds) *Cognitive Psychology in Question*, Brighton, Sussex: Harvester Press.

Shotter, J. (1989) 'Rhetoric and the recovery of civil society', *Economy and Society* 18(2): 149–66.

Shotter, J. (in press) 'Vygotsky's psychology: joint activity in the developmental zone', *New Ideas in Psychology*.

Schweder, R. A. and Bourne, E. (1982) 'Does the concept of the person vary cross-culturally?', in A. J. Marsella and G. White (eds) *Cultural Concepts of Mental Health and Therapy*, Boston: Reidel.

Simon, H. (1981) 'What computers mean for man and society', in T. Forrester (ed.) *The Microelectronics Revolution*, Cambridge, Mass: MIT Press.

Simons, H. W. (ed.) (1989) *Rhetoric in the Human Sciences*, London: Sage,

Sindermann, C. J. (1982) *Winning the Games Scientists Play*, New York: Plenum Press.

Skinner, B. F. (1971) *Beyond Freedom and Dignity*, Harmondsworth: Penguin.

Smedslund, J. (1978) 'Bandura's theory of self-efficacy: a set of common sense theorems', *Scandinavian Journal of Psychology*, 19: 1–14.

Smith, D. (1988) *The Everyday World as Problematic: a Feminist Sociology*, Milton Keynes: Open University Press.

Snell, B. (1982) *The Discovery of Mind*, New York: Dover.

Spence, J. (1986) *Putting Myself in the Picture*, London: Camden Press.

Spender, D. (1980) *Man Made Language*, London: Routledge & Kegan

Paul.

Stacey, J. (1988) 'Can there be a feminist ethnography?', *Women's Studies International Forum* 11 (1): 21–7.

Stam, H. J. (1986) 'The psychology of control: a textual critique', in H. J. Stam, T. B. Rogers, and K. J. Gergen (eds) *The Analysis of Psychological Theory: Metapsychological Perspectives*, New York: Hemisphere.

Stang, D. J. (1981) *Introduction to Social Psychology*, Monterey: Brooks/Cole.

Stanley, L. and Wise, S. (1983) *Breaking Out: Feminist Consciousness and Feminist Research*, London: Routledge & Kegan Paul.

Steedman, C. (1982) *The Tidy House: Little Girls' Writing*, London: Virago.

Steedman, C. (1986) *Landscape For a Good Woman*, London: Virago.

Steinem, G. (1983) *Outrageous Acts and Everyday Rebellions*, London: Fontana.

Stolzenberg, G. (1978) 'Can an inquiry into the foundations of mathematics tell us anything interesting about mind?', in G. A. Miller and E. Lenneberg (eds) *Psychology and Biology of Thought and Language: Essays in Honour of Eric Lenneberg*, New York: Academic Press.

Suppe, F. (1981) 'The Bell and Weinberg study: future priorities for research on homosexuality', *Journal of Homosexuality*, 6: 69–97.

Tajfel, H. (1978) *Differentiation Between Social Groups*, London: Academic Press.

Tajfel, H. (1981) *Human Groups and Social Categories*, Cambridge: Cambridge University Press.

Tajfel, H. (1984) 'Intergroup relations, social myths, and social justice in social psychology', in H. Tajfel (ed.) *The Social Dimension*, Cambridge: Cambridge University Press.

Tajfel, H., Flament, C., Billig, M. and Bundy, R. F. (1971) 'Social categorization and intergroup behaviour', *European Journal of Social Psychology* 1: 149–77.

Tajfel, H. and Turner, J. C. (1979) 'An integrative theory of intergroup conflict', in W. G. Austin and S. Worschel (eds) *Social Psychology of Intergroup Relations*.

Taylor, C. (1979) 'Interpretation and the sciences of man', in P. Rabinow and W. M. Sullivan (eds) *Interpretive Social Science*, Berkeley: University of California Press.

Taylor, D. M. and McKirnan, D. J. (1984) 'A five stage model of intergroup relations', *British Journal of Social Psychology* 23: 291–300.

Taylor, F. W. (1911) *Scientific Management*, New York: Harper & Row.

Taylor, M. (1983) *Growing Up Without Work*, London: Community Projects Foundation.

Taylor, S. E. and Crocker, J. (1981) 'Schematic bases of social information processing', in E. T. Higgins, D. N. Ruble and W. W. Hartup (eds) *Social Cognition and Social Development*, Cambridge: Cambridge University Press.

Thiong'o, N. wa (1987) *Decolonizing the Mind: the Politics of African*

Literature, London: James Currey.

Thompson, E. P. and Thompson, B. (1985) *Star Wars: Self- Destruct Incorporated*, London: Merlin.

Trauer, T. (1984) 'The current status of the therapeutic community', *British Journal of Medical Psychology* 57: 71–9.

Tribe, K. (1976) *Land, Labour and Economic Discourse*, London: Routledge & Kegan Paul.

Tuan, Yi-Fu (1982) *Segmented Worlds and Self*, Minneapolis: University of Minneapolis Press.

Turing, A. M. (1950) 'Computing machinery and intelligence', *Mind* 59: 433–60.

Turner, J. C. (1975) 'Social comparison and social identity: some prospects for intergroup behaviour', *European Journal of Social Psychology* 5: 5–34.

Turner, J. C. (1978a) 'Social categorization and social discrimination in the minimal group paradigm', in H. Tajfel (ed.) *Differentiation Between Social Groups*, London: Academic Press.

Turner, J. C. (1978b) 'Social comparison, similarity and ingroup favouritism', in H. Tajfel (ed.) *Differentiation Between Social Groups*, London: Academic Press.

Turner, J. C. (1981) 'The experimental social psychology of intergroup behaviour', in J. C. Turner and H. Giles (eds) *Intergroup Behaviour*, Oxford: Basil Blackwell.

Turner, J. C. (1982) 'Towards a cognitive redefinition of the social group', in H. Tajfel (ed.) *Social Identity and Intergroup Relations*, Cambridge: Cambridge University Press.

Turner, J. C. (1984) 'Social identification and psychological group formation', in H. Tajfel (ed.) *The Social Dimension*, Cambridge: Cambridge University Press.

Turner, J. C. (1985) 'Self-categorization and the self concept', in E. J. Lawler (ed.) *Advances in Group Processes*, Greenwich, Connecticut: JAI Press.

Turner, J. C. (1987) *Rediscovering the Social Group*, Oxford: Basil Blackwell.

Turner, J. C. and Oakes, P. J. (1986) 'The significance of the social identity concept for social psychology with reference to individualism, interactionism and social influence', *British Journal of Social Psychology* 25: 237–52.

Tversky, A. and Kahneman, D. (1980) 'Causal schemas in judgements under certainty', in M. Fishbein (ed.) *Progress in Social Psychology Vol. I*, New Jersey: Erlbaum.

Urwin, C. (1986) 'Developmental psychology and psychoanalysis: splitting the difference', in M. Richards and P. Light (eds) *Children of Social Worlds*, Cambridge: Polity Press.

Van Kippenberg, A. F. M. (1984) 'Intergroup difference in perception', in H. Tajfel (ed.) *The Social Dimension*, Cambridge: Cambridge University Press.

Venn, C. and Walkerdine, V. (1978) 'The acquisition and production of knowledge: Piaget's theory reconsidered', *Ideology and Consciousness* 3: 67–94.

Vico, G. (1948) *The New Science of Giambattista Vico*, (ed. and trans, by T. G. Bergin and M. H. Fisch), Ithaca, NY: Cornell University Press.

Vico, G. (1982) 'The order of our inquiry', in L. Pompa (ed. and trans.) *Vico: Selected Writings*, Cambridge: Cambridge University Press.

Vygotsky, L. S. (1966) 'Development of the higher mental functions', in A. N. Leont'ev, A. R. Luria, and A. Smirnov (eds) *Psychological Research in the USSR*, Moscow: Progress Publishers.

Walden, R. and Walkerdine, V. (1982) *Girls and Mathematics: the Early Years*, Bedford Way Papers, Institute of Education, University of London.

Walkerdine, V. (1981) 'Sex, power and pedagogy', *Screen Education* 38: 14–21.

Walkerdine, V. 'Developmental psychology and the child-centred pedagogy: the insertion of Piaget into early education', in J. Henriques, W. Hollway, C. Urwin, C. Venn, and V. Walkerdine (eds) *Changing the Subject: Psychology, Social Regulation and Subjectivity*, London: Methuen.

Wallach, M. A., Kogan, N., and Bem, D. (1962) 'Group influence on individual risk taking', *Journal of Abnormal and Social Psychology* 65: 75–86.

Wallis, R. (1985) 'Science and pseudoscience', *Social Science Information* 24 (3): 585–601.

Warren, K. (1988) '"The child as problem" or "the child with needs": a discourse analysis of a school case conference', unpublished B.Sc. (Hons) Psychology project, Manchester Polytechnic.

Weedon, C. (1987) *Feminist Practice and Post-structuralist Theory*, Oxford: Basil Blackwell.

Weisz, J. R., Rothbaum, R. M., and Blackburn, T. C. (1984) 'Standing out and standing in: the psychology of control; in America and Japan', *American Psychologist* 39: 955–69.

Wexler, P. (1983) *Critical Social Psychology*, Boston: Routledge & Kegan Paul.

White, H. (1978) *The Tropics of Discourse*, Baltimore: Johns Hopkins Press.

White, M. J. (1985) 'On the status of cognitive psychology', *American Psychologist* 40: 117–19.

Wilder, D. A. (1978) 'Reduction of intergroup discrimination through individuation of outgroup', *Journal of Personality and Social Psychology* 36: 1361–74.

Williams, J. A. (1984) 'Gender and intergroup behaviour: towards an integration', *British Journal of Social Psychology* 23: 311–16.

Williams, J. E. and Giles, H. (1978) 'The changing status of women in society: an intergroup perspective', in H. Tajfel (ed.) *Differentiation Between Social Groups*, London: Academic Press.

Williams, R. (1976) *Keywords: A Vocabulary of Culture and Society*, London: Fontana.

Wilks, Y. (1985) 'AI and the military again', *AISB: Quarterly Newsletter of the Society for the Study of Artificial Intelligence and Simulation of Behaviour* 53/54: 23–4.

Winnicott, D. W. (1943) 'Delinquency research', *New Era* 24.

Winnicott, D. W. (1972 [1960]) 'Ego distortion in terms of true and false self', *Maturational Processes and the Facilitating Environment,* London: Hogarth Press.

Wittgenstein, L. (1953) *Philosophical Investigations,* Oxford: Basil Blackwell.

Wittgenstein, L. (1980) *Remarks on the Philosophy of Psychology. (Volume I),* Oxford: Basil Blackwell.

Wolins, L. (1962) 'Responsibility for raw data', *American Psychologist* 17: 657–8.

Worchel, S. and Cooper, J. (1976) *Understanding Social Psychology,* Homewood, IU: The Dorsey Press.

Wright, P. (1985) *On Living In An Old Country,* London: Verso.

Zimbardo, P. (1973) 'On the ethics of intervention in human psychological research: with special reference to the Stanford prison experiment', *Cognition* 2: 243–56.

INDEX

243